▼ **MAKING HARD CHOICES
IN JOURNALISM ETHICS**

Making Hard Choices in Journalism Ethics teaches students how to make the difficult ethical decisions that journalists routinely face. By taking a case-based approach, the authors argue that the best way to make an ethical decision is to look closely at a particular situation, rather than looking first to an abstract set of ethical theories or principles. *Making Hard Choices in Journalism Ethics* goes beyond the traditional approaches of many other journalism textbooks by using cases as the starting point for building ethical practices. Casuistry, the technical name of such a method, develops provisional guidelines from the bottom up by reasoning analogically from an "easy" ethical case (the "paradigm") to "harder" ethical cases. Thoroughly grounded in actual experience, this method admits more nuanced judgments than most theoretical approaches.

Making Hard Choices in Journalism Ethics provides a thorough overview of major ethical theories and explains how they can be integrated with case-based strategies such as moral exemplars and case comparisons. Each chapter takes on a different ethical issue in journalism by using practice cases and "walk-through" exercises to sensitize students to the way these issues play out in varying contexts. These exercises also help them to master the basics of the case-based method. The text presents the cases in a developmental sequence, with simpler cases first and more complex cases later, culminating with an extended case for analysis in a realistic newsroom setting.

As today's rapidly changing media landscape is challenging traditional assumptions about journalistic ethics, this text teaches students a method that they can adopt in tandem with traditional ethical norms.

David E. Boeyink is Associate Professor of Journalism and Director of the Journalism Honors Program at Indiana University. His research on the ethics of decision-making in newsrooms is published in *Journalism Quarterly,* the *Journal of Mass Media Ethics,* and the *Newspaper Research Journal.*

Sandra L. Borden is Professor of Communication and Co-Director of the Center for the Study of Ethics in Society at Western Michigan University. She is author of *Journalism as Practice: MacIntyre, Virtue Ethics and the Press* (available in paperback from Routledge), winner of the 2008 Award for Top Book in Applied Ethics from the National Communication Association's Communication Ethics Division.

MAKING HARD CHOICES IN JOURNALISM ETHICS

CASES AND PRACTICE

David E. Boeyink
Indiana University

Sandra L. Borden
Western Michigan University

 Routledge
Taylor & Francis Group

NEW YORK AND LONDON

✓ hft

2865855

070.4
BOE

First published 2010
by Routledge
270 Madison Avenue, New York, NY 10016

Simultaneously published in the UK
by Routledge
2 Park Square, Milton Park, Abingdon, Oxon OX14 4RN

Routledge is an imprint of the Taylor & Francis Group, an informa business

© 2010 David E. Boeyink and Sandra L. Borden

Typeset in Bell Gothic by
Keystroke, Tettenhall, Wolverhampton
Printed and bound in the United States of America on acid-free paper by
Walsworth Publishing Company, Marceline, MO

Library of Congress Cataloging-in-Publication Data
Boeyink, David E.
  Making hard choices in journalism ethics : cases and practice /
  David E. Boeyink, Sandra L. Borden.
      p. cm.
    Includes bibliographical references and index.
  1. Journalistic ethics. 2. Journalism—Objectivity. I. Borden,
  Sandra L., 1963– II. Title.
  PN4756.B64 2010
  070.4—dc22   2009030721

ISBN10: 0–415–98999–X (hbk)
ISBN10: 0–415–99000–9 (pbk)
ISBN10: 0–203–92819–9 (ebk)

ISBN13: 978–0–415–98999–2 (hbk)
ISBN13: 978–0–415–99000–4 (pbk)
ISBN13: 978–0–203–92819–6 (ebk)

For my wife, Karen
D.B.

For my husband, Randy
S.B.

▼ CONTENTS

CHAPTER 1

▼ **HARD CASES IN
JOURNALISM ETHICS**

Sometimes police encounter real murder mysteries when they are called to a crime scene. They don't know who commit7ted the crime or why. They may not even fully understand what caused the victim's death. Without a confession or reliable chronology about what happened, they have no choice but to develop their own "theories" about what took place.

When police face a hard case like this, they rely on their knowledge of forensic science and their experience investigating other crime scenes to know what might be a clue. They also collect and study the evidence systematically. By using an established protocol, they make sure to not miss anything important and to reconstruct their investigation to the satisfaction of other people with an interest in its outcome.

Journalism ethics can seem like a real mystery, too. Sometimes journalists stumble into tough ethical situations that defy simple resolution. They can't "solve" such hard cases by simply consulting the newsroom's code of ethics or falling back on general rules like truth telling. Take the case of Patricia Bowman and William Kennedy Smith. Smith, Sen. Ted Kennedy's nephew, met 29-year-old Bowman in a bar in 1991. After drinks at the Kennedy family mansion, the pair went walking on the mansion's private beach, where Bowman said Smith raped her. She got a ride with a friend to the local police station immediately afterward and got checked out at a hospital for treatment of injuries and collection of forensic evidence.

Within hours, the news media had converged on Bowman, who lived with her 1-year-old daughter. Subsequent news reports questioned her veracity and suggested that she was promiscuous and unstable. Smith, meanwhile, denied the charges, saying the sex was consensual. Most major news media did not name Bowman before she herself went public after the jury's verdict, with the exception of NBC News and *The New York Times*. Bowman specifically requested anonymity until she decided to appear in a post-trial interview with Diane Sawyer on ABC.

For years, *The Courier-Journal* of Louisville, Kentucky, had a policy of not naming persons who told police they had been raped. But the Bowman/Smith case involved such notoriety and such intensive coverage that the editors were uncomfortable with their policy's usual balance between privacy and truth telling. Now they had some questions about the wire stories they were receiving from the Associated Press. They wanted to protect Bowman from a kind of second victimization and perhaps make progress in removing the stigma that is attached to all rape victims. Publisher George Gill reflected after the trial:

> I guess philosophically I subscribe to (the) theory . . . that rape is never going to be manageable, or whatever the word is, as a crime until all the mystery is taken out of it and the guilt is taken out of it and so forth, on the victim's side. And I think, philosophically, I can buy that. It's a little difficult, though, coming down and putting your neighbor's name in the paper without her permission, if she happens to be raped. I mean that's a tough one — a real tough one.

The editors also thought the case deserved coverage since it involved a prominent member of the Kennedy family. Smith's name represented an important part of the truth of this story. Yet the intense nature of the national coverage seemed to the editors to be unfair, as it framed Smith as a rapist day after day. Commenting on the case, then Managing Editor Steve Ford commented:

> And in the end I think that, with varying degrees of enthusiasm, there was kind of a broad consensus of this different kind of case — that this guy, whether guilty or innocent, you know, was being put on the front page of virtually every paper in the country; he was on all the network news shows, and he was there because of his middle name.

This case did not seem to fit the paper's long-standing policy of not naming rape victims. Nor was it resolved by an appeal to ethical rules when three of these rules — truth telling, privacy, and fairness — seemed to conflict. What journalists need in such cases is a way of reasoning that helps them to recognize the moral clues at hand and engage in a proper investigation of what's at stake, morally speaking. Kind of a *CSI* for journalism ethics.

This textbook will provide you with experience using a case-based method for ethical decision making widely used in the Middle Ages and now enjoying a revival in a number of fields, including journalism. It's called *casuistry*. The Bowman/Smith case will provide a touchstone throughout the book as you learn more about the basics of casuistry and how to apply it to "cases of conscience" (Miller 1996: 5) in journalism ethics. But, first, let's get clear on some basic concepts in the study of ethics.

WHY DO JOURNALISTS NEED TO WORRY ABOUT ETHICS?

Some journalists say that there's nothing more to journalism ethics than doing journalism well. Certainly, we expect journalists to perform their jobs competently. A reporter should be able to find out information efficiently and know how to verify it so that he or she can vouch for the information's accuracy and completeness. A good writer should be able to express ideas clearly, describe details vividly and help audiences gain perspective about the world around them. A web designer should be able to arrange text and images in a way that invites audiences to browse, helps them to figure out the most important news on the site, and provides an aesthetically pleasing experience that engages their senses as well as their minds. In short, *technical* excellence is a part of good work.

However, as moral development experts Mihaly Csikszentmihalyi, William Damon and Howard Gardner (The Good Work Project 2007) point out, competence is just part of the equation. Journalists can be skillful and yet fail to perform good work if they do not also do their jobs with *moral* excellence.

Moral excellence consists of performing your ethical responsibilities well:

- All of us have moral responsibilities to be truthful, to avoid harming others, to keep our promises and the like. These are called *general responsibilities*—what we sometimes think of as common decency.
- But sometimes we take on additional responsibilities as members of a religious denomination, profession or some other group that helps to define who we are and what others come to expect of us. These are called *particular responsibilities.*
- We also accept responsibilities as individuals, as an expression of our character, even though nobody "requires" us to define ethical conduct according to these self-imposed responsibilities. These are *personal responsibilities*. Personal responsibilities, of course, can help make our jobs meaningful, which is another characteristic of good work.

Media ethicist Deni Elliott (1986) suggests that general responsibilities, particular responsibilities and personal responsibilities provide the foundations for moral excellence in journalism. Like the rest of us, journalists have the general responsibilities of telling the truth and minimizing harm. However, these responsibilities take on a specific meaning in journalism. Telling the truth is a strong moral imperative because of journalism's mission to help citizens participate responsibly in their communities. All of us should be truthful, but we expect journalists to be especially proactive in seeking and disseminating the truth so that we can participate knowledgeably in public life.

Likewise, all of us should avoid harming others whenever possible. But journalists are in a special position to cause harm because of the power they exercise through the reach of modern media. A picture can sway foreign policy; a blog post can incite virulent attacks on an individual. When you act unethically as an individual, you may risk hurting a few people close to you. When journalists act unethically, they may end up injuring millions. For example, a 2005 brief in *Newsweek* reported erroneously, on the basis of a single anonymous source, that interrogators at Guantanamo Bay had flushed a copy of the Qur'an down the toilet to rattle an Islamic detainee. The accusation appalled Muslims around the world; riots broke out in Pakistan and Afghanistan. Fifteen people died (Thomas 2005).

That's why the first two principles in the code of ethics for the Society of Professional Journalists (SPJ) are "Seek the Truth and Report it" and "Minimize Harm." These principles are in constant tension as journalists endeavor to perform good work — in both the technical and the moral sense. It's precisely because these principles conflict so often that merely appealing to the code is not sufficient for solving the moral mysteries that bedevil even the best journalists.

Elliott notes that journalists also accept certain particular responsibilities by becoming journalists, entering news organizations and joining groups such as the Society of Professional Journalists. By becoming members of the practice and affiliated organizations, journalists agree to the promises that have been made on their behalf by these bodies. If my news organization runs a promo every evening pledging to "be first" with the news, then I have implicitly made this pledge to our audience as well.

One moral hazard is that my organization may make a promise that runs counter to common decency. Will we do anything to be first? Even if it means being insensitive to people in pain or taking advantage of people who are naïve about how the news works? Elliott suggests that general responsibilities have precedence over any particular responsibilities we might accept by virtue of joining an organization. After all, journalists cannot very well keep the lofty promises made by their organizations if they do not first perform their practice's major social functions well.

We often consider "fit" with an organization in terms of whether we will get along with our co-workers or whether the pay will match our credentials. But Elliott's framework suggests we should also consider whether an organization is a good "moral fit" as well.

Elliott says that we have to retain our autonomy as *moral agents* even though our individual actions are constrained by the general and particular respon-sibilities that characterize good work in journalism. To be a moral agent means that you are able to understand the significance of your choices and can be held responsible for them. *Autonomy* is an important condition for moral agency. Autonomy means being able to choose freely without undue pressure or coercion. We cannot just leave our conscience at the newsroom door and claim to be "just following orders" or "just doing our job."

Ethics involves choice at every stage, though sometimes we face very limited options. Our personal responsibilities may direct us to say "no" to an editor — or to go above and beyond what our editor expects of us. CNN reporter Christiane Amanpour, for example, has distinguished herself as a journalist who seeks to promote international understanding. She has gone after stories that normally do not make it onto the radar of today's "hyperlocal" US news media and has traveled extensively to witness events firsthand and to interview people in other countries, even when these actions have placed her in great personal danger. No one "makes" her do these things; these are commitments that she has made herself, as a matter of conviction, and they now define her own personal brand of journalistic excellence.

HOW THINGS ARE VERSUS HOW THEY SHOULD BE

Despite Amanpour's example, however, many commentators have noted that US journalists are remarkably provincial in their reporting. The American press, indeed, has emphasized localism throughout its history, and this trend seems to be only increasing with the capability to tailor media "content" to our individual interests and have it delivered directly to the latest hand-held electronic device.

Localism, in other words, is an enduring value that *describes* the way journalism has been traditionally practiced in the United States. But *should* that be the way that American journalism is practiced? This is a different question that cannot be answered by looking back at the history of American journalism or even by explaining why it is this way. Nor can we simply poll journalists around the country and ask them to tell us to what degree their work has an international dimension and whether they think it should have a larger one. Even now we would only be engaging in what ethicists call *descriptive ethics*: talking about the way things *are* or the values that journalists *actually* believe in.

Anthropologists, historians, sociologists, psychologists — and journalists — do descriptive ethics all the time, telling us about the mores of different societies, the taboos that have existed throughout time, the unspoken rules that tell us "how we do things around here." But to get into the *should* business — to talk reasonably about whether these mores should exist, whether these taboos should endure, whether our unspoken rules should be supported — we have to switch gears and do some *normative ethics*. Normative ethics is the study of the way things *should* be or the values that we *should* believe in.

Of course, no algorithm can figure out what we should do or what kind of person we should try to be. The answers in math are *objectively* knowable:

there is only one correct answer to the sum 2+2. Ethics is not math. Reasonable people can come up with different answers to the question of whether a journalist should honor a promise to a source, and these answers can all have merit. That's the nature of something that is *normatively* knowable. So what does that mean for the study of journalism ethics?

Is Ethics Just Subjective Opinion?

This does not mean that anything goes. Some answers are better than others. Ethics may not be objectively answerable like math, but ethics are not just a matter of taste or preference either. Otherwise, choosing the best answer to an ethical problem would be somewhat like choosing a flavor at your local ice cream shop. I cannot criticize your choice of chocolate over strawberry except on strictly subjective grounds. I like strawberry better, so that's what's good for me. You like chocolate, so that's good for you.

To understand the concept of normative ethics, it's helpful to remember that an answer doesn't have to be *ideal* to be acceptable. Clearly, some things are morally prohibited. For example, sleeping with a source only to obtain information for a news story is obviously unacceptable. We can come to agreement fairly quickly about such actions. On the other hand, there are some actions that are morally required. They are not optional. We must do them or be unethical. If a source has information that is important for the public to know, a journalist must try to obtain the information even if the source is uncooperative. To refuse to do so or to simply "pass" without making any attempt would be unacceptable.

But that still leaves a lot of moral ground to cover. A journalist could try to trick the source into revealing the information by lying about his identity. He could pressure the source by threatening to make her look bad. He could appeal to the source's vanity by flattering her ego. He could appeal to the source's sense of duty by invoking the public's right to know. He could ask for the information and use due diligence to follow up, but not insist if the source is not forthcoming. All of these might be morally acceptable ways to go about the task, depending on the circumstances. But clearly some come closer to the ideal than others—and some come closer to crossing the line.

We can have reasonable discussions about which options rank higher, ethically speaking, and why. This is what it means to say that a certain subject is "normatively answerable." But notice that there isn't just one, and only one, "correct" answer. Reasonable people may disagree about better and worse solutions to moral problems without giving up on the whole idea of normative ethics.[1]

Yet people confronted with the difficult reality of moral disagreement sometimes do give up on normative ethics. Since we obviously don't see eye to eye about ethics, and since moral beliefs seem to change over time, they conclude that ethics are entirely subjective: that there really must *not* be any way to decide. This is a perspective known as *relativism*, which can take several forms (Jaksa and Pritchard 1994):

- In one version of relativism, we simply go along with the social conventions of our culture or group. However "we do things around here" is also the way we *should* do them, although we don't necessarily expect other groups to agree with us. Of course, how we determine what "the group" believes is something of a mystery. It's also unclear whether moral standards should shift along with majority opinion. And what if you're in the minority? Are you just plain wrong—at least until the majority eventually comes around to your view?
- In another version of relativism, we simply appeal to our personal preferences, much as we might defend our choice of chocolate ice cream over strawberry ice cream: This is my opinion about ethics. Take it or leave it. This is what I think, so it's right, at least for me.
- Finally, there is a version of relativism that is sometimes called "situation ethics." In its extreme form, situation ethics claims that every situation is unique and cannot be compared to any other. We make a decision "in the moment" without relying on experience, values, rules or any other ethical concepts brought in from "outside" the situation. As with the other forms of relativism, there is no effort to be consistent. I can decide one thing on Monday and another on Tuesday, even though I faced fundamentally similar situations both times. As we'll see, this is a key difference between situation ethics and casuistry, which uses comparison as the basic structure of ethical reasoning.

Moral disagreement is a fact of life, and we need to reckon with it. But relativism overstates the problem. When we look into matters more closely, it turns out that there are *logical* reasons for moral disagreement. When views about what's right change over time, it's not because there's a "flavor of the day" in ethics. It's because circumstances change enough to neutralize certain moral concerns and (perhaps) give rise to new ones. For example, news policies shielding the identities of rape victims have generally acknowledged that a woman who has suffered rape is likely to feel shame and even somehow to feel responsible for what has happened to her. The reason news organizations tend to avoid telling their audiences the whole truth about such reported crimes, then, is to avoid serious, unjustified harm to women who have already been victimized.

So why did former *Courier-Journal* managing editor Irene Nolan and others who advocated naming Bowman back off this ethical rule? Did they just decide one day, for no particular reason, that rape victims should be thrown to the wolves? Did they wake up one morning with an inexpressible "feeling" that rape was not a serious crime after all? No: they were reconsidering the likelihood that rape victims would be harmed if they were identified in crime reports—for valid reasons.

The term "date rape" had recently entered national public discourse, with the publication of a study in *Ms.* magazine documenting the extent of the problem, the degree to which women and men had trouble making sense of date rape as a crime, and the low reporting rate among victims. The incident at the Kennedy mansion also happened shortly after the well-publicized Senate confirmation hearings for Supreme Court Justice nominee Clarence Thomas, who was accused of sexual harassment (another term that was just gaining acceptance) by a subordinate, Anita Hill. In short, this was a time when feminists and others interested in institutional sexism were talking openly about long-tolerated practices that had historically oppressed women, and they were winning many people over.

In light of this heightened awareness, doubt arose among some journalists regarding news policies that might be, in this new "post-feminist" environment, paternalistic or even unjust. Indeed, perhaps treating rape reports like any other crime might communicate to news audiences that being raped is no cause for shame. Instead of harming rape victims, perhaps identifying them in the newspaper would help them, and indeed help all women. This was part of the argument for naming rape victims that *Des Moines Register* editor Geneva Overholser had made a couple of years earlier in a widely discussed op-ed piece in *The New York Times*.[2]

Of course, many people would disagree with this assessment of the facts. Had society really become so enlightened about date rape that *The Courier-Journal* could be confident about not harming Bowman and other reported rape victims? Would treating rape victims the same as everyone else bring this crime out of the shadows and encourage more victims to report it? If these factual questions could have been answered with certainty, there probably would not have been much need to discuss the Bowman/Smith case.

To take another example of a moral impasse based on a factual disagreement, imagine if there were no question regarding when human life begins. Consensus about this biological fact would dramatically alter the abortion debate. Whether abortion amounts to murder depends on whether we're talking about persons or something else. We don't disagree about the morality of murder. We disagree about whether abortion *is* murder.

Media ethicist Clifford Christians (1997) suggests, in fact, that the sanctity of life is a cross-cultural ethical principle that finds expression in beliefs about human dignity, truthfulness and non-violence shared among all people. These beliefs are expressed in distinct ways depending, once again, on the circumstances. In an individualistic culture like the United States, human dignity finds expression in a reverence for personal liberty. In more communal

MAKING HARD CHOICES IN JOURNALISM ETHICS

cultures like those found in the tribal villages of Africa, human dignity is bound up with group membership.

The point is that, underneath the surface differences that exist across geography and across time, there is more moral agreement than disagreement. We just have to learn to appreciate the underlying reasons for our differences and to consider them seriously when we're trying to sort through solutions to our ethical problems.

WHAT ABOUT RULES IN ETHICS?

In the long-running TV sitcom *Murphy Brown*, the title character was the star reporter of a prime-time news magazine. Although she had her share of personal shortcomings, she was known for her integrity as a journalist. Much to her dismay, she was increasingly surrounded by people who looked good on camera but were not proficient journalists — either technically or morally.

One of these wannabes was Miller Redfield. In the episode "Miller's Crossing," he actually commits the morally prohibited action suggested earlier: he sleeps with a prominent anthropologist to score an interview with her for the newscast. Murphy is livid once she finds out about this journalistic sin. Miller, eager to get into his idol's good graces, proffers an awkward apology. Murphy tries to explain that there are rules journalists must follow. These include not paying sources and not sleeping with them. Miller notes that he has broken both rules, since he paid for the anthropologist's cab fare. Overwhelmed with this new information, Miller asks hopefully, "Wow. Hey, is this stuff written down anywhere, you know, like in a pamphlet or a card I could stick in my wallet?" "No," says Murphy, looking down, apparently resigned to Miller's moral ineptitude. "You just sorta have to *know* it."

We use rules all the time. Most of us try to follow the rules because they're useful. They're the product of many earlier efforts to sort out what works and what's fair. And, as Murphy points out, when we join a practice like journalism, we're expected to know and to follow its ethical norms,[3] which often take the form of rules, or "ethical principles," as ethicists like to call them. However, it's one thing to accept moral rules after reflecting upon their reasonableness and quite another to follow them blindly because they happen to be "written down somewhere."

We also have to be careful that we don't view moral rules as black-and-white mandates that must be followed without qualification. Philosopher Anthony Weston (1997) points out that there are at least three problems with this view of rules.

One problem is that all rules have exceptions. For example, journalists generally shouldn't deceive since they're in the business of seeking and reporting the truth. However, sometimes they use deception to get a story. In 1992, *PrimeTime Live,* a news magazine on ABC, decided to investigate the claims of former union workers at Food Lion stores that the Southern grocery chain was endangering the public. The workers interviewed by ABC said management was directing employees to sell meat and deli products past their expiration dates by repackaging and otherwise disguising the food. The show's reporters used their real names to apply for Food Lion jobs but did not disclose that they were journalists. Once inside some of the chain's stores, the reporters taped fellow employees describing and implementing these unsanitary practices using hidden cameras. Food Lion sued for fraud and won at the trial court stage before that legal opinion was overturned by a higher court.

It's not clear that ABC should have made an exception to the rule against deception in this case. For one thing, the journalists didn't exhaust all truthful alternatives. However, journalists have obtained important information through undercover reporting that could not have been obtained otherwise. A few years before the Food Lion story, in fact, *PrimeTime* used hidden cameras in a widely praised investigation to document safety hazards at some Veterans Affairs hospitals. The report led the Secretary of Veterans Affairs to look into regulatory failures that might be endangering veterans. Such cases remind us that it is not reasonable to simply issue a blanket prohibition against deceptive reporting without considering circumstances that might justify an exception to the rule.

Another problem with rules is that they sometimes conflict. So just identifying a relevant rule doesn't necessarily settle our ethical judgments. Going back to the Food Lion case, the rule "Do not lie" conflicted in that case with the rule "Protect the public safety." What does truthfulness require in these circumstances? Does it mean just giving your real name? Or does it mean that you have to tell Food Lion you're a reporter who wants to observe the chain's food handling practices? What does it mean for journalists to protect the public (as opposed to health inspectors, for example)? Casuists believe that the rules themselves do not contain the answers to such questions.

That brings us to the third problem with "hard and fast" moral rules (Weston 1997: 21): They are too vague to settle specific moral questions raised by particular circumstances. Casuists, in fact, believe you have to figure out the actual content of general rules at the practical level because there is no way that rules can anticipate all possible circumstances. Indeed, casuists think rules can be generalized only to similar cases, and then only as useful guidelines (Jonsen and Toulmin 1988).

This is a lot like legal *precedent* in case law. In civil cases, judges may appeal to a previous court ruling when they are dealing with a legal case presenting very similar legal considerations. In invoking the precedent of the previous case, they compare the established case with the new one to determine if the precedent adequately covers the present case or whether a new precedent revising or expanding the court's previous opinions is warranted.

Casuists believe that moral rules make sense only when we encounter them in practice, just as case law emerges informally from the actual decisions that judges make, one case at a time. Just like precedent in law, ethical guidelines arising from casuistical analysis are subject to revision in light of new circumstances. In effect, the guidelines reflect imperfect knowledge of a rule's scope, which itself is being determined by the details of particular cases.

This is quite different from the top-down way in which most ethical theories apply moral rules. Even theories that take circumstances seriously, as you'll see in Chapter 2, do not allow for the rules themselves to be amended. The rules always remain ''above it all.'' The most that can be said is that the rules may be weighted differently in different circumstances, and then it's through some vague notion of ''intuition.''

This kind of theoretical reasoning in ethics is similar to what judges do when they apply statutory law. In statutory law, a judge has to decide whether a given action conforms to a relevant written law, or statute, enacted by a legislature. The task is mainly one of interpretation: deciding if a given statute applies and if so, how. A judge cannot ''make new law'' or go beyond the written statute in any way. The task is to apply the law to the facts at hand and nothing more—a task that involves all the difficulties discussed earlier when applying rules: dealing with conflicting laws, exceptions, and ambiguity.

We're not suggesting that moral rules and other ethical norms are not pertinent to case-based analysis. They provide some taken-for-granted commitments that help us to ferret out the ethical tensions in a case and to get a handle on the circumstances we're currently facing (Miller, March 1996). However, we cannot *just* appeal to rules if we want to deal responsibly with hard cases.

CASUISTRY: CSI FOR JOURNALISTS

Despite its shortcomings, the process for making a decision in the Smith–Bowman case illustrates how case-based reasoning can help us to achieve the proper balance between theory and cases in journalism ethics. The decision makers took *The Courier-Journal*'s policy against naming sex crime victims as their starting point—a top-down approach—then reasoned through specific cases—a bottom-up approach. Among the circumstances they considered was the publicity surrounding Bowman's accusation and Smith's prominence as a news figure. They also considered whether there was any precedent for naming rape victims at the paper.

This is the way in which medieval casuists reasoned, beginning with general ethical norms that they then specified by working through cases (Jonsen and

Toulmin 1988). Guided by these norms, they agreed on an unambiguous case—the paradigm case—then compared it with increasingly more complicated, ambiguous cases (both actual and hypothetical). Likewise, crime scene investigations use "comparison samples." In this practice, criminal investigators compare physical evidence from the crime scene with "known samples" of objects obtained elsewhere (such as tires).

Case-based reasoning may seem like the perfect ethical decision-making method for journalists, given its concern with the who, what, when, where, why, and how of specific cases (Boeyink 1992). Casuistry, after all, views ethics as a thoroughly practical kind of knowledge. Likewise, the practice of journalism deals with practical, rather than theoretical, expertise—one of the ways in which it differs from its intellectual cousin, science (Borden 2007). Journalists, indeed, will be the first to tell you that they make ethical decisions on a "case-by-case basis."

But case-based reasoning has pitfalls of its own. If we look at how journalists typically practice it, we see that their judgments are often inconsistent from one situation to the next, resembling the arbitrariness of situation ethics. They can also be prone to too much nitpicking, as in the case of a newspaper that has gone through the effort of developing a written policy for reporting Bigfoot sightings. In other words, they get wrapped up in details that don't really matter. "The contemporary casuist must argue that circumstances are important but not too important" (Kuczewski 1997: 66).

At other times, journalists don't pay enough attention to conflicting paradigms when dealing with certain moral cases. For example, *PrimeTime Live*'s producers were probably surprised that a jury awarded damages to Food Lion in its lawsuit against ABC. There are a number of reasons for this, of course, but one is that the journalists had framed the case as one of deception in reporting, while the jury framed the case as one of loyalty in the workplace.

The journalists may have made the same decision to betray Food Lion's trust had they selected a "workplace loyalty" paradigm to anchor their ethical deliberations. But they probably would have thought differently about the ethical factors justifying such a choice and done more to ensure that Food Lion employees were given a fair shake. In other words, the decision would have been more like a whistle-blowing one, rather than an undercover reporting one. In failing to consider the particular responsibilities pertinent to the role of a Food Lion employee, *as well as* those pertinent to the role of journalist, *PrimeTime Live*'s team overlooked an important complexity in its ethical decision.

Unfortunately, once a decision has been committed to the status of a precedent in a newsroom, or even the wider practice of journalism, journalists can be stubborn and thick-headed in repeating their mistakes. Getting slapped with a lawsuit is never pleasant, but, in the Food Lion case, it may have given journalists everywhere a new perspective.

If journalists don't do a good job thinking through ethical issues, they can end up misusing case-based reasoning to rationalize selfish choices—much as "dirty cops" might manipulate evidence at a crime scene to get an arrest warrant they want. Another danger is that journalists may adopt ethical guidelines that merely summarize their own prejudices (Arras 1991).

For example, what other rationale besides the scoop mentality would justify naming Bowman in *The Courier-Journal* because NBC was going to name her first? Although staffers cited fairness as a moral consideration with extra weight in the Bowman/Smith case, it was only with some prompting from one of this text's authors. Did fairness figure prominently in the staff's actual reasoning and discussion about this decision, or was its relevance an after-thought? Perhaps a more explicit acknowledgment of ethical norms might have led to a decision that better balanced fairness toward Smith with preventing harm to Bowman. For example, the paper might have waited until Smith was found not guilty before identifying Bowman. And, of course, the paper was not obligated to run "unfair" wire stories in the first place.

A "neglect of the larger realms of moral ideals," then, can mislead the non-conscientious, as philosophers Albert Jonsen and Stephen Toulmin (1988: 243) acknowledged. On the other hand, seeing all moral rules as "universal, invariable and free of exceptions" leads to either dismissing all exceptions as moral laziness or making ethics so speculative that it has no practical relevance.

It's best not to think of journalism ethics as a one-way street: either top-down or bottom-up. Instead, as Arras (1993: 3) says, it is best to think of the ethical decision-making process we'll be using in this book as a "movement from principles to cases and back again." Although such a method may be less neat conceptually, it is more useful in practice because it permits theory and cases to be called upon as appropriate to reflect different dimensions of human experience. Chapter 2 provides an overview of major ethical theories. But for now we are going to practice reasoning with cases.

EYE ON PRIVACY

To help you learn key ideas from the text, each chapter will conclude with practice cases and "walk-through" exercises, borrowing another term from *CSI*. When investigators first arrive at a crime scene, they survey it thoroughly to scan for potential evidence and determine the kinds of resources they will need for their investigation. They do another walk-through right before leaving the scene to make sure they haven't missed anything. Likewise, to carry out good ethical decision making, you have to make sure you have sized up the situation adequately and that you have not made a hasty choice before declaring an ethical case solved. Therefore, some exercises include "one last look" at the ethical issues at stake in a case.

Each chapter will have an eye on a different ethical issue in journalism, except for the last two chapters. In the spirit of casuistry, we will provide an array of cases that permits a thorough consideration of each issue's complexity in different journalistic contexts and news media. The cases will get longer and more perplexing as you master the case-based method. Chapter 6 focuses on creating guidelines for a variety of ethical issues using case-based analysis, and Chapter 7 presents a complex case for analysis in a realistic newsroom setting.

In this chapter, you will gain an appreciation for how difficult it is to resolve hard cases by relying exclusively on either situational factors or moral rules. The cases at the end of the chapter deal with privacy, continuing the inquiry we began with the Bowman/Smith case. *The Courier-Journal*, by the way, ultimately decided to name Bowman the day after NBC identified her in a prime-time news segment. *The New York Times* followed suit a couple of days later in a profile about Bowman, but later backtracked and kept her name out of subsequent stories, including reports about the trial. Some newspapers continued to withhold Bowman's name even after the trial verdict finding Smith "not guilty."

Privacy as an Ethical Issue

Privacy became a distinct legal concept in the nineteenth century, helped along by a famous law review article by Samuel Warren and Louis Brandeis arguing that people had a legal right to "be let alone" (as cited in Bok 1989: 287). Warren and Brandeis were writing at a time when citizens were becoming concerned about surveillance by an increasingly powerful press, as well as the government. Today, concerns about surveillance extend to advertisers tracking Internet use and parents monitoring web surfing.

Somewhere along the way, privacy also became a means of "being yourself," free from the pressure to conform to social expectations. Privacy, in other words, became a social good, as well as a legal right (Woo 2006). Philosopher Sissela Bok (1989) defines privacy as the moral right to control personal information about oneself. She says it's basic to a healthy identity, as most of us can't imagine living in a world where everyone could know anything they wanted about us whenever they wanted, even against our will. Privacy is an important way for us to exercise our autonomy and dignity as human beings.

Unfortunately, in the course of reporting about important institutions and less important celebrities, journalists often violate people's privacy by:

- Disseminating embarrassing personal information.
- Disseminating embarrassing images.
- Intruding on the peace of a person or her home.
- Exploiting someone's name or likeness for gain.

We'll look at cases illustrating these problematic practices. One thing to keep in mind, though, is that people's right to control their personal information can mean different things. Americans, for example, have historically thought of privacy as a property right. This can be seen in the Constitution's guarantee against arbitrary search and seizure. The quintessential invasion of privacy in the eighteenth century would have been the authorities trespassing onto someone's property and rummaging through private papers and diaries (Rosen 2000). Fast forward to the twenty-first century and the case of former White House intern Monica Lewinsky: To prove she was having an affair with President Clinton, special prosecutor Kenneth Starr subpoenaed the data on Lewinsky's computer hard drive. Among other things, he obtained unsent love letters she had written to the president. These letters ultimately ended up being made public as part of Starr's report to Congress.

Lewinsky's experience illustrates how the notion of privacy as personal property remains relevant. This "property" notion of privacy can be seen in expressions suggesting privacy is a kind of moral space that cannot be trespassed upon: We have a "privacy zone," there are "boundaries" between public and private, and so forth. But the Lewinsky case also demonstrates how difficult it is to shield personal information entirely from public view. Jusik Woo (2006) suggests that it's more pertinent, in today's legal and technological environment, to think of privacy *achievement* rather than privacy *protection.*

Rather than thinking of privacy as the right to keep certain information secret altogether, privacy achievement stresses control over who has access to our information. In this view, privacy is not an either/or proposition, but a matter of degrees (Solove 2007). Bok (1989: 16) acknowledges the complexity of privacy with her thought experiment involving four hypothetical societies, each with different levels of secrecy and transparency. She surmises that we wouldn't want to live in a society in which there was complete secrecy and "all can conceal innocuous as well as lethal plans, the noblest as well as the most shameful acts," nor would we tolerate a completely transparent society in which "surprise and concealment are out of the question."

Instead of thinking there is a "private" zone and a "public" zone, as journalists traditionally do, Livingstone (2008) suggests that we need to think of people as having a *number* of privacy zones reflecting different levels of intimacy. The boundaries that matter, in other words, are social. As Patterson and Wilkins (2007) note, we expect less control over personal information in less intimate circles and more control over personal information in more intimate circles. We feel violated when our information crosses outside the social circle for which it was intended (Rosen 2000).

For example, when you're on a social networking website such as Facebook, you may feel perfectly comfortable posting personal information and pictures for public consumption—as long as you get to decide exactly who "counts" as your public. Facebook lets you do just that, of course, by restricting access to your invited "friends."

But there's more to privacy achievement. Even making already available information more visible can feel like an invasion of privacy, as illustrated by the quick and strong opposition of users to Facebook's "mini-feed" feature when it was first introduced in 2006. Before, people had to actually visit your site to see what you were up to; the new software notified everyone in your network (even virtual strangers you had "friended" on a lark) the instant there was anything new on your page. In response, Facebook gave users greater control over the information going into the mini-feed.

In essence, what we're concerned about is being "judged out of context in a world of short attention spans" (Rosen 2000: 8). When this happens, it inevitably results in oversimplifying who we are and can even reduce us, in a sense, to objects. Barbara Walters alluded to this problem after interviewing Lewinsky. The ABC journalist found Lewinsky to be very different from the cardboard character that had emerged in the press and on the blogosphere after months of "Monicagate": "She is not silly. She is well-spoken. She is intelligent" (Carvajal and Mifflin 1998).

Until she was able to speak for herself in the media, Lewinsky had been reduced to a *quasar*. Film scholar James Monaco came up with the term "quasar" to describe "silent" celebrities who are thrust into the limelight by news events and have no control over their stories or images. They have no voice of their own. Instead, they are made to represent opportunism, or corruption, or suffering. Kyle Reinson (2010) suggests that the increasingly common media practice of creating quasars robs real people of their privacy, identity and dignity. "The public memory of a quasar no longer reflects the true self."

An important ethical problem with the quasar phenomenon is lack of consent. If privacy is essentially about exercising autonomy, then letting someone choose what she shares and with whom becomes crucial. But consent, like privacy, is complicated. Is a legalistic form letter that pops up on your computer screen and must be "checked" before entering a website enough to secure meaningful consent? How about the reporter's quick and urgent "Can I ask you a few questions?" at the scene of a natural disaster? Should journalists let sources and subjects approve quotes and descriptions of themselves? And what if your subject doesn't seem to care enough about her privacy for her own good?

Most people who write about privacy in the media think that you can't violate someone's privacy if you have his or her consent to publish the information in question. Most do not go so far as securing what researchers would call "informed consent" (Lancioni 2003). To be informed, assent must be based on knowledge of all information relevant to your choice, including exactly what is expected and what risks and benefits may result (for example, whether you'll come across as "silly"). To be consensual, assent must be freely given (for example, you can't trick someone into giving an interview or take advantage of them by asking their permission while they're in shock).

When our privacy is wrested from us, we feel violated, exposed—sometimes even humiliated or betrayed. A major moral rule that will be relevant to privacy cases, then, is minimizing harm. As we've seen, though, some ethical problems defy a simple recourse to rules because two or more rules apply— and they conflict. Journalists often have to weigh the harm of invading someone's privacy against the rule of truth telling.

Ethics Codes as Sources of Moral Rules

As noted earlier, the SPJ code highlights the tension between the moral rules, or principles, of truth telling and minimizing harm (Haas 2003). In Chapter 2 we'll take a look at some ethical theories and their suggested rules. But for now the SPJ code is a good place to start our search for moral rules in journalism.

SPJ, founded in 1909, is the largest professional association for journalists in the United States, and its code has provided a template for newsroom ethics policies across the country. After using the code of the American Society of Newspaper Editors for a number of years, SPJ wrote its own code of ethics in 1973. The code has been revised three times since then. A preamble sets out journalism's mission of public enlightenment in a democratic society and leads into four major rules, or ethical principles: Seek Truth and Report It; Minimize Harm; Act Independently; and Be Accountable. Several "standards of practice" spell out specific expectations implied by each principle.

The rules of truth telling and minimizing harm often conflict because telling the truth often hurts people.[4] The truth/harm pair is central to cases involving violation of privacy in journalism. Not only do journalists risk harming those whose privacy they violate, but they risk harming third parties who are not the "story" but get hurt nevertheless.

Given how devastating loss of privacy can be, Patterson and Wilkins (2007) say journalists cannot provide a compelling rationale for violating privacy on the basis of a legalistic *right* to know (I will publish whatever I can get away with under the law) or a pandering *want* to know (I will publish whatever my audience is curious about). Rather, journalists must seriously consider whether the public actually *needs* to know the private information to function well in a democratic society. For example, some ethicists have suggested that, while Clinton could be legally compelled to discuss his marital infidelity, and the public may have found the details of his affair titillating, the only person who really *needed* to know was his wife.

Below are excerpts from the SPJ code related to truth telling and minimizing harm. As you read the privacy cases that follow, consider how well these two rules help you to arrive at a decision. Do they shed light on what's ethically relevant about the cases? Do they tell you how the journalists should have proceeded? Do they tell you which options would be completely unethical? Are they contradictory? Do they cover the most important aspects of the problem? Are they flexible enough to fit the complexities of each case? The entire SPJ code can be found at http://www.spj.org/ethicscode.asp.

Seek Truth and Report It

Journalists should be honest, fair and courageous in gathering, reporting and interpreting information.

Journalists should:

- Test the accuracy of information from all sources and exercise care to avoid inadvertent error. Deliberate distortion is never permissible.
- Identify sources whenever feasible. The public is entitled to as much information as possible on sources' reliability.
- Distinguish between advocacy and news reporting. Analysis and commentary should be labeled and should not misrepresent fact or context.

Minimize Harm

Ethical journalists treat sources, subjects and colleagues as human beings deserving of respect.

Journalists should:

- Show compassion for those who may be affected adversely by news coverage.
- Use special sensitivity when dealing with children and inexperienced sources or subjects.
- Be sensitive when seeking or using interviews or photographs of those affected by tragedy or grief.
- Recognize that gathering and reporting information may cause harm or discomfort. Pursuit of the news is not a license for arrogance.
- Recognize that private people have a greater right to control information about themselves than do public officials and others who seek power, influence or attention. Only an overriding public need can justify intrusion into anyone's privacy.
- Show good taste. Avoid pandering to lurid curiosity.

PRIVACY CASES AND WALK-THROUGH EXERCISES

Case 1: Minor Embarrassment or Major Indignity?

In 2003, he was the tyrannical president of Iraq, who exercised almost absolute power over a terrorized people. In 2005, he was just another inmate doing laundry in his underwear. That's what readers of the British *Sun* and the *New York Post* must have thought when they got an eyeful of Saddam Hussein wearing nothing but a pair of white briefs.

Situational Clues

- Allied troops captured Hussein north of Baghdad in December 2003 when they invaded Iraq. Hussein was hiding in a concealed hole in the ground. He was charged with crimes against humanity and detained for trial.
- The crime Hussein was tried for was the 1982 massacre of nearly 150 Shiite Muslim men and boys from Dujail, a small town 40 miles north of Baghdad. Hussein ordered the massacre as payback for a failed assassination attack that took place while he was in Dujail to make a speech. Hussein was responsible for many other killings of Iraqis during his 24-year regime.
- The two papers ran full-size photos of Hussein in black and white on their front pages on Friday, 20 May 2005. The *Sun* featured only the picture with the headline "TYRANT'S IN HIS PANTS." The *Post*'s headline said, "Butcher of Sagdad: Inside Saddam's prison cell." The photo was labeled "EXCLUSIVE." You can see the front page of the *New York Post* at http://wizbangblog.com/content/2005/05/20/murdoch-tabloid.php.
- The newspapers said they got the photo from a military official who was not identified.
- The photograph was a year old.
- It is not known whether Hussein ever saw the photos or was aware of them.

Walk-Through Exercise: Rules or Circumstances?

1. Were the *Sun* and the *Post* ethically justified in publishing this photo? What situational factors did you consider? Which provisions from the SPJ code did you consider?
2. Does the rule "Seek the Truth and Report It" conflict with the rule "Minimize Harm" in this case? If so, how did you decide between them?
3. Were you unsure which situational factors mattered to your ethical judgment? What additional information would help you make a decision?
4. Another possible source for moral rules in this case is the Geneva Conventions for humane treatment of prisoners of war. Article 13 states

that "prisoners of war must at all times be protected, particularly against acts of violence or intimidation and against insults and public curiosity." How do you think this rule applies to the Hussein photo?

5. Did you consider how this case compared with other embarrassing images in the news media?

One Last Look at Embarrassing Images

1. Does picturing people in embarrassing situations reduce them to objects for others to look at?

2. Both papers are tabloids known for their sensationalism. They belong to Australian media magnate Rupert Murdoch, who also owns the conservative Fox network in the United States. Does this make a difference in whether the photo was ethically justified?

3. Some Iraqis said that the images were insulting to Iraq and the rest of the Arab world because they humiliated a former leader in the foreign press. Other Iraqis got some satisfaction from Hussein's comeuppance. "That's the least he deserves," Hawre Saliee, a member of the Kurdish minority targeted for persecution under Hussein, told *USA Today*. How do the reactions of fellow Iraqis factor into your assessment of this case?

4. Iraq, like most Arab countries, has a large Islamic population. Showing someone in his underwear would be deeply offensive to many Muslims based on their religious beliefs about sexual modesty. How does SPJ's principle of "Minimize Harm" apply?

Case 2: Moment of Death[5]

Hussein's underwear routine had no bearing on his public role as the dictator of Iraq. However, his execution for crimes against humanity certainly did. He was convicted by an Iraqi court on 5 November 2006, about two years after being caught by the US military after the Iraq invasion. He was executed on 30 December 2006 before a small group of witnesses in a compound his own government had used for executions. Days later, his hanging would become an Internet sensation and a global scandal. Not only did the images capture what may be the most personal of moments—the moment of death—but they were graphic in a way that makes the underwear photo seem trivial.

Situational Clues

■ The official video shows a judge reading Hussein's sentence out loud. Hussein had a copy of the Qur'an and asked that a friend receive it after his death. His executioners wore black hoods. He declined to wear one himself.

- The hanging lasted briefly and was not shown on Iraqi TV, which aired only official footage of Hussein being led to the execution chamber and his body wrapped in a shroud.
- However, the actual hanging was filmed without authorization on a camera phone and posted a few days later on the Internet, where news organizations downloaded it. The clip showed Shiite executioners shouting sectarian slogans and insulting Hussein all the way to the end.
- The Iraqi prime minister defended both the sentence and the manner of the execution, suggesting that critics were interfering in domestic affairs and showing insensitivity toward the families of Hussein's victims.
- Major news organizations posted or linked to the footage of Hussein's execution, but cut the video before the actual hanging.
- The edgy online magazine *Slate*, however, posted the whole thing with a "graphic content" warning next to a story reporting the execution. The story was headlined "Lynching the Dictator: On Saturday morning, the United States helped to officiate at a human sacrifice" (Hitchens 2007). In the article, Christopher Hitchens condemned capital punishment generally and the execution of the "father of all hangmen" by "unwashed goons" specifically.

Walk-Through Exercise: Images of Death

1. Which was the more ethical course of action: editing the video to omit the hanging or airing the uncut footage with a warning about graphic content?
2. Which details from the case weighed most heavily in your decision? How does the SPJ code address the significance of these details? Would you add anything to the code to make it "fit" these circumstances better?
3. Some people have suggested that all executions should be shown by the news media, since they are carried out by the state and are, therefore, the public's business. What do you think about that idea?
4. Does it make any difference to you that the video of Hussein's hanging was unauthorized? Why or why not?
5. Many news organizations have policies against showing images of the dead. Do you agree with this prohibition? Do you see any problems with it?

One Last Look at Graphic Content

1. The official video released by the Iraqi government shortly after Hussein was hanged had no audio. It showed a fairly calm man accepting his fate with dignity. However, the unauthorized video raised questions about the handling of Hussein's execution, with many Sunnis angered by the overtones of sectarian revenge. The Sunnis and Shiites are branches of

Islam that have been at odds for centuries over political and religious differences. Shiites were persecuted under Hussein, a Sunni. How does the information from the audio affect the ethics of linking to the unauthorized video?

2. Later, another unauthorized video was posted on a pro-Hussein website showing his body lying on a trolley covered in a bloodstained shroud. Someone uncovers the head, which shows a throat injury that could have been caused by hanging. Foreign news organizations also downloaded this clip. What ethical issues are raised by this video? Are they different from the unauthorized video of the hanging?

Case 3: Cheater-in-Chief[6]

President Bill Clinton began an 18-month affair with 22-year-old unpaid White House intern Monica Lewinsky in 1994 in the midst of two legal scandals going back to his days as Arkansas governor. One scandal involved a land development business in the Ozarks with connections to a shady savings and loan company and the other, an accusation of sexual harassment by a state clerical worker. By the time Clinton had put the Lewinsky affair behind him, he had been forced to air his marital dirty laundry before the world, subjecting himself and his family to public humiliation. He also had to defend himself against impeachment charges of perjury and obstruction of justice.

Situational Clues

- The conservative gossip blog *The Drudge Report* uploads a post on 19 January 1998 to the effect that *Newsweek* is sitting on the story of the president's affair with a former White House intern; the unconfirmed report is soon repeated by a number of mainstream news organizations, a pattern that would be repeated throughout the "Monicagate" coverage. Ironically, *Newsweek* had decided it could not responsibly report the affair without better sourcing.

- On 26 January 1998, the president famously lies about his affair with the words, "I did not have sexual relations with that woman, Miss Lewinsky." He delivers the State of the Union address the following day.

- Some of Clinton's closest advisers, as well as his personal secretary, appear before the grand jury. Even his Secret Service agents are compelled to testify, corroborating Lewinsky's assertions about meeting Clinton in the White House.

- On 17 August 1998, Clinton testifies before the grand jury. He acknowledges having had a sexual relationship with Lewinsky but refuses to provide sexual details. Afterward, he goes on TV to admit he had an "inappropriate" relationship with Lewinsky and to apologize for deceiving everyone, including his wife.

MAKING HARD CHOICES IN JOURNALISM ETHICS

- Special prosecutor Kenneth Starr subpoenas records of Lewinsky's book purchases. Among them, the novel *Vox*, about phone sex. Lewinsky is appalled at what she considers an invasion of privacy, which also included the subpoena of her computer's hard drive.
- Lewinsky secures full immunity for herself and her parents on 28 July 1998. As part of her deal with Starr, Lewinsky produces the "smoking gun" of the investigation: a blue dress she says has traces of Clinton's semen.

Walk-Through Exercise: Gossip About Public Figures

1. The tidbit about the "blue dress" is first revealed publicly by *The Drudge Report* in an unsourced posting. Mainstream news media report the rumor before it is confirmed. The garment is sent to the FBI for testing and comes back with a match. Which principle from the SPJ code would provide ethical justification for reporting the blue dress story before it's confirmed? Which principle would provide justification for holding the story?
2. Only about a quarter of the early stories about "Monicagate" were attributed to named sources; only 1 percent of these stories relied on more than one unnamed source (Haas 2003). Should the threshold for verification be higher when we're dealing with rumors about people's private lives? What are the ethical implications of using anonymous sources for a story like this one?
3. How does this case compare with other stories about public officials' sexual indiscretions?

More Situational Clues

- The House Judiciary Committee formally accepts Starr's report on the Whitewater investigation on 11 September 1998 and releases the first 445 pages to the public. The news media promptly publishes the entire report, which is often sexually explicit. Among other facts, it states that Clinton had 10 sexual encounters with Lewinsky in the Oval Office suite. During one of these, he was talking on the phone about military operations in Bosnia.
- Several days later, the Judiciary Committee releases video of Clinton's and Lewinsky's testimonies. Lewinsky's testimony includes sexual details, such as the couple's use of a cigar as a sex toy. The TV networks broadcast the footage right away.
- More than 70 newspapers call for the resignation of the president, whose sex life had become daily fodder for late-night comedy shows.
- The House of Representatives approves two articles of impeachment against Clinton. The impeachment trial begins in the Senate on 7 January

1999, with Supreme Court Justice William Rehnquist presiding. The trial goes on during US-British bombings of Iraq following Saddam Hussein's refusal to submit to UN weapons inspections.

■ The president is acquitted on 12 February 1999.

Walk-Through Exercise: Intrusive Details

1. Do you think the news media acted ethically in reporting intimate sexual details about Clinton's affair with Lewinsky? Which facts from the case most influenced your decision?
2. Does it make a difference that the details were provided in an official report released to the public? Why or why not?
3. There was real concern at the time that the president's behavior had undermined the dignity of the office. However, there was no evidence that the president's job performance had been negatively affected by the affair (at least not until he became distracted by Starr's investigation). News coverage reflected this, with journalists speculating mostly on the president's political fortunes. So, were the sexual details reported by the news media necessary or just interesting? How do you figure out what the public really needs to know?
4. Whom should the journalists have considered when applying SPJ's principle of "Minimize Harm" in this case? Does anyone deserve special consideration?
5. As a seasoned public figure who had already weathered several scandals during his presidential campaign, Clinton had reason to expect his personal affairs to be scrutinized. But what about Lewinsky? What about people connected to public figures generally, such as family members or friends?

Case 4: Privacy Invasion Goes Viral[7]

Eighteen-year-old Nikki Catsouras died after she wrecked her father's Porsche on 31 October 2006, in Orange County, California. And the Internet hasn't let her family forget it.

Situational Clues

■ Nikki was decapitated in the accident, a scene so horrible that the coroner prevented her parents from identifying her body. Two California state troopers, however, preserved the image of the bloodied teenager with a digital camera. Authorities responding to accidents typically document the scene with photographs.
■ Two dispatchers later emailed some of the pictures to their own family and friends, without authorization. The images went viral, turning up on

24

pornography sites, a fake MySpace page in Nikki's name (where commentators derided her as a "spoiled rich girl" who "wasted" a Porsche) and her father's own inbox. The anonymous email message contained an image of Nikki's injured face and said, "Hey daddy, I'm still alive" (Bennett 2009: 38–39).

- The family is worried that they will stumble upon the wreck photos whenever they go online and are all under psychiatric care.
- *Newsweek* reported on the Catsouras' lawsuit. Although it didn't publish the goriest photos, it acknowledged that its story might prompt readers to seek them out.

Walk-Through Exercise: Survivor Privacy

1. The Supreme Court in 1993 recognized a legal right to "survivor privacy"—the right surviving family members have to control personal information about deceased loved ones for their own peace of mind. The court cited longstanding cultural practices of respecting families' control over death-scene images of close relatives. How does this concept square with the way you think about privacy rights?

2. Nikki was high on cocaine when she was killed. She had taken the drug the night before and was sleeping it off at home in anticipation of an appointment with a psychiatrist the following day. Her parents, Christos and Lesli Catsouras, had taken her to the hospital once before for treatment of cocaine-related symptoms. Do these facts have any ethical relevance? Why or why not?

3. Once again, we're dealing with unauthorized images of a person's death. How does this case compare with the video of Saddam Hussein's hanging?

4. Given the trauma and lack of privacy suffered by the Catsouras, was *Newsweek* justified in calling more attention to the accident photos? Does the family's cooperation affect your assessment? Which SPJ principle provides guidance on this issue? Are there any circumstances in which you would choose against harming someone even if he or she consented to it? Does the SPJ code cover this kind of situation?

5. Law professor Jeffrey Rosen (2000: 19) discusses an alternative to the US notion of privacy based on property. In Jewish law, protecting privacy is about avoiding the injury caused by the "unwanted gaze." The idea is that we are violated by unwanted surveillance, even if it's just a possibility—as when our house window opens up to a common courtyard, or strangers might be getting notifications about the latest activity on our Facebook page. Does thinking of privacy in this way change your view of the Catsouras case?

Case 5: Without a Voice[8]

Terry Schiavo, 41, died on 31 March 2005 under hospice care in St Petersburg, Florida, after a widely reported legal battle between her husband and her parents over what should become of her after a heart attack that left her in a permanent vegetative state. Schiavo, who died cradled in her husband's arms, was in no position to consent or refuse.

Situational Clues

- Schiavo suffered a heart attack in 1990 that deprived her of oxygen, causing severe brain damage. Her husband, Michael, told the press that his wife was bulimic and that her disease may have caused the potassium imbalance that had led to her heart attack.
- Mr Schiavo said he had pledged to his wife that he would not keep her alive with machines.
- Three out of five doctors who testified before the state court of appeals in Mrs Schiavo's case said there was no hope for recovery. Two doctors chosen by Mrs Schiavo's parents said she could improve with treatment. The court ruled that her feeding tube could be removed.
- Under Florida law, the spouse is the legal guardian of incapacitated persons. Mr Schiavo said his wife wouldn't want to live in her condition and asked to have the feeding tube that was keeping her alive removed.
- Schiavo's parents, Mary and Robert Schindler, began fighting Mr Schiavo in court in 1993, citing their daughter's will to live. They fought unsuccessfully in state and federal courts to obtain guardianship of their daughter until the Supreme Court turned down their appeal in 2005. Mrs Schiavo's parents are Catholic. According to Catholic teaching, removing the tube that was nourishing their daughter amounted to starving her to death.
- Mrs Schiavo's plight became fodder for state and national political discourse. Florida's governor intervened in Schiavo's case in 2003 to ensure she continued to be fed via a tube. Pro-life members of Congress decried the "culture of death" as the parents' legal alternatives dwindled. President George W. Bush noted his disappointment when a court ultimately authorized the removal of her feeding tube.
- Besides reporting on the legal milestones, the news media distributed photographs and videos of Schiavo that were criticized as intrusive, undignified and misleading—even obscene. "From the close-ups that relentlessly zeroed in on Schiavo's gaping mouth to the O.J. Simpson-like video of a white van bearing away her body, news coverage has been a lascivious feast of gruesome details," wrote Kay McFadden (2005) in *The Seattle Times*.

Walk-Through Exercise: Private People, Public Policy

1. Which situational factors would you look at if you were deciding whether to invade Mr Schiavo's privacy? Would you look at the same factors when considering the Schindlers? How about Mrs Schiavo herself?

2. Seek out some of the media images of Mrs Schiavo on the Internet. Do you think they are beneficial in any way? To whom? Do you think they are harmful? To whom?

3. Shortly before she died, a probate court in Florida released nine videos of Mrs Schiavo filmed in 2002 for her parents' case before the state court of appeals. Two additional videos were sealed; no reason was given. The videos were soon posted on the Internet, where pro-life advocates pointed to what they saw as evidence of brain activity, including smiling in response to music and laughing at a story her father was telling her about her childhood. However, the autopsy performed on Mrs Schiavo confirmed that her brain damage was severe and irreversible. She was completely blind. How do these facts affect your assessment of the images' harms and benefits? Their relevance to the wider public debate about euthanasia?

4. Do you think the images were used appropriately by the news media? How does the concept of a quasar play into your judgment? Survivor privacy?

Case 6: Without a Vote

Terri Schiavo probably wouldn't have wanted her medical condition to be so widely known, but we'll never know for sure. At any rate, we all assume that, if we get sick, it'll be our choice who knows, how and when. But what if you're a celebrity? Isn't your health automatically "news"? Should you expect to keep your health to yourself? A number of cases have forced journalists to reckon with this question. One of the best known is the "outing" of former tennis star Arthur Ashe.

Situational Clues

- Ashe was the first African American to win Wimbledon and the US Open. He stopped playing tennis in 1979 after suffering a heart attack. He was also well known as an outspoken critic of South Africa's racist policy of apartheid.

- Ashe learns he has AIDS in 1988 when his blood tested positive for the disease during a routine screening in preparation for brain surgery. He thinks he contracted it in 1983 when inadequate screening failed to catch contaminated blood used in a transfusion for his second heart surgery. He told friends and family, but no one else.

- A source tips off *USA TODAY* about Ashe's health condition. When reporter Doug Smith pursues it with him on 8 April 1992, Ashe asks to speak with an editor. When he gets Gene Policinski, managing editor for sports, on the phone, he declines to provide confirmation and asks for 36 hours to make a statment. The paper holds off on the story.
- Ashe calls a news conference the next day and confirms the rumor with the *USA TODAY* reporter in an interview beforehand. *USA TODAY* put the story out on the wire service run by its parent company, which also owns CNN. During the news conference, Ashe complains that he was forced to reveal his illness because someone "ratted" on him. "It put me in the unenviable position of having to lie if I wanted to protect our privacy. No one should have to make that choice" ("Arthur Ashe vows to go forward," 27 April 1992).
- He breaks down while talking about the effect this will have on his 5-year-old daughter, Camera, who will now be forced to deal with derogatory remarks about her father's condition.
- After his "outing," Ashe becomes an AIDS activist and raises money for a cure. He dies of pneumonia less than a year after his press conference.

Walk-Through Exercise: Forced Revelations

1. Ashe claimed during his press conference that he shouldn't have had to reveal his illness because he wasn't running for office or otherwise asking to be entrusted with public business. What do you think of this argument? Does the SPJ code address Ashe's concern? Should it?
2. Did *USA TODAY* invade Ashe's privacy by just asking about his HIV status? Or was his privacy intact as long as the paper did not actually report that he had AIDS?
3. Duke Ellington and other artists over the years decided not to disclose cancer diagnoses to avoid having their bookings cancelled and to keep on working. Sometimes, however, artists willingly disclose serious illnesses. For example, actor Michael J. Fox, then the star of the ABC sitcom *Sin City*, disclosed in 1998 that he had been diagnosed with Parkinson's disease seven years earlier. Former *Charlie's Angels* star Farrah Fawcett announced in 2006 that she had been diagnosed with anal cancer and filmed a documentary about her search for a cure that aired in May 2009 on NBC. How does the concept of consent play into your judgment about the ethics of reporting on the terminal illnesses of celebrities?

One Last Look at Stigmas

1. AIDS was first identified in the United States in 1981. After that, the number of cases quickly multiplied. The disease was a death sentence until doctors developed a successful drug therapy that now allows people

infected with the HIV virus to manage the disease. This therapy, however, did not become widely available until 1996.

2. In the 1990s, the disease carried the stigma of being a "gay disease," since the vast majority of US patients with AIDS were male, and most people diagnosed with AIDS became infected through male-to-male sexual contact. This remains true today, though an increasing number of US women are contracting the virus via risky sex with men, according to the international AIDS charity, AVERT (http://www.avert.or statistics.htm). Sex between men and women is the major transmission route for AIDS in Africa.

3. How do these facts affect your views about the ethics of reporting Ashe's illness? Does Ashe's failure to fit the stereotype of AIDS make his outing more important? And does this override his desire for privacy? Does this case raise similar ethical issues to the case of naming rape victims?

CHAPTER 2

▼ THE ROLE OF ETHICAL THEORY

This book's approach to controversial cases in journalism is a bottom-up form of reasoning. Philosophers call it inductive; classical theorists call it casuistry; you can think of it as *CSI* for journalists.

Take these examples:

■ News organizations often assign African American reporters to stories focused on black communities. These reporters are assumed to have access to black sources that white reporters would not have. They are assumed to have an understanding of the African American culture that will build a stronger story with more context and insight, especially when the stories are controversial or complex. Are such assumptions accurate or racist? And even if true, do the very qualities the black reporters may have (understanding and empathy with other African Americans) undermine their independence, creating a conflict of interest?

■ What about the reporter whose father is an oil company executive? He wants to cover the energy industry he has known from childhood. Does growing up "inside" the energy industry create a unique understanding of the issues or an unconscious bias that threatens his reporting?

Journalists have tended to judge these two situations very differently. Research shows that they are more likely to see the advantage of empathy and access in the case of the black reporter—and more likely to see the potential for bias in the energy reporter (McAdams and Yopp 2003: 192–206).

Whether these journalists were right or not isn't the main point here. The point is that a fundamental question about how journalists protect their independence can't be answered without attention to the details of the case. In fact, resolving either of the cases presented above would take far more information about the reporters, their beats, and the particular stories being reported. Do the black reporters have strong connections to the African American communities in this city or not? Does the son of the energy executive have experience or educational training outside the oil industry that would provide a critical balance to his perspective? Case-based reasoning requires what anthropologist Clifford Geertz (1994: 228) calls a "thick description" of a case before moving toward a decision. As we discussed in the first chapter, this process involves a *CSI*-style "walk-through," gathering all the information we can about the case, then asking what other details we need to know before we draw any conclusions.

However, intense focus on the details of cases does not mean casuistry rejects the use of ethical theory. Indeed, ethical theory is an indispensable part of journalism ethics. This chapter will offer a look at the top-down approach of ethical theory as a valuable complement to the bottom-up approach of case-based reasoning.

TOP-DOWN APPROACHES TO TACKLING CASES

Ethical theory identifies formal ethical norms, such as Kant's categorical imperative, and moral virtues. In the hands of skilled ethicists, these are rigorous concepts that justify our ethical decisions in ways that our common sense does not (Glasser and Ettema 2008). These norms are then applied to cases. This is particularly useful in moments of ethical clarity. In these moments, theory takes over the ethical debate.

For example, at *The Courier-Journal*, this approach shaped the conflict-of-interest policy under Barry Bingham, Jr, in the 1970s. Bingham wanted to protect the independence of the newspaper. So all gifts to reporters, editors, and managers were banned. Gifts that could not be returned were sent to a central office and auctioned off once a year, with the money donated to charity. The newspaper moved out of the free space provided in the statehouse in Frankfort, Kentucky, renting a house for journalists covering state government. Checks were sent to publishers to pay for books sent for review. Bingham even cut his personal ties to the politically active Sloane family (Boeyink 1998: 171–172).

At *The Courier-Journal* in this period, freebies were not a topic for case-based reasoning. The principle—independence—was clear; its application was absolute. Bingham believed this rigid position protected *The Courier-Journal* from conflicts of interest without sacrificing its ability to report.

Given the value ethical theory can play in such cases, let's take a look at some of the options you have in ethical theory. We won't present every possible theory. We will discuss some of the most widely accepted—and useful— options: theories based on duty, consequences, care, and character.

Theories that Focus on Duties

The two dominant approaches to ethical theory over the last century offer radically different visions of the nature of ethical obligations even though they both focus on principles. However, as you will see, the differences for controversial cases in journalism may be less dramatic.

The first of these theoretical approaches focuses on duty. Our ethical obligations are said to be deontological, grounded in the nature of the act itself. Unless you want to impress your friends, you don't need to remember the word "deontology." What you should remember is that this approach claims that certain acts have a quality that makes them right or wrong. When a good friend lies to you, you have no problem telling your soon-to-be ex-friend that lying is wrong. (You might say other things, too, but we can't print those. This is an ethics textbook.)

Immanuel Kant (1956a: 15–16), one of the major proponents of duty-based theory, argued that ethical duties were grounded in reason. To oversimplify Kant's view, certain acts are right because they are not self-contradictory. That is, they can be universalized. Lying, on the other hand, can't be universalized. The person who lies makes a "free-rider" assumption (Bok 1979: 24). The lie works only if others believe it is the truth. The lie gets a free ride on the general expectation that you are not lying. If you universalize the lie, that expectation breaks down and the lie fails to have any effect — except to identify you as a liar. In Kant's words, the lie is inherently irrational. Only actions that can be universalized without self-destructing — like truth telling — are ethically justified.

Kant's general defense of universal ethical principles — and, more specifically, the duty to respect all persons — is an important contribution to the way we think about ethics today. Kant's insistence on the universality of ethical principles pushes against seeing principles as only a matter of personal opinion (individualist relativism) or social convention (conventionalist relativism). His argument that certain principles apply to everyone is needed if we are to have any justification for judging the actions of others.

Moreover, one formulation of Kant's categorical imperative — "Act in such a way that you always treat humanity, whether in your own person or in the person of any other, never simply as a means, but always at the same time as an end" — is widely recognized as a basis for how we should deal ethically with others (Kant 1956b: 96). You can remember this as a simple formula: don't use people. This idea, that all human beings (including oneself) should be treated with respect, has been one of Kant's enduring contributions to ethics.

Unfortunately, Kant's intellectual rigor in the world of reason was not matched by a compelling analysis of conflicts in daily life. Kant argued that the duty to tell the truth was without exception — even if a murderer was at the door asking for the whereabouts of your neighbor, now hiding in your house. Kant was worried that once exceptions were made, it wouldn't be long before all kinds of rationalizations were offered that would allow people to do what they wanted. Fair enough. Yet this inflexibility makes adopting a Kantian system of principles impossible for journalists.

Fortunately, another deontological theory offers a more practical way of resolving complex cases. Unlike Kant, W.D. Ross placed more importance on the real world in which we live. Ross thought that moral duties were created by concrete human interactions. Our nature as social beings places us in contact with others. These contacts, Ross (1930: 19–21) argued, can some-times result in ethical obligations. For example, if you make a promise to a source to keep her name confidential, that promise creates an obligation on you to fulfill that promise. When we encounter a child in danger, our physical proximity to that child creates an obligation to protect him from harm.

Ross offered a list of duties he recognized as morally obligatory in human relations:

- Fidelity (keeping your promises, including the implicit promise not to lie)
- Reparation (repaying others for harm done to them)
- Gratitude (repaying others for services done to you)
- Justice (fairness in the distribution of some good)
- Beneficence (doing good for others)
- Self-improvement (making yourself a better person)
- Non-maleficence (not injuring others, especially the innocent)

One can argue that other duties might be added to this list, such as Kant's "respect for persons." One might also argue that some duties could be deleted, such as the duty of gratitude. (Do we really have a duty to pay back a kindness?) The exact nature of the list is not crucial at this point. What is crucial is Ross' understanding that, in any conflict of duties, these duties may be of variable weight or importance. That gets us out of the uncompromising Kantian view that we can never violate any ethical principle.

Cases involving conflict of interest illustrate the point. Reporter–source relationships are fraught with conflict, especially sensitive beats like the cops. Reporters depend on the police for information (truth). At the same time, this dependence can raise expectations of a quid pro quo: Out of gratitude for police cooperation in providing information, reporters may be expected to keep quiet about a controversy in the department or slant a story in a way more favorable to the police. In other words, the very thing that Ross sees as the basis for our ethical obligations (human relations) creates a conflict of principles.

To handle this conflict, Ross (1930: 18–20) made a distinction between *prima facie* duties and duty proper. *Prima facie* means roughly "at first glance." For Ross, this meant that any act involving truth telling always includes an element that makes that act right. This is his way of affirming Kant's universal principles: Telling the truth is always (*prima facie*) right. Lying is always (*prima facie*) wrong.

However, with principles in conflict, the same act can be both right and wrong at the level of *prima facie* duty. As a police reporter, you may need to choose between continuing to get inside information from the police (truth telling) while cutting the police slack on the rumors of sexual harassment in the department (gratitude) or risk cutting off your sources by digging into the harassment rumors (justice).

This kind of conflict should be expected in all human relations, Ross said. It certainly can be expected in journalism when the telling of important stories means someone could be hurt in the process. The next thing to do is figure out one's duty proper, according to Ross, by weighing the conflicting duties in any case to decide which is most important. That's the actual duty, what Ross called the duty proper. Ross had no magic formula for determining which duty carries the most weight. All he asked is that we think it through carefully in light of the details of the case and make our best judgment.

Interestingly, this intuitive process recommended by Ross, grounded in the details of the concrete case, sounds a lot like case-based reasoning. After all, Kenneth Kirk, one of the great defenders of casuistry in the twentieth century, argued that one important use of casuistry was to deal with cases in which we faced a conflict of principles (Kirk 1999: 110–111). But case-based reasoning offers a stronger methodological approach than "intuition" to deal with this conflict. We'll get to that in Chapter 3. But first, let's look at another approach to ethical theory: consequences.

Theories that Focus on Consequences

Ethical theories based on consequences begin in a very different place. Instead of seeing the basis for deciding what is right in definite circumstances such as past actions, these teleological theories (telos = end) define what is right in terms of the future. An act is right if it produces good consequences. Simple enough.

W.D. Ross also included duties involving consequences. The key difference between Ross and consequentialists is that consequentialist theories argue that consequences are the only basis for deciding what is right. The dominant form of consequentialist theory is utilitarianism. And utilitarianism comes in two main varieties: act utilitarianism and rule utilitarianism. Both are important to understand if you are to make your way through the thicket of ethical theory. So let's begin with the simpler form: act utility.

Act utility argues that, when we face any decision, we should always seek to produce the greatest good for the greatest number. In other words, we should seek to maximize the good at every moment. Consider all of the major alternatives in any situation. Take account of all the people who will be affected by your action. Decide what counts as good (pleasure, happiness, security, health, knowledge, etc.) Then, to the best of your ability, predict which action will produce the greatest balance of good consequences over bad consequences. That's the right action for the act utilitarian.

OK. So it's not so simple. When Jeremy Bentham worked out his system of utilitarianism, he created a hedonic calculus (hedonic because the good he sought was pleasure—sort of like some college students). Acts that produced a greater balance of good over harm were purer and counted for more. Acts that had a ripple effect in continuing to produce good into the future (fecundity) also counted for more. Bentham's calculus had a certain logic to it, but the difficulty was in actually converting ethics into a kind of mathematical formula (Bentham 1948: 29–32). Try it yourself sometime when faced with a tough decision, and you'll see.

And that's not the only problem with act utility. Calculating the consequences of every act we take—or only the important ones—is a daunting task. Sort of like taking a math final every day. More critically, act utility carries the problem of prediction. For the consequentialist, the whole moral universe depends on predicting the future. And how good are you at that? Until we have a computer simulation model for our personal lives, our batting average on knowing the future is rarely good enough to make the major leagues.

Utilitarians have an answer to this, of course. According to this theory, the rightness of an act does not hinge on the actual results, only on a reasonable estimate of what could result. In other words, the proof is not in the pudding but in the recipe. You'll have to decide how that tastes.

Finally, act utility has to deal with the problem of injustice. To be fair to act utility, the greatest good for the greatest number includes the interests of everyone. Each person's good counts in the calculus. That's better than more limited cost/benefit analyses that consider only what's good for oneself, one's company or one's community. But this form of consequentialism doesn't include a principle of distribution. Only the total good counts, not whether one person or group gets more than someone else. Used in a social context, the majority rules. Nothing prevents discrimination against any group or individual for the sake of the greater good.

The 1986 photo of a dead child in Bakersfield, California, illustrates the problem. When photographer John Harte took a photo of a family grieving over the body of a dead son, the journalists in the newsroom argued that publishing that photo could save another child's life by warning parents to be careful of accidental drownings in recreational lakes ("Grief Photo" 41: 17–18, 20). Publishing this photo of a moment of intense grief may harm the family, but the greater good of water safety could be served. The interests of the family in being shielded at this moment of private anguish could be considered, but it was outweighed by the greater good.

Fortunately, many of the shortcomings of act utility are addressed in rule utilitarianism, a form of utilitarianism often associated with John Stuart Mill. Deni Elliott (2007: 105–107) argues that Mill was not proposing some arithmetic calculation for determining what was right. Rather, it was the aggregate good of all concerned that determines what we ought to do. Here's the difference: in contrast to act utility, Mill (1956:14) wanted us to consider "utility in the largest sense, grounded on the permanent interests of man as a progressive being," when we decide what is right. We should consider what kind of society would foster the progress of individuals.

In effect, Mill suggested that we ask what kind of society we want to live in. He sees a society of values and principles (liberty, justice, concern for others, civil rights, a commitment to truth) available to all and binding on all. In the end, Mill still sees utility as the sole ground of morality. But we don't produce the greatest good for the greatest number by calculating it one act at a time.

As Elliott notes, this leads us to a very different judgment of the photo of the grieving family. Whatever value such a photo might have in promoting water safety, the family does not deserve this publicity (Elliott 2007: 109). More important, the exploitation of this family is a concern for the whole society; their vulnerability at that moment becomes our own vulnerability at some unknown time in the future. This is not a case of the interests of the many arithmetically outweighing the interests of the few. This is a case of seeing the interests of everyone in protecting the privacy of that family because that reflects the goodness of the society we want to build.

The strategy here—unlike act utility—is to ask what kind of rules would produce the greatest good, the best society. Mill certainly argued this when he offered a utilitarian justification for gender equality (justice) in nineteenth-century English society (Mill 1956).

In practical terms, then, deontology and rule utility are not as far apart as one might imagine. Both lead us to a set of principles that serve as standards of what is right. We are left with a very different interpretation of why these rules are ethically binding. For the deontologists, such as Ross, ethical obligations are grounded in concrete relations and the nature of the actions we take in these relations. For utilitarians such as Mill, it is the good that results from following these rules that gives them force. It's up to you to decide which account rings true to your sense of ethical obligation.

PERSON-CENTERED APPROACHES TO TACKLING CASES

The ethical approaches discussed so far have focused on principles to determine our responsibilities. The next two approaches focus more sharply on role models for being a good person, not principles. The first approach is an ethics of care; the second, an ethics of character. These approaches are concerned with a different question in ethics. The ethical theories of duty (Kant and Ross) and utility (Bentham and Mill) are concerned with what we ought to *do*; the ethics of care and character ask who we should *be*.

Theories that Focus on Care

Lawrence Kohlberg, a Harvard psychologist, developed a theory of moral development in which an individual's ethical reasoning evolves through a series of stages. At the lowest level, decisions are made based on self-interest: the actions that would avoid punishment or gain some reward are considered the right actions. Later, ethical standards are shaped by the social groups to which one belongs, eventually becoming internalized. At the highest levels, an individual begins to exercise independent judgment, critically evaluating the ethical values of one's society and ultimately acting out of a sense of universal principles (Kohlberg 1969: 376).

Not everyone reached these last stages. In fact, Kohlberg argued that only a few people really lived out an ethic of universal principles. However, men were more likely to reach these stages of independent judgment and universal principles than women. Women, Kohlberg found, were more likely to be clustered among those whose ethical reasoning was grounded in the norms of social groups.

Carol Gilligan, a student of Kohlberg, challenged Kohlberg's conclusion that women tended to be less ethically developed than men (Gilligan 1993: 5–23). She argued that Kohlberg's hierarchical model was built on flawed research design: Kohlberg's early research subjects were males. Based on her own research interviewing women about ethical decisions, both hypothetical and personal, Gilligan did find that women were less likely to appeal to abstract universal principles. However, she interpreted this as evidence of a different way of thinking about ethics, not evidence of women's second-class moral status.

In our culture, males are more likely to see ethical choices in terms of black and white, not grey, Gilligan argued. A choice is clearly right or wrong because it supports or violates some universal principle. On the other hand, women are more likely to be concerned about how a decision affects the relationships and feelings of the people involved.[1] How will a decision to get a divorce in the face of infidelity affect the children? Will the publication of a shoplifting charge against a gifted schoolteacher alter her relationship to her students? Women tend to turn to natural models of caring in their own lives for guidance on how to deal with such questions, instead of principles. They tend to act from a caring disposition, striving to be responsive to the needs and feelings of others, instead of limiting their response to what is required by principle.

This ethics of care is part of a growing tradition of feminist research. Gilligan's work has been supported and extended by many others, including Mary Belenky and her associates (1997), who documented the different ways men and women approach learning, or popular authors such as Deborah Tannen (*You Just Don't Understand*) and John Gray (*Men are From Mars; Women are From Venus*).

A word of caution: Gilligan's argument is cultural, not biological. Men can be caring and nurturing; women can reason from universal principles. Indeed, Gilligan sees these two ways of thinking about ethics as complementary, not contradictory—just as we are arguing that case-based and theory-based approaches combine for a more complete ethical strategy. All Gilligan argued is that the tendency for men and women to reason ethically in different ways is part of our culture.

It would be easy to dismiss an ethic for journalism grounded in caring. Based in particular relationships, care-based ethics seems to condone partiality. The key ethical question is what action will sustain those relationships in which we find ourselves, especially with family and friends. Most journalism is practiced in institutional settings, not interpersonal settings. Institutions require rules to ensure that all sources are treated fairly. Everyone's arrest gets published on the records page. Policies are set for the naming of rape victims. Rules governing freebies and memberships in organizations protect journalists from conflicts of interest. At first glance, an ethic of care looks like a round peg in a square hole for journalists.

Care-based ethics also emphasizes feelings as legitimate considerations in moral reasoning. That's clearly different than the rational focus of deontology and utilitarianism. Indeed, standards of objectivity in journalism seem to impose a rigid moral neutrality in which journalists leave their personal values at the door. Strike two.

But this analysis is short-sighted. In some cases, an ethic of care can support the most basic goals of good journalism. In other cases, an ethic of care can temper or even challenge rigid journalistic positions. Consider these examples:

- Traditional reporting often involves covering official meetings and interviewing official sources—the people with power to make decisions. What happens when the reporting is not top-down, but bottom-up, talking to the people about the effect that official decisions have on their lives?

Twin Cities Public Television's documentary, "Living with a Hole in Your Pocket," brings us voices of people struggling to get out of poverty, only to be blocked by the rules of the bureaucracy ("Living" 2008).

- Journalists are charged with reporting on the whole community and writing for the community. But how can journalists report on diverse communities if they cannot empathize with them? How can journalists "talk across difference" if they are not able to reach across difference and understand how we are different and how we are the same?
- Why is it that surveys of audiences repeatedly show that people don't think journalists care whether they hurt people or not? Is it because objectivity creates that moral distance?
- Despite digital manipulation, the photograph is still recognized as one of the most objective pieces of information in the media. In a concrete way, that objectivity is reinforced by the camera that stands between photographer and subject. But when Cindy Brown (1998) explored the link between photographer and subject in her doctoral dissertation, she found that many subjects of photos felt an important relationship with the photographer that was more meaningful to them than the image reflected into the camera.
- Edward R. Murrow's classic 1960 broadcast, "Harvest of Shame," documented the plight of the migrant worker in America. Although the documentary included facts about the average wage of the migrants, one of Murrow's aims was to create a relationship between these workers and his audience. Early in the documentary, he says, "I want you to meet some of the people responsible for making us the best-fed people in the world" (Murrow 2005).

Here's the key point: Journalism's commitment to principles does not need to be abandoned, but neither does an ethic of care need to be ignored. To take an ethic of care seriously is to emphasize the value of empathy for others in reporting and the value of human relationships and community in writing. That would not jeopardize journalism; it could enrich it.

Theories That Focus on Character

If an ethic of care focuses our attention on the subjects of reporting, an ethic of character focuses attention on the journalist. In a nutshell, virtues are enduring traits of character. If a friend consistently acts in a considerate way, we may conclude that she is kind. We could be wrong, of course. She could be feigning concern for others to fool them. But the more evidence we have over time, the more we can trust it to be a true quality of her character.

As children, we looked up to people we could trust. Often these would be parents or religious leaders. Perhaps they were just kindly neighbors who seemed to care about others. And it wasn't always a matter of what they did.

They were just good people. Character, like care, focuses less on principles and more on role models.

As young journalists, you may have identified one or more role models. Perhaps it's Carol Marin, who led a bold experiment in bringing substantive news to Chicago's WBBM late-night news. Perhaps it's I.F. Stone, who proved long ago an individual working alone could break political news in Washington, D.C. Or Murrow, whose courage in standing up for migrant labor and against Joseph McCarthy was legendary. All of these journalists did the right things, but we admire them for something more—the idea of what they stand for.

Character says something about the whole person, not just what she does. Character can promote the right action, but that's not the whole story. Character also focuses on a *telos*, or end. But unlike utilitarianism, the *end* is the good of a whole human life (Borden 2007: 16). In other words, character is holistic. It focuses on our history as a lifelong narrative: our will, our feelings, our thoughts (MacIntyre 2007: 204–205). Virtue is nothing less than our moral identity.

Even though it is helpful to distinguish judgments of character (who we are) from judgments of obligation (what we should do), these theories are connected in important ways.

- First, who we are affects what we do. An honest person is more likely to tell the truth. A courageous person will take action in the face of opposition. An important part of what we mean by character is the will or motivation to do what is right. As Sandra Borden (2007: 17) has argued, "[v]irtue theory's emphasis on the habitual disposition to do the right thing also takes morality out of the realm of calculations and into the realm of moral responsiveness." The result is a greater guarantee of constancy, even under pressure.
- Second, we can become virtuous—or vicious—through our actions. Aristotle argued that habit produces moral virtues. If we were raised to tell the truth, over time these actions turn us into honest people, even when we are not looking. The same applies to lying. We often say that the first lie is harder than the second. And if the lies become a way of life, we become dishonest people.
- Third, we can become better people—and act more ethically—by reading and thinking about ethics, just as you are doing now. Aristotle said reflection and experience produce intellectual virtues. The moral virtues help us know what's good; the intellectual virtues help us to recognize virtuous means for attaining what's good. Thomas Lickona (1992) has documented the positive effect on character and behavior that follows academic study in ethics.

In his "I Have a Dream" speech in Washington, D.C., Martin Luther King, Jr (1963) dreamed of the day when people would be judged by the content of their character, not the color of their skin. So what would we find when we look for the content of a person's character? The classical Western virtues are temperance (moderation), prudence (wisdom), fortitude (courage) and justice (giving others their due). That's not a bad list for starters. If all people were wise, courageous, fair, and moderate, this would be a good world.

Yet this list may not capture everything we admire in others. Wikipedia lists more than 120 virtues ("Virtues and values"). Here are 12 Wikipedia entries in the virtue sweepstakes: altruism, creativity, discernment, empathy, flexibility, forgiveness, honesty, humor, loyalty, nonviolence, self-awareness, and tolerance. Many of these add dimensions to character not easily captured by the big four. This multiplicity of virtues has important advantages. What we treasured about our grandfather was his humility. What we seek in a trusted friend is a forgiving spirit. In the same way that we need to define what counts as good for a utilitarian journalist, we need to define what counts as good for a journalist of high character.

Although honesty, bravery and compassion are all good generally, the relative importance of these and other character traits is certain to vary, depending on our role or profession. A good judge needs impartiality and wisdom more than others. A good soldier needs courage and commitment more than others. A good journalist needs honesty and . . . ? How you finish that sentence will say a lot about the kind of journalist you want to be. What are the ends journalists ought to seek? And what virtues are best suited to help us reach those ends? Is empathy or detachment next on your list? Fairness or flexi- bility? Idealism or pragmatism? We'll argue later that specific virtues are essential to the work of journalists, especially in making ethical choices. If you can't wait, see Chapter 6.

The alternatives posed above raise an interesting issue for our understanding of character. Not all traits of character listed by the diverse contributors to the Wikipedia site fit easily together. Can one be both compassionate and fair? Do loyalty and cooperativeness threaten creativity and candor? Alasdair MacIntyre (2007: 218–220) argued that unity was an essential quality of the moral life. We recognize this when we see someone who "has it all together." A moral exemplar would not be both wise and unjust. The people we admire are a complete package. Whatever character traits you choose as a virtuous journalist, they need to form a cohesive whole. And if possible, the character you foster as journalist needs to fit the character you bring to your personal life and your life as citizen. This unity of character is what virtue theorists call "integrity."

The question of character is particularly relevant to the approach of this book. By advocating a bottom-up approach to ethics—focusing on the details of controversial cases—we gain more flexibility in reaching ethical judgments about individual cases than if we simply applied principles from the top down. As Kant feared, the casuist has more room for rationalization, for basing decisions on the particulars of each case. This means that the casuist needs to be someone of good character: wise, creative, focused, consistent, and above all, discerning.

If any quality of character has been seen to rise to the top of the heap for case-based reasoning, it is discernment (Jonsen and Toulmin 1988: 9–10). Discernment allows the casuist to see which features of the case are ethically relevant and which are not. Discernment allows the casuist to sort out which cases are similar and which are not. Case-based reasoning is not for the faint of heart. Weak character will lead to bad casuistry. Only someone who has the tools to engage "with discernment" in the complexity of controversial cases need apply. The goal of this book is to help you to do just that.

WHY PROFESSIONAL ETHICS MATTERS

This chapter has focused on the place of ethical theory in the context of a case-based approach. In doing so, we have reviewed a handful of the major ethical theories you will find useful in resolving ethical issues as a professional journalist. However, you also need to understand that approaching controversial cases as a professional journalist alters the landscape of ethical theory in two important ways. First, professional ethics alters the priority of ethical norms. Second, professional ethics alters the meaning of ethical norms.

Imagine for a moment that you are a physician. What are the most important ethical goods you value when you head to work? If you think like a utilitarian, the good that is central to your work is health. If you carry W.D. Ross' duties into the examining room, you might remember the injunction, "Above all, do no harm." In a similar way, a lawyer or judge would see justice is the ultimate ethical principle driving the legal system.

For the professional journalist, the answer also seems clear. We are in the communication business. We traffic in the truth. If we can't live up to that ethical norm, we have no value as journalists.

But you can go even further in exploring the priority of ethical norms as a journalist. Not all journalists think of their profession in the same way. A documentary videographer will still be committed to the truth. But justice may be equally important for her understanding of journalistic work: showing us the consequences of illness without health insurance, the abuse of illegal immigrants, or discrimination against gay couples. In other words, the ordering of ethical norms will vary, depending on the way you understand your role as a professional journalist: objective gatherer of information, watchdog on government, or advocate for social causes.

Being a professional journalist can also shape what we mean by ethical language. Both lawyers and journalists use the language of confidentiality. But the meaning of this professional obligation of lawyer to client and journalist to source is exactly reversed. For the lawyer, confidentiality means keeping the client's information secret. For the journalist, it means keeping the identity of the source secret while broadcasting the information to millions.

In a similar way, the obligation to tell the truth means something different to a journalist than to a non-journalist. Normally, the obligation to tell the truth to another person is limited to not lying when we speak. A person may have information—even information someone wants—but is often under no obligation to provide it.

Edmund Lambeth has articulated the richer—and more rigorous—obligation of the journalist to the truth. If the information we have is important to the public, we are required to publish it. And it isn't enough to provide accurate information; we also need to give our audience the context that provides meaning for the facts. In all, Lambeth (1992: 24–27) outlines five separate dimensions to truth telling, including the obligation for journalists to prepare themselves to understand the fields they cover. In the code of ethics for the Society of Professional Journalists, the principle to "Seek the Truth and Report It" contains 17 separate provisions. To be committed to truth telling as a journalist means more than not lying.

This expanded and enriched meaning of truth telling (and other ethical norms) stands at the very heart of casuistry. As we noted at the beginning of this chapter, ethical theory can identify basic ethical norms, whether they be principles, role models or something else. But sifting through the evidence of the controversial cases, like *CSI* investigators solving a crime, provides critical content and meaning to these norms. Without that understanding, the journalist will be no better equipped than the person on the street to address the ethical issues emerging from the maelstrom of the journalist's daily work.

This book will give you those tools, leading you through the steps of casuistry. By the time you are finished, you should be able to explore cases with an experienced eye for detail, sorting out relevant and irrelevant facts, seeking paradigm cases and looking for similar (analogous) cases, and creating precedents and guidelines for future cases.

This same kind of discerning eye also needs to be applied to ethical theory in the context of our profession. It is not enough to have a list of ethical norms; you need to sort out how these norms should be prioritized within your own conception of the profession. And it is not enough to be committed to truth telling or justice. You need to know exactly what that commitment means for you as a professional journalist.

The Bowman/Smith Case Revisited

As you learned in Chapter 1, the case of Patricia Bowman and William Kennedy Smith will be used throughout this book as an example for each of the steps in case-based reasoning. Ethical norms play a pivotal role in this process, either as a beginning point when they are clear or as they emerge from the case-based process that future chapters will explore. The Bowman/Smith case is no exception.

The naming of rape victims has been a settled issue at many news outlets for decades: they don't do it except in unusual circumstances. This general consensus among journalists masks a basic ethical conflict between truth telling and doing no harm. Providing the name of an adult crime victim is standard procedure for journalists. The name of the victim is an important fact in the story—part of the truth. However, the personal nature of the assault causes many women to feel shame. Publishing their names in accounts of the crime or the trial would cause them emotional harm—a second victimization. For the most part, news organizations have concluded that the harm caused outweighs the partial omission of the truth.

Attempts have also been made to introduce a rule-utilitarian argument into the issue. As you saw in Chapter 1, Geneva Overholser (1989), one-time editor of *The Des Moines Register*, thought naming rape victims could destigmatize rape, treating it as a crime of violence, not a crime of sex. Seeing women who had been raped as crime victims like any other victim would counter any belief that they were now damaged, should be ashamed, or worst, were at fault. The consequences would be good for our culture, especially for the women who were raped. Ultimately, it might even result in more women being willing to report rape, bringing the crime into the open. *The Des Moines Register* gained significant attention when it published the name of Nancy Ziegenmeyer, but it was only done because Ziegenmeyer requested it, not as a new policy. Overholser's argument has not gained much footing in journalistic practice, in part because another utilitarian argument argues for a continuation of existing policy: publishing the names of rape victims, with the existing threat of stigma, may actually result in fewer women reporting rape, driving the crime underground and letting more rapists escape punishment.

From the perspective of ethical theory, the Bowman/Smith case introduces an additional principle to those already mentioned: justice as fairness. *Courier-Journal* editors David Hawpe and Steve Ford both thought that withholding Bowman's name while publishing repeated trial stories that identified Smith created a presumption of guilt that was unfair, given the notoriety of the case.

STRENGTHS AND LIMITS OF USING THEORY

Think of an ethical problem you faced as a journalist or a media controversy you have read about. How would you begin to sort through the case? One way would be to figure out what ethical theory might be relevant to the case. This top-down approach, like everything else, has strengths and weaknesses. Here are a few we can see. You may have others.

Strengths:

- Beginning at the top with ethical theory guarantees a clear connection to the ethical norms that will be an important part of any controversy. Knowing what these norms are provides clear guideposts through the analysis. For example, it doesn't take a genius to know that membership in a community organization risks jeopardizing a journalist's autonomy. That, in turn, could undermine the credibility and even the truth of the story. Having that ethical concern in front of you can help to sort through a variety of hypothetical or real situations in which the risks to autonomy are too high.
- A top-down application of principles and other ethical norms can be quicker, especially in uncomplicated cases. Identifying a key ethical norm can beam you to the core of the controversy. Remember the diamond earrings the reporter brought back from her interview? Can you say "compromised"?
- This also means you are less likely to be sidetracked by irrelevant details. It won't be as easy to rationalize your way to a more comfortable solution. That offers a high likelihood of consistency from case to case. When *The Herald-Times* of Bloomington, Indiana, created an ethics committee, a key concern was a political writer who was good friends with a local politician. Ultimately, that reporter got reassigned. But the sports editor who was a close friend of Indiana University's basketball coach, Bob Knight, stayed in his post (Boeyink 1992: 118). What might have happened if more attention had been placed on the norm of autonomy, rather than on the convenient journalistic advantage of having an inside source into the basketball program?
- Ethical theories are central to any resolution of controversial cases. If that's true, why begin with features of the case that are less important?

Limits:

- In some cases, the ethical norms may not be clearly identifiable in the beginning. Moreover, framing the case based on a particular norm may short-circuit the exploration of the case, as when police reach a premature judgment of guilt or innocence. Like the experts on *CSI*, you may need to suspend judgment on what ethical norms are really at stake until you get all the facts. In the publication of the controversial photo of the drowned child and grieving family, some people reach a quick conclusion that the ethical issue is water safety. The photo warns parents to be more careful around pools and recreational lakes. Only after more discussion do they see that this utilitarian argument can't be sustained without violating Kant's duty to respect persons because the parents here are used only as a means to an end.

■ Unlike clear-cut cases, complex cases sometimes resist easy resolution by appeals to theory. If the answer is so clear, we wouldn't need to spend time figuring out what to do. And that will take more work than laying claim to a principle, declaring the case solved, and breaking for lunch. The Bowman/Smith case has that kind of complexity.

■ No one is denying the central place of ethical principles. However, it can be that a conflict of two or more principles is the issue. And theory won't help you resolve that; only attention to the details of the case can. That's because the circumstances will help determine which of the principles has more weight in each case.

EYE ON CONFLICT OF INTEREST

Any approach to resolving controversies in journalism will have strengths and limitations. Finite human beings use these tools. Journalists bring their own experiences and beliefs to any controversy. That changes how they see the case. Facts may be interpreted differently; ethical norms may be defined differently. That's why casuistry pays attention to the qualities of the person doing the analysis. We'll discuss this more in Chapter 6.

However, that's also why the best ethical methodology will include both top-down (deductive) and bottom-up (inductive) strategies. As John Rawls (1971) suggested with his idea of "reflective equilibrium," these strategies are complementary, not contradictory. (For more on Rawls, check out Chapter 5.) The trick will always be to maximize the strengths of each approach while minimizing the weaknesses. So where should we begin: with theory or with facts? Well, as a good casuist might say, it all depends on the circumstances. Let's look at some of those circumstances in a few cases involving conflict of interest.

Conflict of Interest as an Ethical Issue

The cases in this chapter focus on conflict of interest. This issue offers a good field in which to apply the ethical theories discussed in this chapter. However, the cases themselves will also illustrate the pivotal role that circumstances play in a variety of controversies.

Among the most common conflict-of-interest controversies are free gifts and memberships in community organizations. Both of these are frequently debated in newsrooms because the ethical problem is so clear. Taking freebies offers the simplest case. When a journalist takes a free gift from someone who is or could be a source in a news story, a red warning signal ought to be triggered on your mobile phone: "Warning: Your autonomy as a journalist is being tested." Small gifts, such as a cup of coffee, are innocent enough. But any gift of substantial value can be viewed as an attempt to compromise your independence. And that can undermine the ethical principle on which your profession depends: truth telling.

In its worst form, the gift can actually influence the story, leading the reporter to leave out negative information on a company or highlight positive information. The reporter doesn't have to lie, but the truth can be shaped based on what information gets put in the lead—or what information gets left out.

When this is a conscious decision, the ethical problem is obvious enough. But it isn't always that simple. How do you know if you have been unconsciously affected by the free dinner at an expensive restaurant or the free gear from your trip to the Super Bowl? It's easy to deny being influenced; it's harder to know for sure what effect a well-chosen gift—say a product from the company you are profiling—has on the final story. Remember W.D. Ross' list of duties? One of these is gratitude, the feeling we get that we owe something to someone who has done us a favor. If the gift fits, don't take it.

Even if you are convinced you have not been influenced, free gifts raise one final problem: appearances. Imagine that you are a travel writer and have been given a chance to take a whitewater rafting trip free of charge. You were ready to write a truthful, balanced account of your experience for your magazine readers. But the truth is that you had a great time. And you think your readers would, too. Your story reflects that. But a reader of your story who takes your account to heart has a terrible time. She contacts you by e-mail and asks if you paid for your trip. When you tell her "no," she responds, "I thought not." Should you worry about this, even if your account was accurate? If you take seriously our account of the role of character in journalism, the answer is "yes." The relevant virtue here is trustworthiness. As journalists, we need our audiences to believe we are giving them the best account of events we can provide. If we give our audiences reason to doubt our character, we have lost the ability to inform them—even when we are providing what we believe is the truth. That's why the appearance of independence is important, even when we feel uncompromised.

The same ethical analysis applies to the question of belonging to community organizations. Both the reality of conflict and the appearance of conflict can be at risk. However, what is different in these cases is that membership in a community organization can be less closely tied to our work as journalists. You may belong to the parent-teacher organization where your children attend school. But as the health and science reporter, the potential for conflict is very small. One could even argue that the issue here was not membership in an organization, but involvement. The education writer—who also has children in the school—might want to be a member of the PTO, but could avoid being an officer in the organization or—perish the thought—the media liaison. In short, the exact nature of one's professional responsibility, the organization's mission, and the extent of involvement could all be factors that would need a careful case-based analysis before we knew how much—if any—autonomy were at risk.

Journalists could protect their autonomy by refusing all gifts and memberships in organizations. But journalists who gather information need good working relationships with sources. These relationships can themselves be a double-edged sword, according to Jeremy Iggers (1995):

> [N]ews-gathering involves an inextricable inter-dependence between reporters and sources. Reporters must cultivate sources and are keenly aware that future access to information depends on how they handle today's story. Sources, in turn, cultivate reporters. The most valuable gifts that reporters and sources can exchange—scoops and favorable coverage—simply aren't recognized as gifts.

These relationships can threaten one's independence. They certainly complicate the ethical choices. Covering the police beat is notoriously difficult. Reporters depend on the police for access to important stories, but the police are sensitive to any negative reporting, however factual. Knowing what you can report—and when—is part of the intricate dance of reporters and sources.

From an ethical perspective, that dance has an added dimension: promise-keeping. While the journalist is committed to the truth of any story, he or she needs to relate to many people on the beat. These interactions inevitably include explicit and implicit promises. Human interactions are complicated, especially when the people in these interactions often need each other. That can create a kind of social contract with reciprocal obligations, often unspoken. The ethics code from *The New York Times* says it this way:

> Relationships with sources require sound judgment and self-awareness to prevent the fact or appearance of partiality. Cultivating sources is an essential skill, often practiced most effectively in informal settings outside of normal business hours. Yet staff members, especially those assigned to beats, must be aware that personal relationships with news sources can erode into favoritism, in fact or appearance. Editors, who normally have a wide range of relationships, must be especially wary of showing partiality.

Following the lead of the *Times,* one might even want to frame this ethical concern in the context of friendship. Inevitably, some reporter/source relationships are friendly. The stories may not require controversial information; the journalist and the source hit it off. But here, we would be wise to heed Aristotle's (1925: 195–196) warning. Some friendships are built on utility, and others are built on character. In the former, we find the friendship useful; in the latter, we are friends because we seek only the good of the other. Only a friendship between people of good character can be trusted. Aristotle's distinction is fundamental to evaluating any reporter/source relationship.

One might think editors and news directors would be off the hook on this issue. They could, like Leonard Downie, Jr, former editor of *The Washington Post*, even avoid the civic action of voting to avoid involvement in the political process. And because their work is usually broader (not limited to specific beats), the same ascetic approach can be taken to involvement in community. Autonomy is clearly preserved. That does, however, leave open one ethical question: How can one edit the news about one's community if one does not participate in that community? How does an editor develop the important virtue of empathy without any significant ties to the community's social organizations?

A final level of concern is corporate conflict of interest. It's always been true that the corporate interests of a media company could conflict with its journalistic purposes. Many have commented on the lack of coverage given to the passage of the 1996 Telecommunications Act by the national networks—the corporations who stood to gain the most from the relaxation of ownership rules on media groups (Gilens and Hertzman 2000).

However, the potential for conflict has escalated with the growth of conglomerates that swallowed up many companies, including media. The reason is simple: the potential for a story to touch on the corporate interests of a newspaper's parent company is greater the more products and services the conglomerate provides. So when ABC News conducted a four-month investigation that showed Disney, owner of ABC, had hiring practices that allowed the employment of convicted pedophiles in the Magic Kingdom, Disney executives raised concern over the story. The story never ran on ABC.

This conflict could have been defused if Disney had stuck to its pledge not to interfere with the newsgathering role of ABC News. Instead, then-Disney Chairman Michael Eisner turned the reality of the conflict on its head, arguing that it would be better for ABC News not to report on Disney "to avoid a conflict of interest." (Stevens 1999: 95). Unfortunately, that would not avoid a conflict of interest; it would only bury it—with the truth-telling mission of ABC News dead in the cold ground. As corporations become larger and more complex, look for this kind of conflict of interest to continue to grow. Unfortunately, the evidence for this kind of ethical conflict is often hard to find. Like the black holes in space, you may find that conflict only in the darkness of the stories that are never done.[2]

CONFLICT OF INTEREST CASES AND WALK-THROUGH EXERCISES

Case 1: The Borgata Hotel[3]

In January 2003, the Borgata Hotel Casino & Spa in Atlantic City, New Jersey, contracted with M Booth & Associates, a public relations firm from New York City, to generate publicity for the new hotel. The dual goals were to pitch the Borgata and revive the declining tourism revenues of Atlantic City. The plan devised by the firm would test the independence of the journalists invited to the extravaganza.

Situational Clues

- The Borgata was more than a hotel and casino. Along with the gambling, visitors could eat at 11 restaurants, relax at a 50,000-square-foot spa, and shop at a number of stores. A theater and several nightclubs offered entertainment. All of this was packaged around marble floors, fountains, and spacious rooms with hot tubs. Las Vegas was coming to Atlantic City.
- M Booth & Associates decided to showcase the Borgata with a grand opening for media professionals, inviting more than 350 journalists within a range of 100 miles to the grand opening. The journalists were offered the entire deal free of charge. They could even bring along a friend. The only requirement was to take a "Borgata 101 tour." They had to use their own money for gambling, but everything else—meals, nightclubs, spa, room—didn't cost a dime.
- On 3 July 2003, the journalists who accepted the invitation got a tour of the facility at 5 p.m. and dined at a restaurant of their choice between 6 and 9 p.m. Singer Michael Buble performed a free concert. VIPs from Vegas were in attendance; Joe Pantoliano from "The Sopranos" made an appearance. Gambling was available after midnight.
- A reporter for a New Jersey weekly accepted the invitation and brought her husband to the event. She said she enjoyed the evening. She did not see any ethical problems. "In PR you want to get your message out to people in the fastest way that doesn't cost too much," she said. She believed this event was nothing out of the ordinary in public relations.
- Amy Rosenberg, another reporter who attended the event, gave the Borgata high marks in *The Philadelphia Inquirer*. She wrote, "Here the chefs are personalities, the all-you-can-eat buffet features hand-painted ceilings and Tuscan inspired décor. . .and floors give a feel of a classy, luxury hotel."
- The Borgata Hotel was the first casino to open in Atlantic City in 13 years. In August 2003, Atlantic City's casino revenues jumped 11 percent, according to *Business Week*.

- After 160 national and local print stories, rooms at the hotel were booked through 2004 with convention business reaching into 2010.

Walk-Through Exercise: Self-Interest

1. If you had received the invitation to attend the Borgata grand opening, would you have gone? What situational factors would be critical to your decision?
2. What additional information would help you make a decision? How would this information shape your decision?
3. This chapter has offered a number of ethical perspectives that can be used by journalists in making decisions. In your mind (or on paper if you have any short-term memory issues), sketch out how you would reason through this case using an ethic of duty. Now do the same with an ethic of utility, an ethic of care, and an ethic of character.
   a. Which of these ethical perspectives works best in bringing you to a solution?
   b. Would you combine any of these in your argument?
   c. Would you reject any?
4. Compare your use of the theories with those of others in your class. Look for ways that others may have used the theories differently, and explore these differences. These differences may signal some misunderstanding of how the theories should be applied.
5. Several theories might lead you to the same conclusion in the case. What do you make of that? How much should you judge the adequacy of the theory by the outcome? How much should you depend on the strength of the theory itself, without regard to the outcome in a specific case?
6. Does the argument of the New Jersey reporter that this is standard practice in public relations change the ethics of the decision for the journalist? Keep in mind the difference that being in a particular profession makes.
7. The Borgata grand opening contains some free events (tour, dinner, entertainment, hotel). Are the ethical problems of some events greater than others for a journalist?

One Last Look at Freebies

- An account coordinator for a public relations firm in Chicago said that the press needs to get the full experience of the product: "How could one write a story about a hotel and its services if they had never experienced it?" Do you agree with this assessment? Does it make accepting the invitation more ethical?
- Is it OK to take a friend? You might argue, as an extension of the Chicago account coordinator's argument, that you would have a better idea of the

experience if you shared it, as many of the people reading your story would want to do.

■ One easy resolution of this case is to get the news organization to pay for the journalist's costs. Given the current downturn in revenues for traditional news media, especially newspapers, it isn't too much of a stretch to believe that a newspaper would not want to pay the costs at an expensive casino and hotel. Do you think it is ethical to attend the event if your news organization says it can't afford to pay? Does the value of your report to your audience override any ethical concern you have?

■ The journalists who attend these events are sometimes contractors (freelancers) who do not work full-time for the publication. The New Jersey journalist was one of these contractors, hired by the weekly to cover the event. Often, contractors do not have to follow the guidelines of major publications. Do you think being a contractor makes a difference in the ethical decision? Is she part of the journalism profession? Is she part of the weekly newspaper? Or is she only an independent contractor? Why might her ethical obligations vary depending on the context in which her work is seen?

■ The New Jersey journalist noted that she did not leave with any free tangible gifts, only the experience. Would accepting gifts to take home have made this event less ethical? In other words, is there a difference between being given the experience and between being given a freebie?

Case 2: Friends as Sources

Human relationships, such as those between journalists and sources, can be complicated. Sometimes, journalists get close to their valuable sources over time, creating potential conflicts when a controversial story involving that source arises. But it can also happen the other way around: friends become sources. It happened that way to Dave Boeyink, one of the authors of this book. Here's his story.

Situational Clues

■ David Adkisson attended the same graduate school as Boeyink. When Adkisson went back to his hometown to look for work, he talked with the publisher of the paper. The publisher liked Adkisson's perspective on public issues, especially his knowledge of ethics. So the publisher tried to hire him for the editorial page editor's job. Adkisson turned him down. He was interested in a career in politics, something the newspaper position would not make possible. So he passed the word on to the graduate school. Boeyink, who was completing his degree in ethics, heard about the job, applied and started work in June 1978.

- Adkisson and Boeyink didn't know each other that well in grad school. As a teaching assistant, Boeyink had graded a few of Adkisson's papers.
- But Adkisson was there when Boeyink interviewed for the job. He invited Boeyink and his wife to a social gathering with his friends that weekend. And when the Boeyinks moved to Owensboro, he invited them to the church his family attended.
- The Boeyinks joined that church. And they attended the Sunday School class to which Adkisson and his wife belonged. That class became a major social circle during their nine years in Owensboro. Their families became friends; their children played together.
- None of this seemed to be a problem at first. Adkisson worked in the local Chamber of Commerce as projects manager while Boeyink wrote about the issues facing the local community. But it wasn't long before Adkisson was promoted to CEO of the Chamber of Commerce. Now he was much more visible in the community—and in the newspaper.
- Their friendship didn't change during this period. In social settings, over coffee or lunch, Boeyink and Adkisson sometimes talked about community issues. In fact, Adkisson was smart and connected. His insights into topics on which Boeyink wrote were often helpful.
- Occasionally, Boeyink wrote about projects in which the Chamber of Commerce was involved. But he rarely had occasion to disagree with the progressive direction Adkisson was taking. When an interview was needed from Adkisson, Boeyink made clear that they were on the record.
- Adkisson's next career move was more problematic. Remember Adkisson's political ambitions? After four years as CEO of the Chamber of Commerce, Adkisson became a field agent for US Sen. Wendell Ford. Adkisson was headquartered in Owensboro, Ford's hometown. Boeyink's job included writing editorials on national and international issues on which Sen. Ford had an important voice. And he wrote on Kentucky issues, a state for which Ford was a vigorous advocate in controversies such as tobacco, coal mining and clean air. Adkisson was Boeyink's most accessible source on many of these issues.

Walk-Through Exercise: How Close Is Too Close?

1. They say that a frog can be placed in a pan of cool water, placed over a fire and never seem to notice the difference in the rising temperature of the water until it's too late to save its life. Do you think Boeyink was like that here? At what point should he have noticed the rising temperature caused by the changing professional relationship with Adkisson and gotten out of the hot water? And what should he have done before he got cooked?
2. What do you see as the ethical issues at stake in this case? Describe these in terms of the ethical theories discussed in this chapter. Which ethical theory is the most compelling here?

3. Care-based theory is grounded in the nurturance of relationships. How, if at all, does that theory help you understand this case? Conversely, how does this case inform the way you think about care-based theory?

One Last Look at Source Relationships

1. When Barry Bingham Jr took over as the editor of *The Courier-Journal* in Louisville, he cut off all ties with Harvey Sloane, a long-time friend, because the Sloane family was politically active. (Sloane had been mayor of Louisville twice and ran for governor and the US Senate.) Was Bingham's strategy for dealing with friendship a better one than Boeyink's? Is there a third strategy that would be better than either?
2. Aristotle argued that only people of good character can be friends in the best sense because each wants what is best for the other and won't use the friend for any selfish purpose. Boeyink thought Adkisson was a person of high moral character. And while Boeyink refused to make the same claim for himself, he did say he had never been indicted. Joking aside, does good character make sustaining the friendship easier in the face of professional tension? How would you do that if you were Boeyink?
3. Now it gets messy. In his last years at the *Messenger-Inquirer*, Boeyink was a member of the Citizens Committee on Higher Education, a group dedicated to expanding low-cost higher education in the community. He took this community position with the encouragement of the publisher, who chaired the committee (the newspaper had campaigned for access to low-cost higher education for years on the editorial page). In the mid-80s, that committee had enough financial support to hire a part-time director. Adkisson, who wanted to run for mayor of Owensboro (another part-time job), applied for the committee's position. He was, far and away, the best candidate. What does Boeyink do now to extract himself from this mess?

Case 3: Special Perspectives, Special Problems[4]

Every journalist brings unique experiences to the job. In some cases, a reporter's special perspective is viewed as an asset to the reporting; in other cases, it is labeled a conflict of interest. For two female journalists at the *San Francisco Chronicle*, getting married became the flashpoint in determining whether they could continue to cover a major national story right in their backyard.

Situational Clues

■ Rachel Gordon covered City Hall for the *San Francisco Chronicle*. A major story on her beat was same-sex marriage, a controversy triggered by the invitation of Mayor Gavin Newsom to gay couples to exchange marriage vows at City Hall. Not surprisingly, news coverage went national.

- Thousands of couples, including Gordon and *Chronicle* photographer Liz Mangelsdorf, accepted Newsom's offer. Mangelsdorf had also covered the same-sex marriage story.
- Their marriage set off a series of intense discussions in the newsroom to determine whether Gordon and Mangelsdorf should continue to cover the same-sex marriage controversy.
- In a newsroom memo on 12 March 2004, Phil Bronstein, executive editor, said that the integrity of the journalists was not the issue. He had complete confidence in their professional ability. The issue for Bronstein was the credibility of the paper, particularly in the perception of a conflict of interest by readers. His memo quoted Tom Rosenstiel, director of the Project for Excellence in Journalism: "How would this look if people did know?"
- For Bronstein, a key fact in the case was the action taken by the couple to formalize their relationship at City Hall. "[B]eing personally involved in such a specific way" and having a personal stake in the outcome meant that they should not also cover that story, Bronstein said in the memo.
- Gordon and Mangelsdorf were taken off the story.
- A slightly different perspective on the couple's marriage was offered by Dick Rogers, the *Chronicle*'s reader representative. In a published column, Rogers noted that the Gordon/Mangelsdorf marriage was not an act of civil disobedience (after all, the mayor had extended the invitation). And it wasn't meant to attract attention. The couple did not get married on the first day when more publicity was likely.
- San Francisco's Human Rights Commission also weighed in, protesting the decision of the newspaper to remove Gordon and Mangelsdorf from coverage of this story. In a letter to Bronstein, the commission said the two women had "already demonstrated their ability to report on and photograph the story before they got married." The commission saw this decision in the context of its mandate to protect San Franciscans from discrimination based on sexual orientation or marital status.

Walk-Through Exercise: Is Integrity Enough?

1. If you had been in Bronstein's shoes, what facts from this case would be most relevant to you in making a decision? Why?
2. If you apply the theory of W.D. Ross, at least two ethical principles are in conflict here. On the one side is autonomy, linked to the credibility of the newspaper. On the other side is justice for Gordon and Mangelsdorf. Which of these has more weight for you in this case?
3. One other ethical component plays a role: character. As we noted, the editors were unflinching in their support of the integrity of Gordon and Mangelsdorf. The concern was over what readers would think. In the end, that concern trumped their assessment of character. Do you agree with

that choice? Would communicating the editor's support of the journalists to readers have been a better way to deal with this than taking them off the story?

4. Gordon and Mangelsdorf were in a same-sex relationship prior to their marriage. Assuming the newspaper editors knew about the relationship, should that have been enough to consider taking them off the story? Or should their sexual orientation have been viewed as a plus, as it often is in assigning stories focused on race to reporters who represent a racial minority? In our discussion of character, we suggested that character was holistic, the narrative of one's life. In that context, how should editors deal with reporters capable of bringing unique perspectives to stories because of who they are?

5. A key point of dispute is the meaning given to the action taken by Gordon and Mangelsdorf to formalize their relationship in a same-sex marriage. For Bronstein, getting married was an action that put them at the center of the controversy and disqualified them from participating in coverage, while being gay did not. Do you agree?

6. Kelly McBride of the Poynter Institute argues that everyone has a stake in this issue, including straight journalists. What questions should be asked about a straight journalist who would be assigned to this story? And should the marital status of all reporters and photographers covering the same-sex issue be reported, as the San Francisco Human Rights Commission recommended?

One Last Look at Personal Biases

1. McBride believes that all journalists should be asked to inventory their conflicts of interest to answer the question: "What is it about my beliefs or experiences that might compromise my ability to be fair?" What would be on your list of biases?

2. When the Hearst Corporation considered buying the *Chronicle*, reporters with a stake in the outcome wrote about it. How is this case different than the coverage of same-sex marriage?

3. Pamela Strother, executive director of the National Lesbian and Gay Journalists Association, said that if you see a same-sex marriage as a political act when it is legal, then just being lesbian, gay, bisexual or transgendered is also a political act. Do you agree?

4. As we noted above, one of Bronstein's key arguments is that getting married put Gordon and Mangelsdorf in the center of the same-sex marriage controversy. What actions, if any, would an African American reporter need to take to disqualify her from covering a story about slavery reparations? If she knows she's a descendant of slaves? If her family has suffered discrimination in the past? If she has joined an organization dedicated to documenting the effects of slavery on African Americans?

5. Can you think of any alternatives to removing reporters or photographers from coverage because of a possible conflict of interest?

Case 4: Naming of the *St. Pete Times* Forum[5]

Conflicts of interest can arise when the economic interests of a media organization and the journalistic standards of the same organization clash. That happened in 2002 when the *St. Petersburg Times* put its name on a local sports arena. No one, including newspaper executives usually committed to aggressive reporting of such information, was willing initially to say how much the deal was worth.

Situational Clues

■ The Tampa Bay area is host to one of the more vigorous newspaper competitions in the country. The *St. Petersburg Times* (283,000 daily circulation) and *The Tampa Tribune* (195,000 daily circulation) are duking it out on the streets and online. Though the cities are separated by Tampa Bay, neither is timid about trying to build circulation in the other's home territory.

■ In 2002, the *Times* completed a 12-year deal (with an option for another 12 years) that made it the first newspaper in the nation to have its name on a major sports stadium.

■ The name "St. Pete Times Forum" was installed on the top of the Ice Palace arena on three sides. Anyone buying a ticket to an event at the forum sees the newspaper's name on the ice and on the ticket. Ice Palace Drive has been renamed "St. Pete Times Forum Drive"—all this in the heart of Tampa.

■ Paul Tash, editor and president of the *Times,* hailed the deal as a sign that the *Times* was the premier newspaper in the area.

■ Hillsborough County Commissioner Jan Platt wanted to know the financial terms of the deal between the *Times* and Palace Sports & Entertainment. The Ice Palace was constructed with public and private money. And another surcharge of about $3 per ticket was due to kick in to help keep up with debt payments on the Ice Palace. Platt thought the public had the right to know what the deal was worth and what effect it would have on any proposed increase in ticket prices.

■ Tash said this was business information he didn't want *The Tampa Tribune* to know. He also said part of the deal was that the financial terms of the arrangement were not to be disclosed. He said he would not object if Palace Sports gave the county the figures, but the *Times* was bound by the agreement. "We keep our word," Tash said in a *Times* story.

■ Reasons for the secrecy are not completely clear. Lucy Morgan, a member of the *Times* board of directors, didn't think Palace Sports insisted on it. She concluded this was about the paper's competition with *The Tampa Tribune.*

Walk-Through Exercise: A Business Decision

1. The *St. Petersburg Times* was clearly making a strategic business decision in competing with *The Tampa Tribune* for newspaper supremacy in the Tampa Bay area. Do you think the business of a news organization should be subject to the same level of openness as its editorial operation? In other words, can secrecy for business purposes ever override journalistic obligations?
2. Which of the facts above seem most relevant to you in deciding how the *St. Petersburg Times* should respond to Platt's request for information? Would it make a difference if the request came from a reporter for *The Tampa Tribune?*
3. What do you see as the ethical issues at stake in this case? Use the ethical theories discussed in this chapter to check whether you have identified all the ethical components.
4. Tash believed he was bound by a promise. Does this promise trump the commitment of the newspaper to telling the truth (the cost of the deal)?
5. Are there also obligations to the taxpayers in Hillsborough County here? In what ethical framework can these be best expressed?

One Last Look at Covering Yourself

1. One of the disputes in the case was over what was standard practice in such naming-rights deals. Tash said the deal, including the non-disclosure of financial terms, was similar to other marketing arrangements. But Dean Bonham, a consultant on stadiums, said financial terms in most naming rights deals were disclosed. Does standard practice make a difference here? Is it relevant that, unlike other deals, one of the partners in the naming deal is a media company?
2. The *St. Petersburg Times* is known for its commitment to open records. In fact, the *Times* successfully got the records opened on contracts for suites at another stadium owned by the Tampa Sport Authority. Does the action of the *Times* in the previous case make a difference in the ethical argument? Why or why not?
3. This case contains a clear case of public interest because the Ice Palace was built in part with public funds and because debt payments affect the cost of the tickets. Assume that the Ice Palace was a private facility, built without public money. Would that change the obligation of the newspaper to disclose how much it is paying for naming rights?
4. Three days after the controversy broke, officials with Palace Sports & Entertainment disclosed that the naming-rights deal was worth

$30 million. Do you think Tash released them from the promise of the confidentiality agreement by saying he would not object if they released the figures? Was this the best ethical solution possible to this conflict?

Case 5: Pedophiles in the Magic Kingdom[6]

As news outlets become part of large conglomerates, the potential for conflict of interest between journalism and the corporate whale that has swallowed it grows exponentially. ABC, a news property owned by Disney, found that out when its news division pursued a story that led higher up the food chain. You heard about the case earlier in this chapter. Here are more details.

Situational Clues

- Since 1996, ABC has been a small part of the large Walt Disney Company. In the late 1990s, when this controversy is brewing, annual revenues at Disney topped $20 billion.
- When Disney's acquisition of ABC was announced in 1995, *The Wall Street Journal* reported that Michael Eisner, chairman of Disney, told ABC News employees that he "wouldn't screw around with news, especially ABC News." And a year before this controversy, Richard Wald, ABC News' senior vice-president for editorial quality, told a crowd at the Columbia Journalism School that ABC News would not censor itself. "We do not play around with the integrity of the central question of our lives, which is to report fully and fairly what we know," Wald said.
- Brian Ross, an aggressive investigative reporter for ABC News, wanted to develop a story on pedophile employees at theme parks. The focus was on Disney's theme parks, where most of the problems seemed to be centered.
- David Westin, president of ABC News, initially approved the story idea. Westin was a corporate lawyer with no previous journalism experience who had just taken over the position. Westin reportedly approved the story on the condition that the story be broadened to include an investigation of competing theme parks, such as those run by Disney's rival, Universal Studios.
- Ross led a four-month investigation into Disney hiring practices that allowed convicted pedophiles to be employed in its theme parks. The story, according to *Brill's Content,* documented cases of crimes against children by Disney workers. Two of the sexual assaults were on Disney property.
- According to Ross' story, Disney did not have a policy of running criminal background checks on new hires. Disney World employed 51,000 workers at the time.
- The story was vetted and cleared for broadcast by Disney lawyers.

- Law-enforcement sources contacted by Elizabeth Stevens of *Brill's Content* said Disney was less helpful in combating the problem than other parks, a claim that Disney spokesman Bill Warren disputed.
- In an interview shortly before the final decision was made on this story, Eisner said he would prefer that ABC News not cover Disney: "[B]y and large, the way you avoid conflict of interest is to, as best you can, not cover yourself."
- Four months after approving the story—and days after Eisner's comment, Westin saw a draft of the story script. Westin killed the story. In a written statement, he said the story did not meet editorial standards at ABC News, that senior journalists concurred in that judgment and that the focus of the story on the Walt Disney Company did not influence the decision. Westin's claim that others were involved in the decision to kill the story was disputed by an unnamed Disney executive quoted in *Brill's Content*.
- After the controversy, Disney began screening for criminal records in new hires.

Walk-Through Exercise: Hands Off?

1. In the discussion of conflict of interest, three possible sources for the conflict were discussed: self-interest, journalistic interest, and corporate interest. Can you identify ways in which each of these played a role in this case?
2. What are the key facts in the case that shape your decision about what should have been done? What details of the case point to mistakes made in the process that made the conflict of interest worse?
3. Eisner's solution to avoiding a conflict with ABC News was for ABC not to report on Disney. In fact, other news organizations might be better able to report on Disney without conflict of interest. Do you agree with Eisner's solution? If not, what are the problems?
4. Clearly, no one is likely to reverse history and take ABC and other major news organizations out of the corporate world. Given that, what do you think would be the best strategy for maximizing autonomy and/or controlling the inherent conflict of interest in this case? What kind of ethical argument, based on the theories presented in this chapter, would you make?
5. This case includes several controversial people:
    a. Michael Eisner, Disney's chairman, made contradictory statements about the relationship of Disney and ABC News.
    b. Brian Ross, an aggressive reporter with a reputation for taking stories beyond the facts, used tactics that resulted in several major lawsuits.
    c. David Westin, head of a prestigious network news operation, was named to his post with no previous journalism experience.

How much of your judgment in this case depends on your assessment of the virtue or character of these key players?

5. After Westin kills the case, can Ross ethically leak this story to a competitor? What would the ethical arguments be for and against that strategy? How would you support them with theory?

One Last Look at Corporate Conflicts of Interest

1. *Brill's Content* asked 21 ABC News employees this question: "Would you be comfortable working at ABC News if Brian Ross' story about Disney was killed because of Disney's connection with the story?" Two-thirds of the journalists—including Peter Jennings, Barbara Walters, Ted Koppel, Diane Sawyer, and Sam Donaldson—declined to comment. As nationally known journalists, should they have spoken out? Or were they right to keep quiet?

2. In response to that same question, Chris Wallace said, "I don't comment on other reporters' work." Does this suggest a broader concern for conflict of interest—that journalists shouldn't report on each other? What do you think of that argument? And what implications does this have more generally for reporting on the media? (Remember the example of non-reporting by many media organizations with a financial interest in the passage of the 1996 Telecommunications Act.)

3. This case involves a news organization reporting on its corporate owner. But what would you think about this story if Ross were investigating pedophile employees at the theme parks of Universal Studio, Disney's rival? Would that be better? Or would it also be a conflict of interest since Ross works for Disney?

4. And what about a story documenting the expansion of Disney's global holdings—a story that effectively promotes Disney's image? Can ABC News do that story without a conflict of interest problem, assuming the story is as accurate as the pedophile story?

Before You Go

If you are like most students, working through the cases is more fun than talking about ethical theory. But the goal of the cases in this chapter is to help you apply ethical theory and critically analyze theory's role in decision-making. Here are a few questions that might be interesting to discuss now that you have worked through both the theory and the cases in this chapter:

1. The chapter lists several strengths and limits for ethical theory. Did you experience these in applying theory to the cases? What were your own conclusions on the strengths and limits of ethical theory?

2. Which of the theories did you find more helpful in resolving the cases? Did your judgment change depending on the case?

3. In the chapter, we argued that being part of the practice of journalism—
    a part of the profession—means that your ethical obligations are
    different than those of non-journalists. The priority of your obligations
    will be different; so will the meaning of the ethical terms you use. Did you
    find evidence of that in the cases? In what way?
4. The conflict-of-interest cases offered a range of conflicts, from self-
    interest (freebies) to journalistic (reporters and sources) to corporate
    (naming rights and Disney). Rank these three general types of conflict in
    terms of the usefulness of ethical theory in resolving the cases. Why do
    you think conflicts are not all created equal when applying theory?

CHAPTER 3

▼ THE PARADIGM CASE AS ETHICAL STANDARD

Jayson Blair's name is infamous among journalists. Over the course of six months in 2002 and 2003, at least half the articles he wrote for *The New York Times* were inaccurate, plagiarized or made up. Not by accident or out of a misguided attempt to accomplish a greater good. On purpose. For fun. In fact, he told an interviewer he laughed out loud at his most elaborate fiction: a completely fabricated backdrop of "tobacco fields and cattle pastures" for the West Virginia home of Pvt. Jessica Lynch's family—a POW in Iraq who, ironically, became a celebrity herself as a result of deceptive government propaganda (Associated Press 2003).

It was only after the *Times* launched an investigation into Blair's reporting that management discovered he had never even talked to the Lynch family or seen their house. And that was the tip of the iceberg. There were many, many more such instances. Blair resigned after he was found out, but he was unrepentant. In fact, he seemed to take pride in "fool[ing] some of the most brilliant people in journalism" and signed with a literary agent soon afterward (Associated Press 2003).

Blair's actions were roundly condemned as exemplifying the worst in journalism. In casuistical terms, the fraud he perpetrated upon his editors and readers is a *paradigm case*. The paradigm case is like a known sample in a *CSI* investigation. When police investigate a crime scene, they compare evidence from the scene to known samples obtained elsewhere. For example, they might compare a shoe print from the scene to the sole of a known shoe brand. If the samples match, the police can establish that the print from the scene was made by same shoe brand as the known sample.

Likewise, journalists who use case-based reasoning engage in a comparative analysis that often starts with a case presenting known ethical qualities. This case is called the paradigm case. It is essentially an ethical no-brainer; in other words, people can easily agree on whether or not it presents an ethically acceptable situation. Thus, the paradigm serves as a clear-cut moral standard that can provide guidance for deciding more ambiguous cases. For example, the Blair case is a clear instance of unethical fabrication in journalism. Journalists can use this paradigm to decide more problematic examples of made-up facts in news stories.

For example, a couple of years after the Blair scandal, novelist and sports columnist Mitch Albom filed a column on a Friday stating that two NBA players were at a game on Saturday for the *Detroit Free Press'* Sunday sports section. (Confused yet?) Albom had interviewed the NBA players separately, and they had said they would attend the game together at their old alma mater, Michigan State University. Albom, however, was not in a position to physically observe the two players at the game or otherwise confirm their attendance before his deadline. He was counting on luck to make his account "true" a day later. Unfortunately, the two players ended up not going to the game after all.

One way to figure out whether Albom's decision was unethical (or *how* unethical it was) is to compare it to what Blair did. This process helps us to figure out why exactly we think making up facts in journalism is wrong. For example, would it have made a difference if the players had shown up as predicted? (Would Blair be in the clear if he had guessed right about the tobacco fields and the cattle at the Lynch house?)

Casuistry provides a bridge between the particular and the general in ethics. Bottom-up reasoning may consist of the following processes, which we've listed from the lowest level of abstraction to the highest. But keep in mind that you won't necessarily go through each process when you're actually doing case-based analysis or even perform them in this sequence (sorry; ethical reasoning is messy):

■ Identification of the situation's morally relevant characteristics.
■ Classification of the situation under an established paradigm case or a hypothetical one if no precedent has been established.
■ Comparison between the hard case and analogous cases, including the paradigm.
■ Development of provisional guidelines that reflect your practical experience comparing these cases.
■ Reflection on the ethical norms you found pertinent to the case.

This chapter focuses on the first two processes; let's put them under the microscope.

TOOLS OF THE TRADE: IDENTIFICATION AND CLASSIFICATION

Case-based reasoning typically moves between the particular and the general in a way that defies strict separation of these two levels of analysis. At *The*

Courier-Journal, for example, editors initially approached the Bowman/ Smith decision in terms of the paper's existing policy against naming *any* rape victims. There were certain features of that particular case that prompted the editors to question how well the paper's policy "fit" the situation. But they also experienced doubt because of former managing editor Irene Nolan's proposed new policy of naming *all* rape victims. In other words, perplexing circumstances potentially covered by competing ethical policies could not be reconciled: the classic conditions for a hard case in ethics. In true casuistical fashion, the paper's decision makers moved back and forth among newsroom policy, previous cases they had handled in their experience as editors, and the particular details of the Bowman/Smith situation. Let's take a closer look at how to sort through these various aspects of case-based reasoning.

Recognizing Situational Clues with Moral Relevance

Forensic examiners rely on tested tools for systematically identifying and classifying the evidence in a forensic investigation. This protocol helps them to draw defensible conclusions about what crime was committed, how it was committed, and by whom. Casuists, likewise, follow a number of steps to make sure they understand what's at stake in an ethical case, how best to evaluate that case, and how to interpret all the "evidence" at hand to draw reasonable moral conclusions.

Deliberation about a hard case requires casuists to immerse themselves in the particular details, much like forensic examiners looking at the clues at a crime scene: What do we have here? What kind of case is this? It is only after we've gotten a handle on such questions that we can settle on a relevant moral model. Put another way, we have to become familiar with the moral territory before we can figure out its most important features and how these should be represented in a paradigmatic map (Jonsen and Toulmin, 1988: 307).

But how should journalists proceed when dealing, usually on deadline, with the layered complexities of real-life ethical problems? Once again, they can borrow a page from forensic science. Forensic examiners trying to solve a crime can't examine every single speck of dust, every shred of fabric, every paint chip, every computer file. They have to narrow things down by relying on their expert knowledge of what sorts of materials have yielded usable evidence in the past, by trying to match items at the scene to known samples, and by understanding what sort of evidence is pertinent to a legal deter- mination. In short, they have to focus on *relevance*.

Journalists trying to solve a moral problem, likewise, possess expertise regarding the sorts of stories, subjects and sources that warrant special moral consideration: they have knowledge of other situations in which these factors were ethically significant, and they understand how these factors relate to the larger moral commitments journalists have made to society. In short, sound case-based reasoning is not just a matter of technique; it involves discernment about what's relevant, which, in turn, requires a good understanding of the case at hand and its larger context.

Forensic examiners determine relevance through the process of *identification*. "Identification" in forensic science refers to the accurate description of items that may be used as evidence in a crime case. What counts as evidence, of course, will depend on the crime: If the charge is drug possession, merely identifying a plant as marijuana is sufficient identification.

However, identification can be much more complicated. Perhaps investigators have to demonstrate collusion among a group of suspects. In that case, they will have to identify relevant phone numbers, for example, and establish frequency of contact and other indicators of collusion. In other words, what they're after are not just *any* facts, but key facts in the context of evidentiary rules in court. They must describe them with the specific purpose of legally proving an allegation (evidence that may be used in a court of law is known as *probative evidence*).

Some characteristics are especially crucial. In *CSI* parlance, such characteristics would be called *dispositive evidence*. Certain features of ethical cases can cinch our moral judgments about them, just as a DNA match or the proverbial "smoking gun" can cinch a legal prosecution. For example, if President Clinton had given Monica Lewinsky access to classified documents, that fact would have been dispositive evidence for the journalist using case-based reasoning. The ethical decision whether to report the details of their affair would have been simpler.

Just as some items you might find at a crime scene are not relevant to a criminal investigation, not all features of a journalism ethics case are relevant to a moral analysis. Only those features with some relation to ethical norms, such as truth telling and fairness, are going to count as "probative evidence" for making a moral determination. These are known as the *relevant characteristics* of a case. In Chapter 4, we'll look at the different ways in which relevance plays out when we compare analogous cases. Relevance, as you'll see in Chapter 5, can ultimately be grounded in theoretical considerations. But, for now, let's look at how another important forensic tool called *classification* relates to the use of paradigms in case-based ethical reasoning.

What Kind of Case Do We Have?

"Classification" refers to the way in which forensic examiners are able to categorize, say, a gun as belonging to a particular caliber, or a shoeprint as traceable to a particular shoe manufacturer. In other words, this process pegs an object as belonging to a certain "class." Similarly, casuists need to classify hard cases as belonging to a certain moral "type" before they can identify a suitable paradigm case and other analogous cases.

But the "classification" step can be especially tricky in jobs such as medical diagnosis, forensic examination or journalistic reporting. Because of the very nature of these tasks, our understanding of the situation evolves gradually. We may think we've identified a suitable paradigm for the ethical problem confronting us, for example, only to figure out partway through the discernment process that we have to abandon the first paradigm we chose.

This was the situation faced by reporters for the *Kalamazoo* (Michigan) *Gazette*.[1] In February 2008, teenager Calista Springer of Centreville, Michigan, died of smoke inhalation in a house fire. It was front-page news in the *Gazette*, a daily newspaper based in a city about an hour away from the small town of 1,500 residents where the fire occurred. The *Gazette* reported on the fire itself and on the reactions of the family and people who knew Calista in the community. In other words, they reported the story the way they would any fire fatality involving a minor, demonstrating the sensitivity that would be expected toward Calista's grieving parents.

Within a couple of days, however, it became clear that this was not just another story about a teenager's accidental death, like others the paper had covered. Quoting anonymous sources at first, the *Gazette* reported that state troopers and firefighters had found Calista chained by her hands and feet to her bed in a second-floor bedroom. A recent picture showed a girl who was very underweight, looking much younger than her 16 years. She was wearing only a T-shirt and sweatpants in the deep of winter, with no pillows, sheets or blankets on her bed. Further reporting revealed that Calista's adoptive parents, Anthony and Marsha Springer, had been investigated by state child welfare officials at least four times since 1997 and that Marsha Springer had sought a restraining order against her husband in 1999 in fear of his violent temper.

After Calista's death, her parents were finally charged with child abuse and neglect, and their two other daughters were removed from their home. Attorneys for the defendants argued that Calista's parents restrained her at night for her own safety, for Calista was disabled and tended to wander away from home.

As the *Gazette*'s coverage turned toward reporting the circumstances of lifelong abuse that ultimately trapped Calista in her hopeless situation, it became clear that this was not the kind of case the *Gazette* had assumed it was. Calista's parents were not the innocent victims of a cruel fate, but irresponsible agents of their child's own demise. The moral implications of the situation were drastically different from what the journalists initially had supposed. To proceed with the original paradigm and its moral presumptions would have been an ethical error.

A paradigm case, as we've said, is especially useful to the casuist. The beauty of a paradigm case is that it "loads up" a situation with all the moral factors we think matter to our evaluation of a given problem and makes clear how these factors relate to each other. As templates for viewing exemplary cases (R.B. Miller March 1996), paradigm cases are similar to the grids used by *CSI* investigators to "map" the evidence at a crime scene. Certain features of the case at hand "stand out" as moral evidence because of the template provided by the paradigm case. These features can then be used as comparison points with similar cases.

Remember, the structure of casuistical reasoning is analogical. Casuistry avoids the inconsistency of situation ethics by treating similar cases similarly. We may be able to arrive at a moral judgment by comparing our case to other ambiguous cases, but working with a paradigm gives us confidence that our analogies are on target. That's because a paradigm strips a moral problem down to its essence. If we are able to identify or construct a paradigm, we'll have more luck zeroing in on what's morally relevant and what's not.

USING PARADIGM CASES IN JOURNALISM ETHICS

There are two major kinds of paradigms: exemplars of right action and exemplars of wrong action. Paradigms that function as exemplars of right action may provide a model for "doing everything right" so that there is no moral controversy. For example, we could analyze a case in which the journalist "did everything right" when it came to promising confidentiality. As another option, an exemplar of right action might exemplify circumstances that justify making an exception to a strongly held moral commitment. For example, we might ask what sort of situation involving anonymous sources presents us with a clear justification for disclosing their identity.

Once journalists have settled on a suitable paradigm, they need to spell out how exactly rules, codes and so forth shed light on what's ethically relevant about the situation. Then they have to judge how these ethical norms "fit" the circumstances. Notice that this strategy is the opposite of how traditional ethical theories approach the task: those theories try to determine how cases *illustrate* general ethical norms; "applied ethicists" judge new cases based on their consistency with these norms. In casuistry, novel cases provide occasions for exploring the meaning of those ethical norms and even for *revising* them; it is the norms themselves that are being judged based on whether they are consistent with our moral judgments about cases. It is the rules that must bend to the cases, not the other way around.

The Bowman/Smith case provides an example of how this process works. Interviews with the editors who were involved in the decision to name Bowman in *The Courier-Journal* suggest that they viewed this case from the outset as a possible exception to the paper's policy against naming rape victims. Therefore, most of their reasoning took place at the level of particular circumstances, rather than at the level of general norms. In other words, the Bowman/Smith case mainly provided an opportunity for what casuists call *specifications* of the policy's scope.

Courier-Journal staffers concluded that the Bowman/Smith case was substantially different from the paradigm of a sex crime involving non-prominent parties and, hence, a justifiable exception to the paper's policy. In explaining their reasoning, they mentioned a number of moral presumptions underlying their judgment that the policy of not naming rape victims was sound overall. By going back and forth between general ethical norms and the particular circumstances of this case, the paper's editors gained a new appreciation for just how far *The Courier-Journal*'s deference to rape victims should extend.

The paper's policy on naming rape victims was effectively revised to incorporate specific exceptions based on the Bowman/Smith case. Editors treated this case as a precedent when three other women came forward before Smith's trial, saying they would be willing to testify that he had also raped them several years earlier.[2] Now applying their revised policy top-down to these women, the editors judged their cases to fall under the same exceptions as Bowman's and published their names as well.

Although certain paradigms function as exemplars of right action, others serve the opposite purpose. Exemplars of wrong action may either provide a model for "doing everything wrong" so that there is no doubt it is morally prohibited (like the Jayson Blair case), or they may exemplify circumstances that do not meet the threshold for justifying an exception to a strongly held moral commitment. Which kind of paradigm case is most useful depends on the moral problem at hand. Are we contemplating the violation of an important ethical norm, such as protecting anonymous sources? Or are we trying to figure out whether we should offer the guarantee of anonymity in the first place?

For some decisions, it may help to have a paradigm for right action and also a paradigm for wrong action. This may be a good idea, for example, when we're trying to analyze a series of cases and "rank" them: The more a case resembles the right action paradigm, the more ethical it is. The more a case resembles the wrong action paradigm, the less ethical it is. In effect, anchoring your casuistical reasoning this way allows you to place hard cases on a continuum from most ethical to least ethical. This could be a good way to get clear on the meaning of a newsroom policy or to tease out the implications of a principle stated in an ethics code. This process can also help you to identify extremely ambiguous cases that do not clearly resemble either paradigm case. We will get into such issues in more detail in Chapter 4.

Settling on an Exemplar

A key step in casuistry, then, is to find the right paradigm case. But where exactly do you find paradigm cases? Sometimes, you'll be able to remember a straightforward moral decision from your own experience when you're trying to resolve a difficult ethical case. For instance, members of a committee appointed to draft an ethics code for the newsroom at *The Herald-Times* in Bloomington, Indiana, discussed cases in trying to figure out where to draw the ethical "line" in accepting gifts from news sources. They quickly settled on an obvious example of unacceptable practice from the newsroom's past: The case of the former reporter who scored some diamond earrings after an interview with a diamond company official (Boeyink 1992).

Journalists do not have to rely solely on their own newsroom experiences to supply possible paradigms, however. Journalism ethics cases that get widespread publicity, such as Blair's fabrications or *PrimeTime Live*'s undercover story on Food Lion, provide exemplars for all journalists to discuss and to use as paradigms in their own practice.

But what if there isn't a handy case out there to invoke as an ethical standard when a hard case comes up? Perhaps the hard case you're dealing with literally has no precedent, or (more likely) you are simply not familiar with any other case like it. What do you do?

Let's return to the Bowman/Smith case for a moment. Whatever case or cases gave rise to *The Courier-Journal*'s blanket policy against naming rape victims had long disappeared from the paper's institutional memory. When discussing the newsroom's longstanding practice, the editors invoked certain ethical norms embedded within the policy, including respect, autonomy, fairness, and preventing harms. These norms gave form to what would have otherwise been a vague notion of the typical (and paradigmatic) case at *The Courier-Journal*: one in which the accuser was a local resident and neither she nor the accused was a prominent figure in the community. The editors were thus able to appreciate the morally relevant characteristics of any situation they would consider paradigmatic.

The Courier-Journal editors already had some working presumptions they could flesh out in their discussions. This process might have helped them to remember a case in the newsroom that possessed the relevant characteristics (though we have no evidence this happened). However, they also could have brainstormed some relevant characteristics first and *then* developed a hypothetical paradigm case possessing the appropriate details.

Let's practice the hypothetical strategy with another class of ethical cases that continually perplexes journalists: news photographs portraying images of grief. Say you're the city editor of a metropolitan daily newspaper, and one of the paper's photographers has just phoned in to say she's caught a compelling image of a mother rushing up to the firefighter who's carrying her dead son out of a burning apartment complex. She warns you that the child's face is easily recognizable in the picture and that the mother's expression is heart-breaking. You're uncomfortable already even without seeing the picture.

You decide to go looking in the archives to see whether the paper has published such a picture before. There is a precedent for publishing photos of house fire victims surveying the damage and firefighters cleaning up at the scene. In a couple of cases, the victims and the firefighters are upset, but not distraught. There is no precedent for showing an identifiable body.

The photographer is back and has uploaded the picture she told you about. It's stunning in its composition and detail, telling a story in a way that could never be matched by words. The emotional impact is wrenching. As far as technical excellence, this is an award-winning photograph. But you look at the child, and you look at the mother's face, and you can't imagine being in that kind of pain as a parent yourself. There's something obscene about looking at this moment.

You ask the photographer, her supervisor, the reporter working on the story, and the managing editor to join you in the conference room to discuss this problematic case. How do you all begin to work through this case without an actual example for comparison?

One way to proceed is to think about what would make your decision easier. If the victim were an adult, rather than a child, the photograph would be less disturbing. If the body were not identifiable, that would pose less concern for the victim's privacy, regardless of age. If the body were not in the photograph to begin with, it would be even more straightforward because you wouldn't have to be concerned with disrespecting the dead. If the mother's expression were less pained, the photo would be less intrusive. If you could obtain the consent of the mother and the firefighter, you would have fewer reservations about traumatizing them with this image and about stepping on their right to be left alone at such a time.

In essence, you could construct a hypothetical paradigm by imagining characteristics that would make this particular picture—and by analogy any other picture in its "class"—ethically acceptable. The more of these characteristics a picture possessed, the more certain you would be that it was OK to publish. If the photograph you're looking at is too dissimilar from the hypothetical paradigm you've constructed, you could ask the photographer for alternative shots that have fewer objectionable features.

However, imagine that the reporter now tells the group that this apartment has been cited multiple times for fire code violations and that the mother had asked her landlord at least twice in the past year to repair the fire alarms in her unit. Is this feature of the case significant enough to warrant an exception to your hypothetical paradigm? This fact makes the photo much more newsworthy—and, therefore, more consequential—in terms of public safety and public policy. The hard truth of this photograph may be something your readers have a right to see, even over the subjects' objections. The mother's expression is no longer a simple cry of grief, but a cry for justice.

Now you have a situation that may more closely resemble Charles Porter's famous photograph of the Oklahoma City bombing in 1995. In this Pulitzer Prize-winning picture, firefighter Chris Fields lovingly cradles the bloody body of 1-year-old Baylee Almon. A police officer, not sure whether the baby was dead or alive, had pulled her out of the rubble of the destroyed federal office building and handed her off to Fields. This photograph was published widely and hailed as an iconic image that captured both the horror and the compassion that marked that day. Although the photograph you're evaluating does not have the same historical significance as Porter's, it gives you an important handle for considering what might cause a "paradigm shift" in your thinking.

To summarize, there are two ways to find paradigm cases. You can "start at the bottom" by recalling a suitable case, then teasing out the characteristics that make it paradigmatic. Alternatively, you can "start in the middle" by brainstorming the characteristics *any* case would have to possess to be paradigmatic, then either recalling an *actual* case or imagining a *hypothetical* case that has these characteristics, perhaps "tweaking" an actual case to fit your parameters.

Making the Right Distinctions is Crucial

Just as journalists around the world were united in their condemnation of Jayson Blair, they were united in their support of another *New York Times* reporter, Judith Miller, when she went to jail in 2005 for refusing to name the source at the center of a federal leak investigation. After all, protecting anonymous sources is considered to be a virtually non-negotiable ethical norm in journalism,[3] just as reporting fact rather than fiction is.

Miller ultimately served 85 days in jail for refusing to comply with a subpoena to testify before a grand jury looking into the "outing" of CIA agent Valerie Plame Wilson. Wilson's role as a CIA agent was first disclosed publicly by Robert Novak in one of his syndicated columns. Wilson's husband, diplomat Joseph Wilson, accused the Bush Administration of a smear campaign against him for disputing the White House's assessment of the threat posed by weapons of mass destruction in Iraq. Deliberately exposing a covert agent is a federal crime.

Miller never actually wrote a story about Valerie Wilson, but was subpoenaed by the federal grand jury investigating the leak, along with several other journalists. She refused to comply even after her source signed a waiver form prepared by special prosecutor Patrick Fitzgerald, worried that the waiver did not express her source's true wishes. Miller's source turned out to be the vice president's chief of staff, I. Lewis Libby. She testified only after Libby phoned her giving her explicit permission to cooperate.

At this point in the story, we seem to have a rather easy ethical call. Although Libby did not seem to be exposing wrongdoing with his "leak" of confidential information, in all other respects this situation seemed to be a paradigmatic example of when reporters should protect source confidentiality. Sometimes the only reason that the public ever finds out about governmental and corporate wrongdoing is because insiders choose to come forward with privileged information that would otherwise never see the light of day. These insiders are called whistleblowers, and the risk of retaliation is so high that they often insist on anonymity. That is why most newsrooms have policies allowing for the limited use of anonymous sources.

The Miller case had several morally relevant features, including:

■ Miller had given Libby her word that she would not name him in any story reporting the information.
■ Miller's reporting could be seriously hampered in the future if she proved untrustworthy, since sources for national security stories are notoriously reluctant to go on the record.
■ By limiting her cooperation with the federal investigation, Miller also avoided giving the impression that the *Times* was an arm of law enforcement, rather than an independent watchdog of the government.
■ Miller's account did not seem directly relevant to the special prosecutor's investigation into the leak, so she would not be seriously impeding justice.
■ Even if she *were* throwing a wrench into the proceedings, there was widespread doubt about the seriousness of the offense in question. In fact, the grand jury did not ultimately charge Libby with breaking the law that makes it a crime to intentionally blow the cover of a covert government agent.[4]

However, after Judith Miller was released from jail and provided details about her interviews with Libby, many of her colleagues inside and outside *The New York Times* criticized her. The editor of the journalism trade magazine *Editor & Publisher* went so far as to call for her dismissal (Mitchell 2005), and her own editor, Bill Keller, apologized for her actions. Why the sudden change of opinion? Some journalists objected to Miller's testifying at all in the belief that the commitment to protect anonymous sources is absolute. However, many more were miffed because she refused to help reporters at her paper piece together her role in the leak investigation and because her own accounts of the Libby interviews raised new ethical concerns.

Among other things, the veteran national security reporter revealed that she agreed to refer to Libby as a "former (Capitol) Hill staffer" instead of a "senior administration official" (J. Miller 2005). Although technically accurate, it was an attribution that did not begin to reflect Libby's actual position in the Bush Administration.[5] Keller also acknowledged that editors at the *Times* never knew what Miller and Libby had talked about—a troubling disclosure considering that, a few months earlier, the paper had acknowledged failing to thoroughly check Blair's sources. Miller, whose reputation had already taken a beating for her part in the paper's gullible coverage of the supposed threat of Iraqi weapons of mass destruction (WMD), finally reached an agreement with the *Times* to retire from her job.[6]

The *Times*, like many other US newspapers, has adopted strict ethical guidelines for the use of anonymous sources. Although the paper's ethics guidelines specify standing authorization to grant anonymity on the national security beat, they also state that reporters should promise anonymity only when they are confident in the newsworthiness and reliability of the information and when there is no other way to get it into print. Further, the guidelines insist that attributions accurately convey the qualifications and motivations of anonymous sources, and they forbid any "coy" devices that may deceive readers (*The New York Times* 2000). Miller insisted that she followed these guidelines in her reporting, but her colleagues weren't so sure.

In hindsight, Miller's case of protecting anonymous sources may not have been paradigmatic after all. Yes, she gave Libby her word that she would conceal his identity, but it is not clear that such a promise was justified. The information seems at best to have been a malicious leak, not something essential for the public to know. In agreeing to use a misleading attribution, Miller maintained her relationship with Libby, but, seemingly, at the expense of the public, her colleagues and her paper.

The Judith Miller case illustrates the complexities involved in identifying relevant characteristics. We may not be privy to all the relevant details of a situation, or perhaps the significant consequences of a decision don't become evident for some time. Correctly classifying a hard case is also imperative. Using the wrong paradigm to do ethics is similar to a judge using the wrong precedent to settle a legal case. In a court of law, such an error would be grounds for appeal; in ethics, it would be cause for moral disapproval.

The Bowman/Smith case illustrates the problem. The editors at *The Courier-Journal* took the paper's policy against naming rape victims as the starting point for their ethical deliberations. This policy placed a premium on preventing harms to women who were raped and presumed that the full truth would make these harms worse. But what if the editors had started out with the new rule that Nolan advocated—that is, name all rape victims? In interviews, they acknowledged various ethical norms that would justify such a policy:

- It would allow the paper to give its readers the truth without making any judgment about guilt or innocence.
- It would be fairer to the accused by treating him and his accuser the same.
- It might eventually contribute to the removal of the stigma attached to rape.

This alternative starting point would have put a premium on fidelity to the public; it would have presumed that the full truth would mitigate harms to the accused and to women who were raped.

When entertaining this policy shift in interviews, the editors mentioned some paradigmatic criteria:

- The victim would be an adult.
- Her identification would not perpetuate stereotypes in news coverage.
- She would not object to being identified in the paper.

If *The Courier-Journal* editors had started with such a paradigm, the burden would have been on women to demonstrate why they should *not* be named in the paper when reporting a rape to police, rather than the burden being on the paper to demonstrate why it *could* sometimes identify such women.

As Albert Jonsen and Stephen Toulmin (1988) point out, where you end up in ethics depends a great deal on where your start. Experience with similar cases and expert knowledge of a moral decision's context are crucial because they help you to choose well no matter how you start your analysis of a case's relevant characteristics: with a paradigm, with ethical norms, with a code, or with analogies to other ambiguous cases.

EYE ON DECEPTION

The cases at the end of this chapter focus on deception in journalism. The exercises will sensitize you to the ethical issues presented by the use of deceptive practices in journalism and provide practice identifying paradigm cases. Before we look at the cases, let's think a bit more about truth telling and deception and why these are key ethical norms in journalism.

Deception as an Ethical Issue

We've already noted the premium that the SPJ ethics code places on the truth. But journalists haven't always been so straight-laced about the truth. In the mid-1800s, newspapers often perpetrated harmless hoaxes on their readers, who willingly suspended disbelief for fun—much the way we might approach a fictional novel or movie today (Tucher 1994).

But later in the same century, journalists began to equate truth with gathering facts unaffected by partisan sympathies. They developed science-like procedures for verifying and selecting these facts that readers could inspect for themselves if they wished. This stance toward truth telling, known as objectivity, continues to distinguish mainstream journalism from other media occupations, despite criticism of objectivity's limitations in recent years.

Deaver (1990) has suggested that being truthful means different things depending on a number of factors. These include a media occupation's primary intent (for example, to inform without bias) and audience expectations (for example, complete and accurate presentation of facts and information). When we consider what truth telling means for different media, it becomes clearer why no one seems particularly upset at the *National Enquirer* or some conspiracy blogs, with their Elvis sightings and their far-fetched theories. These media outlets have the same playful orientation toward the truth as the penny papers of the 1830s, and their readers expect no more and no less. However, if CBS News or the *Los Angeles Times* started tricking its audiences, there'd be a scandal.

But why is truth telling a big deal? And is it a big deal for everybody or just for journalists? To get to the bottom of the ethics of deception, philosopher Sissela Bok adopts a casuistical approach in her influential book *Lying*. She acknowledges that there are lots of ways to deceive—through strategic gestures, silences and imagery, among others. But a lie, which she defines as "any intentionally deceptive message that is *stated*" (Bok 1979:14), is the most blatant. If we can figure out the ethics of lying—the paradigmatic form of deception—then we can be more certain about the ethics of distortion, deflection, omission, and other deceptive methods. Fabrication in journalism is equivalent to lying: The journalist makes up quotes and other statements, passing them off as the truth by placing them in news stories. As the most blatant form of deception in journalism, fabrication is easily condemned.

To those who would try to change the subject by claiming that absolute truth is an unattainable ideal, Bok says, "Get over it." We don't expect people to have perfect knowledge; we just expect them to make a good-faith effort to communicate what they believe to be true. She calls this common-sense notion *truthfulness*. We know that people sometimes make mistakes. For example, when a reporter gets the date for the next City Council meeting wrong due to a typo, we don't think of that falsehood as a lie, but an error. And, while we may worry about her reliability if she's habitually sloppy, we don't judge her to be a liar whose motives can't be trusted.

Bok (1979) says that society as we know it would be impossible without a strong expectation of truthfulness. We wouldn't be able to make plans, agree to contracts, or place any confidence in our educations. In short, there would be no basis for social trust. Given that social trust benefits us all, it's not fair gaming the system as a "free rider," using other people's trust in us to take advantage of them. We also place a high value on truthfulness because we want to make informed decisions as citizens.

Being able to make decisions freely, with our eyes wide open, is essential to autonomy. A major reason why lying has a moral strike against it from the get-go is that it always interferes with the autonomy of the deceived. When we lie to others, even if we're telling a white lie to spare their feelings, we are robbing them of the opportunity to make informed choices for themselves and their communities. Bok (1979) goes so far as to compare the coercive aspect of lying with violence, saying that lying assaults another's free will.

A journalist's job is to make sure we have access to the best information we need to make autonomous choices as individuals and as members of our communities. That's why a major ethical principle in journalism is to "Seek the Truth and Report It." In fact, Borden (2007) has suggested that journalism's mission makes it an intellectual practice like science or teaching. Like scientists and teachers, journalists strive to discover the truth and communicate it responsibly to others. Therefore, moral excellence in journalism (like science and teaching) entails an especially high standard of truthfulness. Not being able to trust journalists to be truthful would be like not being able to trust judges to be fair. The very idea of journalism would be thrown into question.

Besides, lying causes a world of hurt. Bok (1979) notes that the consequences of lying are overwhelmingly negative, a fact we are most likely to appreciate from the perspective of the deceived. Who among us has felt "lucky" or "special" when we found out we were on the receiving end of a lie? More likely, we felt betrayed, violated or patronized. Even the liar pays a price, Bok reminds us, as his character becomes corrupt from lying. And one lie often begets another, so we can't just worry about particular lies. We have to think about how one lie here and one lie there add up to entire practices of deception, like government propaganda or get-rich-quick schemes—or alien hoaxes in the *National Enquirer*.

Because of the importance of truthfulness, Bok (1979) proposes the Principle of Veracity, which states that truthfulness should be the default setting for human communication. We expect people to be truthful except in rare circumstances. And, even then, they must make a reasonable argument for departing from this important ethical norm. One way to do this, as we've seen, is to identify a paradigmatic example of when we might be justified in lying. If we choose a clear enough example, and can successfully pinpoint its relevant characteristics, we can make a good case for allowing the lie. A compelling example will be one that satisfies all those potentially affected by lying, not merely the liar—who'll be too willing to *justify* any lie—nor the deceived—who'll be too unwilling to *excuse* any lie.

Bok (1979) thinks we should actually test our rationale for lying. For this, we must at least imagine (if it's impossible to solicit actual feedback) how our rationale would stand up to public scrutiny. How would reasonable people generally—not just people who share our circumstances or who would benefit from our lie—react to our reasons for lying if they knew about them in advance? Would they buy our reasons, or would they call us out for being self-serving or controlling? Bok calls her method the Test of Publicity. If you think about it, any form of ethical justification has to meet this threshold. If we arrive at a decision using casuistry that we don't think we can defend to other reasonable people, we have cause to doubt the quality of our reasoning.

For example, say a TV station located in a state with no laws against surreptitious taping decided that it would routinely tape sources during interviews without their knowledge. Legally, the station would be in the clear, but what sorts of reasons could it offer outside the newsroom that would justify this practice ethically? Comparing cases of when we think surreptitious taping is justified could help us to isolate these reasons—or they could end up showing us that surreptitious taping is best saved for extraordinary circumstances. Instead of testing out a policy of routine surreptitious taping, we might instead test one that spells out the limited circumstances in which we may tape someone without his or her knowledge.

How could the station test its reasons for the surreptitious taping policy? Whom should it consult? Certainly, we would expect the perspective of sources to be represented since they would be most directly affected. (Who else should be consulted?) Bok's argument is that, whenever possible, consultation through focus groups, working committees, town halls, and similar venues can help us to adopt practices that respect the Principle of Veracity's regard for truthfulness while recognizing that we occasionally may be justified in lying.

However, lying should only be a last resort. Bok (1979) says you have no business even going so far as to test your rationale on a public of reasonable persons unless you've exhausted all truthful alternatives for accomplishing your aim. Truthfulness is that important. Any paradigm for justifying a lie or a deceptive practice would have to possess this feature. If your aim is to have an accurate record of all interviews, think of how you can do this without misleading your sources. For example, you could inform them that you will be taping interviews. If you're worried that warning them will squash their candor, think of how you can help them to be comfortable with recording. (What are some of your ideas?)

Getting a lie past multiple perspectives is a lot tougher than getting it past just us or our peers. This will be true of any decision that violates a widely shared ethical norm. Sometimes, it's so obvious our action would never survive public scrutiny that deliberation is not needed. At other times, the situation is more ambiguous, and we have ourselves a hard case crying out for casuistical analysis.

Besides fabrication and surreptitious taping, a number of ethical problems arise in journalism involving deception, including:

- *Plagiarism.* Using another author's reporting or writing without any acknowledgment, making it look as if it were your own.
- *Staging.* Setting up a photo or video instead of shooting things as they actually happened.
- *Digital manipulation.* Removing or adding visual elements to an existing image.
- *Literary license.* Using composite characters and other literary techniques that are not "literally true."
- *Sensationalism.* Exaggerating the truth for effect.
- *False empathy.* Giving a source the false impression you will write a positive story.
- *Over-specificity.* Deceiving or offending by means of literal accuracy.
- *Undercover reporting.* Deceiving in order to find and report the truth.

As you can see, some of these practices, such as digital manipulation and sensationalism, just "shade" the truth a bit by distorting reality. Others manage to deceive while sticking to the facts. Others use creative means to tell a "larger truth" that's not obvious when you look at "just the facts." All of these are ethically problematic, but some come closer to fabrication—the exemplar of wrong action—than others. The practices of undercover reporting and surreptitious taping, meanwhile, involve outright lying, but the journalists involved lie to their sources, rather than to their audiences. As you consider ethical issues related to deception in the following cases, consider how you might "rank" these practices in order of least ethical to most ethical and why. How is your ranking informed by paradigm cases?

DECEPTION CASES AND WALK-THROUGH EXERCISES

The first set of cases is designed to help you identify a paradigm case. One case is morally clear-cut regarding the acceptable use of deception in undercover reporting; the other cases are less obvious. After you've worked on identifying a paradigm, we'll take a closer look at some specific ethical issues raised by undercover reporting.

Case 1: Participant Observation in Prison[7]

Ted Conover spent almost a year working as a correctional officer at New York's maximum-security prison, Sing Sing. He told no one he was a journalist working on a book about the lived experience of being a prison guard. He published the results of his reporting in his 2001 book, *Newjack: guarding Sing Sing* (from the term used to describe rookie guards).

Situational Clues

■ Before resorting to undercover reporting, Conover tried for two years to get the story in other ways: by interviewing state officials (who refused), by obtaining access to another New York prison with the help of the guards' union (the guards froze up), and by doing a profile on a guard in training (the academy turned him down).

■ After agonizing about the use of deception, Conover applied for a job as a guard, passed an entrance exam and went through seven weeks of demanding training at the academy. Two years later, working at Sing Sing, he had to deal with the same fear, brutality, confinement, and family stress as the other prison guards. The experience gave him a whole new understanding of the nation's huge incarceration system and how it affects the people who live their lives within it.

■ In his book, Conover explained his reasons for going undercover and exactly what he did and did not do while he was a participant-observer. He carefully considered what to put in his book and left out those details that, in his judgment, would endanger the guards. He used pseudonyms to protect the privacy of those about whom he wrote. When his investigation was done, Conover disclosed his deception to several guards; two months before his book's publication, he let the Sing Sing Prison superintendent know about his investigation.

■ At first, prison officials were hostile to the book: it became a forbidden item inside New York prisons and later was censored. The guards' union, however, was happy with it, and dozens of officers showed up at a public reading of the book at a library near the prison. Several guards asked Hanover to sign their copies of the book; some stayed afterward to get their pictures taken with him.

■ "For all the time I spent in an officer's uniform, one poignant reality of the life had only begun to sink in, and that was the depth of the stigma they felt, the pain of society's disregard," Hanover wrote in an afterword to *Newjack*'s paperback edition. "The antidote was recognition, and an appreciation of the job's unique difficulties. This *Newjack* seemed to provide" (Conover, n.d.).

Walk-Through Exercise: Identifying Paradigms

1. Do you think Conover's use of deception was ethical? Why or why not?
2. Which of the facts above seem most relevant to you in deciding whether Conover acted ethically? Explain why you think they are morally relevant.
3. Could these features of the Conover case be used to assess the ethics of other cases of undercover reporting?
4. Do you think this case is clear-cut enough to be used as a paradigm case? If so, what kind—an exemplar of right action or an exemplar of wrong

MAKING HARD CHOICES IN JOURNALISM ETHICS

action? If not, how would you change the case to make it a paradigm case?
5. Does the case have any features that are morally ambiguous? If so, what are they?
6. If the guards had reacted negatively to Conover's book—say, by accusing him of betrayal or sensationalism—would that change your opinion of this case?

Case 2: The Dictator's Advocate Who Wasn't[8]

Ken Silverstein pretended to be "Kenneth Case," a consultant for a fake energy company called The Maldon Group, to catch Washington lobbyists taking money to popularize a dictator. Presumably, "Case" wanted to launch a PR campaign to improve the image of Turkmenistan, an Eastern European country where his London-based client did business. And, in fact, a couple of lobbying firms took the bait, offering to plant op-ed pieces in newspapers, orchestrate bogus conferences and other dubious services for fees climbing as high as $1.5 million. Silverstein, the Washington editor of *Harper's Magazine*, published a first-person account of his sting in a 2007 cover story for the magazine.

Situational Clues

- Silverstein made sure his client was unsavory. The reason he chose the natural gas business was because of the documented corruption in the Turkmen-Ukraine gas trade and the suspected role of middlemen in hiding the profits. The reason he chose Turkmenistan was because it had a neo-Stalinist regime.
- To carry off his deception, Silverstein made up some business cards, gave a fake address, created a barebones website, and recruited a friend to accompany him to meetings he set up with lobbyists in Washington.
- Silverstein's deception resulted in a close-up view of the depths to which lobbyists will stoop for money and the privileged access they enjoy thanks to their success in hiring former public officials, and to lax enforcement of disclosure laws.
- Silverstein, who had reported on Washington lobbying for several years, defended his deception by citing the public interest involved in the story and the impossibility of obtaining the same information without misrepresenting himself.
- "In my case, I was able to gain an inside glimpse into a secretive culture of professional spinners only by lying myself," Silverstein (2007a) wrote in a *Los Angeles Times* op-ed responding to his critics. "I disclosed my deceptions clearly in the piece I wrote (whereas the lobbyists I met boasted of how they were able to fly under the radar screen in seeking

to shape US foreign policy). If readers feel uncomfortable with my methods, they're free to dismiss my findings."

Walk-Through Exercise: Identifying Paradigms

1. How is this case similar to the Conover case? Are there important differences? Explain, making reference to the relevant characteristics you came up with earlier.
2. Which case is a better candidate for a paradigm case: this one or the Conover case? Why?
3. Although they weren't as colorful as Silverstein's piece, earlier news stories had documented similar deals with repressive governments using similar PR strategies. Does this affect your assessment of this case?
4. How could you defend Silverstein's deception publicly? Whom should you consider in making your defense?
5. Let's consider the Conover case a paradigmatic example of ethically justified deception. What do you conclude about Silverstein's use of deception when you compare it to the Conover case?

Case 3: Packing Chickens—and a Punch[9]

Tony Horwitz, a reporter for *The Wall Street Journal*, got hired at poultry processing plants in Mississippi and Arkansas for a 1994 series investigating working conditions at dead-end jobs, "9 to Nowhere." Following his paper's strict no-deception policy, he used his real name on his application, gave his real credentials (a college degree from Columbia University) and his real employer, Dow Jones & Co., the parent company of his newspaper (though he did not say what he did for Dow Jones). He was hired on the spot without questions because of the high turnover rate in the industry.

Situational Clues

■ In the model of Upton Sinclair and his undercover investigation of the meat-packing industry, *The Jungle*, Horwitz experienced the same filth, stress, hazards, and dehumanizing labor conditions as the others packing chicken parts.
■ When it was all over, he tried to return a week's pay, but the company told him to keep it because he had earned it.

Walk-Through Exercise: Identifying Paradigms

1. How is this case similar to the Conover case? To the Silverstein case?
2. If there are important differences between this case and the earlier ones, what are they?

3. Do you conclude that Horwitz' use of deception was ethical? Why or why not?
4. Which case was closer to the Conover case? The Silverstein case or this case? How would you rank these cases from most to least ethical?
5. One reason the Food Lion jury was unsympathetic to ABC was because the reporters had been "disloyal" to the grocery chain by taking time out of their paid jobs as meat packers and deli workers to film and interview co-workers about unsanitary food-handling practices. Horwitz didn't film, photograph or interview anybody at the poultry-processing plants while he worked for $5.10 an hour (though he did conduct numerous interviews before and after going undercover). Does this affect your assessment of his actions?
6. Horwitz' "9 to Nowhere" series won the 1995 Pulitzer Prize for national reporting. Does this affect your assessment?

Case 4: Black and White[10]

A black church in Philadelphia—a large church with about 5,000 members—had been built by a dynamic leader who was retiring. His spiritual sons had been given control of the church, but they began feuding, contending for power. *The Philadelphia Inquirer* decided it would have to infiltrate the church to figure out what was happening.

Situational Clues

■ One reporter was sent to the church on the up and up to get the story, but that reporter (who happened to be white), was thrown out.
■ The paper asked Kim McLarin to go. McLarin is black.
■ All the women in the church dressed in white. Besides hiding the fact that she's a reporter, she would have to dress completely in white in order to escape detection.

Walk-Through Exercise: Identifying a Paradigm Case

1. Is this case more like the Conover case or the Silverstein case? Which features of this case seem most relevant to your comparison? How could you explain their moral relevance to a colleague?
2. Silverstein wore a suit and fake prescription glasses to "look" like a consultant. Conover and Horwitz dressed the same way as the workers they were observing. How is this different from the way you would have to dress in this case to mask your identity as a reporter? If it's significantly different, how much does it matter ethically?
3. Do you conclude that it would be ethical to attend this meeting, dressed in white, without disclosing that you're a reporter? Justify your answer,

making reference to the relevant characteristics you came up with for the Conover case.

4. If you refuse to go, what would you say to your editor?

One Last Look at Undercover Reporting

1. Pam Zekman, an investigative reporter for the local CBS station in Chicago, went undercover many times when she wrote for the *Chicago Sun-Times*, including a role in the Mirage Bar sting. During a panel discussion about undercover reporting on the National Public Radio program *On the Media* (air date 17 October 2008), she said:

    I have always been a believer that the undercover technique, when there's no other way to get the story, is a truer way of getting at what's happening in an abusive area, and a more credible way for the viewer or for the reader because they can see and hear what's happening. They don't have to trust that these anonymous sources exist. They don't have to make that leap of faith.

2. What do you think of this argument? Are audiences better off trusting reporters than, say, anonymous sources whom they cannot evaluate?

3. Many undercover reports are written in the first person. Does this increase the credibility of the reporting or diminish it?

4. Horwitz got in there and worked side by side with the people he was observing and developed empathy for them. Is empathy an appropriate response for a reporter? In Horwitz' case, perhaps it was natural that he would identify with exploited workers. Conover dealt with prison guards who were sometimes brutal and not always easy to like. Yet he grew to care about his subjects as well. Is this OK?

5. Compare the features of Case 1 with the ethical guidelines for journalistic deception developed by the Poynter Institute's Bob Steele, posted at http://www.poynter.org/content/content_view.asp?id=866. How closely do they match? Would you modify any of Steele's guidelines based on the Conover case? Based on any of the other undercover reporting cases we've looked at?

The next set of cases is designed to help you classify cases as being of one "type" versus another. Remember, this is important for settling on an appropriate paradigm.

Case 5: To Catch a Murderer[11]

In 2003, *The King County Journal*, a 39,000-circulation newspaper in Washington state, knowingly printed a fake arson story at the request of the county prosecutor's office and the sheriff's department. Steven Sherer had hired his cellmate at the state penitentiary to torch the home of his former mother-in-law, who had taken in his teenage son after Sherer was convicted of murdering his wife. The cellmate's payment: $17,000 in hidden jewelry.

Situational Clues

- The arson was supposed to be a trial run for Sherer's next project: killing the four kids of the prosecutor who had put him in prison. Officials got wind of the plot from a prison informant and confronted Sherer's cellmate upon his release.
- The cellmate told them that Sherer wanted a newspaper article reporting the arson as proof that he had followed through with their agreement.
- The sheriff's office staged the fire, and the paper printed a brief article on 23 March 2002, reporting that the fire department was investigating a possible arson at the targeted house.
- The article was mailed to Sherer in prison, and he followed through on his deal with the cellmate. As a result, authorities were able to charge him with solicitation to commit arson.
- The *Journal*'s editor cited the paper's responsibility to the community and the extraordinary circumstances to defend its decision to publish the fake news story.

Walk-Through Exercise: Classifying a Case

1. Look at the list of problematic journalistic practices involving deception earlier in the chapter. What kind of case is this?
2. Are there additional ethical issues besides deception that affect your judgment about this case? If so, what are they?
3. If there are additional issues besides deception, do they change the way you would classify this case? If not deception, then what?
4. Sherer had tried to have his son and mother-in-law murdered before, but authorities did not have the evidence they needed to charge him. Does that make a difference in whether you think the *King County Journal* acted ethically?
5. Would the *Journal* have been justified in complying with the sheriff's request if Sherer had not specifically demanded that the proof be a newspaper article?
6. Fort Collins, Colorado, police—among other departments—have admitted to occasionally planting fake stories in newspapers to draw out criminal suspects. Would the *Journal* face any ethical problem if the sheriff's department had planted the story without the paper's knowledge?

Case 6: To Catch a Predator

NBC's prime-time news magazine, *Dateline*, has been airing a regular segment called "To Catch a Predator," featuring correspondent Chris Hansen, since 1994. Hansen works with members of an online watchdog organization to set up men who solicit minors for sex in Internet chat rooms. These paid "consultants," pretending to be as young as 12, lure suspected pedophiles to houses equipped with hidden cameras. The investigations have taken place in several different states.

Situational Clues

■ Some predators have shown up naked; one showed up with his 5-year-old son. First, they are greeted by a young-looking decoy who pretends to be the boy or girl the man was chatting with online. Then Hansen comes out, notebook in hand, to interview the surprised men. He does not identify himself as a journalist or inform them at this point that they are being recorded.

■ Hansen confronts the suspects with explicit transcripts of their online chats ("Picture this—picture this: you lying back I straddle your chest"). A camera crew emerges, and the men find out they are on a news program.

■ Police await outside, where the men are arrested, on camera, after emerging from the house (unless there is reason to intercept them en route).

■ To date, more than 250 people have been charged with sex-related crimes as a result of this ongoing sting operation. "When we catch somebody who has committed a sexual assault in the past, especially when you talk about the sexual assault of a child, to me, I think that's satisfying to expose somebody like that," Hansen said in an interview posted on *Dateline*'s website (Hansen 2007: 'Frequent viewer question #4: Why keep doing these investigations?').

Walk-Through Exercise: Classifying Cases

1. Is this case more like Case 5 or more like the undercover reporting cases?
2. How would you classify this case? Could you use Case 1 as a paradigm case for comparison purposes, or does this case involve substantially different ethical issues?
3. Sometimes, local law enforcement deputizes members of the Perverted Justice group that *Dateline* works with so that they can use what the group has found out as evidence in their criminal investigations. Does cooperating so closely with Perverted Justice and the police hurt *Dateline*'s independence? Is the arrangement appropriate as long as no one from NBC gets deputized and the network shares only previously broadcast or posted footage for use as evidence?

4. In 2000, police in Newark, New Jersey, pretended to be photojournalists by taking the cameras of TV photographers to fool a father who was holding his 9-year-old son hostage at gunpoint. The Radio-Television News Directors Association (RTNDA) condemned the action, citing the need to maintain press independence from law enforcement and the dangers created for real journalists who might be suspected of being police officers (Steele 2000). Is this a reasonable position? If there is reason to think that such cooperation may be justified as a rare exception, what conditions would you place on the practice?

Case 7: Explosive Footage[12]

In a 1992 segment about General Motors' C/K pickup trucks called "Waiting to Explode," *Dateline NBC* told viewers about the potential for the trucks to catch on fire in side-impact collisions. The network hired safety experts to run a test to see what would happen when one of the trucks was hit in the side. The experts installed small rockets under one of the vehicles that would ignite should any gas leak from the tank during the crash. NBC did not disclose this to viewers.

Situational Clues

■ The carmaker had been fending off allegations from consumers and advocacy groups that the "side-saddle" design of the gas tanks was unsafe because it caused post-crash fires. National traffic safety officials were contemplating a recall of the trucks.
■ After the segment aired, GM said that the tank in one of the cars did not rupture, as reported, and that the vehicles were going faster than suggested, among other problems. As part of a defamation lawsuit settlement, NBC apologized on air for the factual errors and for the "inappropriate" demonstration.

Walk-Through Exercise: Classifying Cases

1. Is staging a worse form of deception than fabrication? Than undercover reporting?
2. If *Dateline* had informed viewers about the "extra help" they had in ensuring a test crash would result in a fire, would that have taken care of the deception problem?
3. Here, NBC is not cooperating with an arm of the government, but with a private business known for providing expert witness testimony about car safety defects. GM accused the network of hiring a contractor with an ax to grind. Is that a fair criticism?

4. How independent can journalists be when they rely on outside consultants to conduct tests, reel in subjects or perform other tasks that "make" the news?

5. Is deception the key issue here or independence? Based on your answer, how would you classify this case for purposes of ethical analysis?

6. Which case discussed so far is the most similar to this one? Which features of this case matter most to your answer?

The next pair of cases deals with digital manipulation. We'll look at some specific ethical issues raised by alterations made to news photographs and video. You'll also get some practice developing a hypothetical paradigm case.

Case 8: Dueling Covers[13]

The arrest of football star O.J. Simpson on suspicion of murdering his wife and a friend was big news in 1994. Both *TIME* and *Newsweek* magazines decided to run the mugshot taken of Simpson when he was booked into jail on their June 27 covers. Yet the photos looked drastically different.

Situational Clues

- *Newsweek*, with the headline "Trail of Blood," ran the original image taken by police.

- *TIME*, however, decided to go with a more "artsy" treatment of the photo, adjusting the color so that it was noticeably darker, and shrinking the size of Simpson's prisoner ID number. The cover ran with the headline "An American Tragedy." The magazine did not tell readers about the changes made to the photograph.

- *TIME's* managing editor said the intent of the photo adjustments was to convey the tragedy of a fallen hero, but critics accused the magazine of racism by making Simpson look darker and, by implication, evil.

Case 9: Dueling Skaters[14]

Tonya Harding shot into the national spotlight after she admitted covering up the role of her ex-husband and her bodyguard in ordering an attack on her rival, Nancy Kerrigan, during practice at the 1994 US Figure Skating Championships. Kerrigan, who was hit on the knee, had to withdraw from that event, which Harding won. Olympics officials contemplated disqualifying Harding from the 1994 Olympic team, but relented after she threatened to sue. As the Olympics got closer, anticipation was building for the showdown between the two divas. The Long Island, New York, paper *Newsday* obliged.

Situational Clues

- The paper ran a photo illustration on the front page apparently showing the two rivals skating together.
- The headline was "Tonya, Nancy to meet at practice."
- The cutline said, "Tonya Harding, left, and Nancy Kerrigan, appear to skate together in this New York *Newsday* composite illustration. Tomorrow, they'll really take to the ice together."

Walk-Through Exercise: Hypothetical Paradigms

1. Is deception the key issue in *TIME*'s alteration of the Simpson photo, or is it racism? Based on your answer, how would you classify this case for purposes of ethical analysis? How does your classification affect your ethical assessment of this case?
2. Do you think *Newsday*'s composite picture of Tonya Harding and Nancy Kerrigan was ethical? Which features of the case do you think are most relevant to your assessment?
3. What are some key differences between the Simpson case and the Harding/Kerrigan case? What are some of the key similarities?
4. Develop a hypothetical paradigm that exemplifies the unethical use of digital manipulation in the news. You may use the case characteristics you thought were most relevant in assessing Case 8 and Case 9, or you could take the case you thought was the most unethical and "tweak" it to make it the very model of irresponsibility. When you're done, go to http://www.nytco.com/company/business_units/integrity.html and check out *The New York Times'* policy on "Photography and Images." How does your paradigm compare to this policy?

One Last Look at Digital Manipulation

1. Although *Newsweek* didn't alter Simpson's mugshot, Deni Elliott (2004) has pointed out that the headline "Trail of Blood," has the same effect of demonizing the athlete as *TIME*'s photo illustration. Do you agree?
2. Does the potential for reinforcing stereotypes—such as the stereotype of black men having criminal tendencies—make certain editing techniques acceptable for some groups and not others?
3. One of the best-known cases of fabrication in journalism history was that of Janet Cooke, a *Washington Post* reporter who had to return her Pulitzer Prize in 1981. She admitted that Jimmy, the 8-year-old cocaine addict featured in her award-winning story, was not a real person, but a "composite" of several persons she had learned about in her reporting on Washington's drug problem. In what ways is a written composite such as Cooke's "Jimmy" similar to a composite image such as the photo of Harding and Kerrigan in *Newsday*? In what ways is it different?

4. *Newsday*, unlike *TIME*, acknowledged that its photo was only an "appearance" of reality. What difference, if any, does that make ethically? Is the *Newsday* photo misleading despite the explanation in the cutline?

5. Are there different standards of truthfulness for words rather than images in journalism? For newspapers rather than television? For "legacy news media" rather than "new media"?

CHAPTER 4

▼ # USING CASE COMPARISONS TO MAKE ETHICAL CHOICES

A news story has always been the creation of a reporter, assembling the facts the reporter discovers into an order that tells a story. The photo always had a stronger claim to accuracy. The light through the lens burned the negative and became the print. Only dodging and burning (lightening and darkening) specific areas of the image were allowed. And that was only to produce a more accurate picture—to highlight details in the photo the eye itself would have seen.

That was the paradigm case for ethically responsible photojournalism. Now, the photojournalist can easily darken the blue of the sky, sharpen elements in a photo that are out of focus, or remove objects protruding from the subject's head. Ethical news photography has become more problematic.

This chapter explores this shift into more problematic cases. We'll learn how to use the relevant characteristics from a paradigm case to draw conclusions about the ethical acceptability of complex cases. The paradigm case provides a search pattern—like the grid used by *CSI* investigators to "map" the evidence at a crime scene. Certain features of the new case at hand "stand out" as moral evidence because of the template provided by the paradigm case. As in crime scene investigations, various scenarios can play out when performing a case-based comparison in journalism ethics.

USING CASE COMPARISONS IN ETHICS

At *The Herald-Times* of Bloomington, Indiana, a committee of reporters and editors considered what to do about free gifts that reporters sometimes received from sources (Boeyink 1992: 108–109). The conversation began with quick references to two paradigm cases. You have already read about one of the paradigm cases: the reporter who went to interview a diamond company official and came back with a set of diamond earrings. For all members of the committee, this was out of bounds, a clear violation of ethics. You can't take diamond earrings without risking your independence as a journalist and, consequently, undermining the confidence a reader—or an editor—has in the truthfulness of your story.

Almost as quickly, one of the committee members offered the second paradigm case: "But what's wrong with accepting a free cup of coffee? I can't be bought for a cup of coffee." (This conversation took place before the $5 skinny cinnamon dolce latte, but never mind that!) Again, everyone agreed. The boundaries of the paradigm cases were established. What happened next moved the committee members to another key step of casuistry: analogous cases.

Back to the committee's conversation. . . "Fine," said another reporter. "Free coffee is OK, but what about coffee and a donut?" "What about a free lunch?" asked another. "At what kind of restaurant?"

The committee members were testing one of the paradigm cases with similar (analogous) cases to see whether consensus held or dissension reared its tasty head (journalists with a love of free food are a particularly contentious lot). In effect, they were exploring the middle ground between one paradigm—let's call it "the gift" (diamond earrings)—and a second paradigm—let's call that "courtesy" (free coffee). At what point does a freebie become a gift? At what point is the freebie only a matter of common courtesy? In other words, does the freebie in question fit the courtesy paradigm or the gift paradigm?

As the value of the gifts rises, the paradigm will ultimately shift from "courtesy" to "gift." The task of the casuist is to find that tipping point in looking at each case.

The problem with any kind of case-based reasoning is that the cases are never exactly like the paradigm case. The details of every case are different. The journalist needs to decide when the differences matter and when the similarities outweigh the differences. The devil is in sorting through those details. Analogous cases help do that sorting. And to be honest, it can be fun.

For example, what counts as the truth in publishing a quotation? Again, two clear paradigms emerge. We can all agree that publishing the quotation exactly as spoken would be right. And completely fabricating the quote would be wrong. But what about these analogous cases?

- The speaker stutters periodically. Do you include the stutter?
- The speaker uses incorrect grammar. Do you correct it? Does it matter if the speaker is a governor or a private citizen?
- How about when the speaker said "hemming and guffawing" and should have said "hemming and hawing"?
- Should you capture dialect in the quote if that's the way someone speaks? Under what conditions?
- Should you eliminate clauses that obscure the meaning of the sentence?

A comparison of these kinds of analogous cases (and others you can think of) is likely to help us figure out what policy we ought to have on statements that we put in quotation marks. More important, that comparison could well expose some of the reasons why we feel the way we do about altering quotations. For one thing, we are likely to disagree based on the way in which we define "truth." Truth as accuracy will push us closer to the paradigm of "no changes." Truth as meaning will allow us to consider more options— though obviously far short of fabrication.

Other factors can also emerge from the use of analogous cases. Some differences in the analogous cases will be based on unique factors, not the central paradigm's key ethical norm (truth). For example, grammar problems raise new ethical questions about respect for the source. Readers may wonder if we are mocking the source when we keep the grammatical errors in place. Dialect may turn on differences in our expectations for spoken language and written language.

In short, we don't always know exactly what the analogous case will add to our analysis. The comparisons could be straightforward, problematic or just plain ambiguous. Let's take a look at these different outcomes of analogous cases.

Straightforward Comparisons

Sometimes ethical analysis turns a simple problem into something complex and confusing (they teach that in graduate school). But the results of some comparisons can be very straightforward. This happens when the case under analysis matches up with virtually every aspect of the paradigm case.

Many smaller newspapers think of themselves as newspapers of record. In that context, they have established policies on the publication of official information from public agencies such as the police or the courts. For example, the policy for police records (often a paradigm case) might be that all arrests for shoplifting will be published as long as the alleged shoplifter is an adult and the value of the goods taken is more than $100. When the police reporter picks up the latest report and finds an arrest for shoplifting by a female, aged 35, of a stuffed animal valued at $112, the comparison to the policy is straightforward. This may even be an unusual case in that the woman is a well-known local teacher. She may call the newspaper, pleading that publication of her arrest will ruin her reputation and risk the loss of her job. But for the purposes of deciding whether to publish her name on the records page, the only relevant features are her adult status and the value of the alleged theft. End of story.

The good thing about cases like this is that they are relatively simple, even if the cases aren't a perfect match in all their details. Journalists need to make dozens, perhaps hundreds, of decisions each day. Most of them will be simple, perhaps not even rising to the level of conscious analysis. But the importance of this kind of comparison should not be overlooked. This comparison of new cases with the paradigm case assures a level of consistency and fairness in the handling of news. As Aristotle argued, we should treat similar cases similarly. And although some details of the new case are different, they may not be important differences.

The use of the straightforward comparison is important in a second way. Once you have made a decision on a tough case, you have set a precedent. That is, you have established a standard for future cases that are similar. Neither case will be a paradigm case, but the goal will be to be consistent in the way you make decisions about all cases. Let's go back to the Bowman/Smith case.

As we have seen, the Bowman/Smith case itself is a hard case, not a straight-forward one. The involvement of a prominent person (William Kennedy Smith) and the intensive media coverage of the trial raised a new issue for some news outlets such as *The Courier-Journal*. So the editors decided to name Patricia Bowman along with Smith in their coverage of the trial as a matter of fairness. In effect, they were creating a new paradigm for what came to be called "celebrity" rape cases. That established a precedent for similar cases in the future.

So when Desiree Washington accused boxer Mike Tyson of raping her in an Indianapolis hotel, the editors at *The Courier-Journal* did not hesitate to name Washington. Managing editor Steve Ford was clear about why that decision was made: this case was like the Bowman/Smith case in all the key features that made that case an exception to their policy. Tyson was a prominent celebrity, and the trial coverage would be extensive—just like Bowman/Smith.

Obviously, these cases are not identical. William Kennedy Smith was part of a prominent political family (though not himself in political office); Mike Tyson was a professional boxer with a reputation for violence. But this was a difference that didn't make a difference to the editors. For them, the cases were similar enough in their key features to be handled the same way. In other words, even though the Bowman/Smith case was not straightforward, the Washington/Tyson case was. Once the precedent had been set, the application to this new case was clear.

Problematic Comparisons

At other times, one or more characteristics of the paradigm case do not apply in a straightforward way to the case being analyzed. The differences between the paradigm case and the new case are more significant than a few details. Before we head into that territory, keep one thing in mind. No one can predict exactly how any comparison will work out. As we noted earlier, that's why your preparation as a casuist is so important. You will need to decide for yourself how best to deal with these cases. Practice with the cases in this book will help. So will talking with others.

However, we can predict some of the strategies that may be helpful in these problematic comparisons. Learning these will help you choose the best course for your own analysis.

Strategy 1: Think Relevance

You know what the crucial features of the paradigm case are. Like the grid from the *CSI* crime scene, these factors are neatly laid out. But each new case is different in some way. The trick is to decide which of the similarities and which of the differences are relevant.

Let's go back to the use of quotations. We can agree with the paradigm case: quoting someone using her exact words is clearly right. However, in the real case before us, the governor stumbled over a word, stuttering slightly. Should we reproduce her stutter in the quotation? Or should we conclude that the paradigm case is about accuracy in reproducing the exact words, not accuracy in reproducing every sound made? If the latter, you have made a decision about the irrelevance of the stutter. It is a difference that does not make a difference.

But what if the governor makes an error in grammar? She says, "These new regulations governing the state lottery is a major step forward." Is the grammatical error irrelevant because we recognize the different standard for spoken language and written language? Or is it relevant because of the governor's public standing and experience in dealing with the media?

Relevance is also a key question when the case becomes more complex. The use of deceptive techniques in gathering information is a perfect example. It's one thing to assert that journalists are committed to telling the truth to audiences. But what about misrepresenting oneself as a way of gathering information? Years ago, the *Chicago Sun-Times* wanted to write a story about corruption among the city's public safety inspectors. Restaurant owners and others would tell reporters off the record about being forced to bribe officials to get certified as meeting health and fire safety standards. But the *Sun-Times* wanted to get that information attributed to real people, not just anonymous sources. So they set up a bar, deliciously called "The Mirage," staffed it with journalists, and waited for the inspectors to demand payoffs. The plan worked perfectly, allowing the *Sun-Times* to publish a series of 25 stories on government corruption in Chicago ("1978: Bribes" 2008).

But when the project was nominated for a Pulitzer Prize, the Pulitzer board did not give the *Sun-Times* the award. Undercover reporting has been discouraged by Pulitzer judges. As Bill Bradley, former executive editor of

The Washington Post, said: "I don't think reporters should misrepresent themselves. Period" (Paterno 1997). The argument was that the method of gathering the information was relevant to one's ethical judgment on the story itself. Deceptive means were relevant to judging the story unethical, even when the information was true. Is Bradley right? Must journalists tell the truth (not misrepresent their identities) in gathering information as well as when publishing it? Or is the journalist's commitment to the truth limited to what is written in the story? How you decide these questions of relevance will clearly shape your views about the way this case fits—or does not fit—the truth-telling paradigm.

Strategy 2: Look for Conflicts of Ethical Norms

Often, when a case is more complex, the complexity may introduce other ethical norms. This creates tension with the paradigm case. For example, the question of whether to alter the grammar in a quote from a private citizen not used to interacting with the media introduces a tension between truth telling (accuracy in the quote) and the harm that quote could cause the source in the form of public ridicule.

Or take the case of a reporter at a major regional newspaper. He was told to do a background story on a political candidate running for mayor. The broader framework of this story meant that more than the current political campaign would be included in the story. The reporter needed to find and include any past information that voters would need to know in order to choose among several candidates. The reporter failed to uncover a family business scandal involving the candidate's brother and father. The scandal had taken place more than eight years earlier. Although the candidate had done a small amount of legal work for the family firm, he had no part in the corruption and was not a part of the firm.[1]

Let's imagine that the reporter had found this information. Should he have included it? Clearly, the focus of the reporting about this candidate is broad. The goal is to present a rich, contextual truth about the life of this candidate. But a rehearsal of the scandal involving his father and brother, even if presented accurately, runs the risk of raising questions about this candidate's trustworthiness. This story isn't just about telling the truth anymore; it is also about another ethical norm: fairness. In that context, decisions about the relevance of that information have the potential to frame the ethical debate as a conflict of ethical norms.

Cases involving more than one ethical norm are at the heart of journalism ethics. A significant number of cases you will face in a journalism career involve a choice among ethical norms: tell the truth, but subject someone to harm; protect your autonomy at the price of compassion; keep a promise to a source and rob your audience of the crucial knowledge of where you got the information.

These conflicts are likely with any ethical framework that offers more than one ethical basis for making ethical choices. That's the key problem we discussed in Chapter 2. No one can tell you which norm is more important without the details of the case. That's why casuistry pays so much attention to the details. The facts matter in knowing whether the truth of the story to be told is more important than the harm that may be done to the source.

That's also why casuistry pays close attention to relevance. We need to get the facts right, but the real question is whether the facts are relevant to our judgments about what is right. Only close attention to the facts and their relevance will provide the clues to which ethical norm has more weight in any particular case.

Strategy 3: Consider New Paradigms

Up to this point, we've been exploring how to deal with increased complexity in relation to the paradigm case. However, some cases will be so different that they will force us to consider revising the original paradigm or even finding a new one, as we saw in Chapter 3. One of the most valuable aspects of analogous cases is that they can expose weaknesses in the earlier paradigm. As a consequence, we may develop new guidelines, modifying our earlier mistaken—or oversimplified—paradigm.

In the case of quotations, the analogous cases presented earlier in the chapter challenge one of the paradigms: truth telling as accuracy in quoting sources. Some of the analogous cases (the quote with bad grammar) may cause us to refine our paradigm: use accurate quotes, but correct for grammar to avoid embarrassing sources.

In other cases, the effect on the paradigm could be more radical. For example, one of the analogous cases involves an important quote that is too full of digressions to be clear. In addressing this analogous case, one nationally known journalist argued that our ultimate obligation was to the audience. If stripping away the unneeded clauses clarified the meaning of the quote, then that was the right thing to do. What seems to be happening in his argument is a shift in the paradigm: from truth as accuracy to truth as meaning. If the new paradigm holds, we would clearly make very different decisions about what we could do with quotations.

But remember this: The shift of paradigms is always an ethical choice, just like defining the relevant details of the case (strategy 1) and resolving conflicts of ethical norms (strategy 2). You can see this clearly in the case of truth telling. If we shift from a paradigm of truth as accuracy to a paradigm of truth as meaning, journalists would have much broader latitude in dealing with quotes. Where does that latitude stop? Jeffrey Masson sued journalist Janet Malcolm over her story about Masson, charging that she fabricated some of the quotes attributed to him. Although the case is complicated, a key element in the court's judgment was that Malcolm was not required to prove that her quotes were accurate. In fact, the standard applied by the court was that "a deliberate alteration of the words uttered by a plaintiff does not equate with knowledge of falsity. . . unless the alteration results in a material change in the meaning conveyed by the statement."[2]

But even if Malcolm's quotes were legally protected, were they ethical? Under a paradigm of truth as accuracy, the clear answer is "no." Under the truth-as-meaning paradigm, the answer is not so obvious. In other words, the shift in paradigms has ethical consequences.

Ambiguous Comparisons

It's time for a confession. Case-based reasoning, like any other ethical decision-making method, provides no guarantee that you will reach the one and only "correct" conclusion in a controversial case. As we noted in Chapter 1, ethics is not math. A number of acceptable solutions to an ethical problem are possible, and reasonable people may disagree about which is best. You cannot do normative ethics without exercising a considerable amount of judgment.

Here's what case-based reasoning *will* do: Paying attention to the case details will help you understand the case, and it will help you sort out the relevant details from the irrelevant facts. Using case-based reasoning, you can identify paradigm cases, resolve conflicts of ethical norms and create guidelines and precedents to help you in future similar cases.

But it won't make you infallible. Some cases will challenge you from beginning to end, no matter what tools you apply. Ethics cannot be reduced to a computer program. Let's look at a few ways this ambiguity of outcome can arise.

When the Case Matches Only Some of the Paradigm Characteristics

Case-based analysis may lead you to conclude that a given case is sufficiently ambiguous to preclude judgment about whether it crosses the line (just as the police may declare that a case cannot be solved).

Think of it this way: we believe seven characteristics are relevant in the paradigm case for right action, but the new case matches only five out of seven relevant characteristics. Normally, that's enough grounds to conclude the case is essentially similar to the paradigm, but maybe not as ethical. On the other hand, if you have two matches out of five, you can reasonably conclude that your case is, in fact, pretty unethical (albeit not completely awful). Being able to articulate our judgments with this kind of precision is one of casuistry's advantages.

Of course, even one key moral difference may be enough to shift your judgment about a case entirely (usually because it has a domino effect on other characteristics or is in itself definitive of a moral problem—what we compared to dispositive evidence in forensic science). Realizing this can be useful because it helps us to grasp what is truly at the heart of our decision.

The Bowman/Smith case illustrates this phenomenon because the nature of a "celebrity" rape introduces only one new dimension—intensive national coverage—to the case. The relevance of that? Fairness. For the Louisville *Courier-Journal* editors, this raised the question of whether the old paradigm still applied, just as case-based reasoning would predict.

One way to arrive at this insight is to "tweak" a case to see how many differences, or which differences, "flip" a case from ethical to unethical or vice versa. This strategy can help us find an alternative that neutralizes the most important ethical liability we're facing. Or it can help us figure out when an exception is warranted to a paradigm whose characteristics still capture what we consider to be the relevant moral presumptions for the kind of case we're dealing with.

When We Have Unresolved Doubt and Uncertainty

Doubt can arise from any number of factors. We lack all the facts when government documents are confidential—or we have so many documents we are drowning in a complex web of information. We can't predict the consequences of publishing a controversial photo. We are unsure about the relevance of old information to a current case. The ethical norms in conflict in the case (truth telling and promise keeping) seem evenly balanced.

The case of Dan Cohen and the *St. Paul Pioneer Press* illustrates several of these ambiguities. Reporter Bill Salisbury promised Cohen anonymity in return for Cohen's information about Marlene Johnson, a candidate for lieutenant governor in Minnesota. The information documented three charges of unlawful assembly and one charge of petty theft against Johnson. But Cohen was an adviser to the Independent-Republican candidate for governor. Salisbury's editors overrode his promise and published Cohen's name as the source of the information.

This case leaves us with plenty of room for doubt. Did Salisbury have the authority to grant anonymity? His editors said he needed to check with them first. That wasn't Salisbury's understanding. Is the charge against Johnson for stealing $6 in sewing supplies more than a decade ago, and now expunged from her official record, relevant to the voters in the campaign? What would the consequences be of publishing this last-minute charge during the final days of the election? Is keeping the promise to the source while outing Johnson more important than breaking the promise to tell what the editors thought was a more important story: dirty tricks by a Republican operative? Any one of these factors gives us cause for doubt about our ethical choice (Salisbury 1991).

When We are Faced with Complexity

The Cohen case already offers a hint of this final source of ambiguity. The bigger the case, the more important the case, the greater the complexity. And complexity can complicate ethical judgments. We have ended this book with a case that has that kind of complexity. But virtually any in-depth, investigative reporting will result in tough choices. The well-documented decisions made in the Watergate coverage by *The Washington Post* certainly qualify for that kind of complexity.

So do the recent decisions about how producers should treat those children, from the worst slums of Mumbai, who starred in the movie *Slumdog Millionaire*. For one month's work, the children were paid three times the annual wage of an adult in that neighborhood. But with movie revenues of more than $300 million and rising, is $1,000–3,000 enough to pay the children? The producers have focused on long-term benefits for the children, enrolling them in school and promising trust funds to pay for their college education. But the children still live in the slums, one with only a tarpaulin for a house, the movie money gone to pay for his father's tuberculosis treatment (Nelson 2009). Their roles in the movie have given them a moment of fame, money, and a different perspective on the world than they had before being plucked out of the slums. That kind of upheaval threatens to reshape their lives and the lives of their families. Knowing what responsibility the producers have to children they have both helped and made more vulnerable is no easy task.

Making the Best Choice

But that's not the final word. Recognizing these problems is only the first step in finding the best possible solutions. And casuistry is well-suited to help you search for the best ethical solutions. You will find analogous cases useful in several strategies for resolving ethical controversies.

Strategy 1: Look for the Most Fitting Solution

Hard cases are found on a continuum between the exemplars of right action and the exemplars of wrong action. This may mean that the best course of action available is one that involves tough choices. Just as a crime investigation may warrant a charge of involuntary manslaughter rather than first-degree murder, ethical judgments often are a matter of fitting the decision to the facts at hand. In other words, case-based reasoning can offer grounds for concluding that one decision is more ethical than another, even when a perfect choice is not available.

The editors at *The Courier-Journal* made a compromise with their paradigm of not naming rape victims. Because the Bowman/Smith case raised questions of fairness, they made an exception, naming Bowman in their news stories. But they kept their basic policy of not naming rape victims in the usual cases where fairness to the accused was not as central to the story.

In a similar way, online journalists have to adjust the traditional meaning of truth telling to the Web's demand for speed. Not every online news story needs to be instantaneous, but the nature of the Web—and the expectations of the audience—foster a push for immediacy. Stories cannot always be complete and in context before posting. But the obligation to be accurate can be the gold standard, combined with a commitment to develop a more complete story over time.

Strategy 2: Search for Alternatives

Too often journalists are caught up in either/or debates. Yes, choices need to be made. But alternatives can sometimes provide better solutions if we look for them. When Michael Gartner became editor of *The Courier-Journal*, the newspaper was working on a story about corruption in the basketball program at the University of Kentucky. The ethical choices had been framed in the usual way: to do this story, they would need to use anonymous sources. They believed that without anonymity, the basketball players and other key sources will never talk. So the reporters were prepared to sacrifice a piece of the truth (the names of the sources) for the larger truth (the story of a corrupt program). Gartner disagreed. He wanted all the sources on the record. No compromise. Surprisingly, the reporters were able to do what Gartner asked. The story was told with all sources on the record.[3]

When *PrimeTime Live* went undercover with its cameras inside Food Lion supermarkets, the program exposed questionable food-handling practices. To accomplish that, several producers had to misrepresent themselves, omitting their connections to journalism on their resumes to get hired (Andron 1997: 15–16, 19–21). The decision was framed as a choice between full disclosure (and no video for verification) or deception and inside access. But *PrimeTime*

Live's team had alternatives to verify information. They already had interviews with many former employees and a current employee. They could also have purchased food and had it independently tested. They could have obtained records of health inspections. They could have interviewed customers (McMasters 1997: 18–19). Going undercover, with all its ethical costs, wasn't the only option—and, upon reflection, perhaps not the best one.

Strategy 3: Search for a Different Paradigm

Sometimes we don't know what kind of case we are dealing with. In such cases, one of the alternatives may be to find a different paradigm. For example, one of the accepted standards for journalism is that our obligation to the truth is not only for accuracy, but also for context and completeness. But should this standard be applied to online journalism, where speed is so important? Can we be ethical in reporting online when we acknowledge that doing it fast will mean making more errors? Does the "marketplace of ideas" paradigm (eventually getting to the truth) fit online journalism better than either the accuracy paradigm (get it right the first time) or the meaning paradigm (report the facts in context)? Finding the best paradigm can often be a critical step in moving toward a good decision.

Strategy 4: Talk to Others, Including Those Familiar with the Case

Casuistry focuses on the details of the case. Conversations with others may provide factual information you don't have. More important, others can offer perspectives on the case you do not have. A key part of casuistry is discernment—making judgments of relevance. Discernment will be addressed more fully in Chapter 5. But for now, the simple point is that people can differ about these judgments. Like the journalists at *The Herald-Times* of Bloomington, Indiana, other voices will provide analogous cases that test our judgments and our paradigms.

One night a reporter and photographer from the *Messenger-Inquirer* of Owensboro, Kentucky, went on a drug raid with the sheriff's department. In the course of a drug bust, pictures of a young woman being booked were taken. Several of the photos showed her son, taken to the station because he could not be left home alone. Should the newspaper run a photo showing the child with his mother? If so, should it be the one with his face visible or the one showing only the back of his head? The newsroom debated these choices for more than two hours that night. Everyone from the managing editor to the obituary clerk offered opinions.[4]

Group discussions are no guarantee that the best decision will be made; but the involvement of multiple perspectives heightens the chance that all the relevant facts will be on the table, that a variety of options will be considered, and that analogous cases will be offered to challenge any potential decision.

EYE ON TRUTH TELLING

Anyone interested in journalism knows something about truth. If you are in the business of communication, truth is (almost) always relevant. That's why we have already explored several dimensions of truth throughout the book.

■ We discussed the special obligation of journalists to truth telling based on professional duty (Chapter 2). As you remember, we argued that being a professional journalist heightened the priority of truth telling in relation to other ethical norms. And it expanded our commitment to truth telling far beyond "not lying."

■ Part of that conversation in Chapter 2 was also about different models for the truth; ranging from the minimalist "marketplace of ideas" expectation (where truth was the outcome of multiple versions over time), to a sharp focus on facts and accuracy, all the way to a richer understanding of truth as meaning. Edmund Lambeth's (1992) five dimensions of truth offered a multifaceted definition of truth for journalists.

■ Chapter 3 also raised questions about the relationship between truth and deception for journalists.

Truth Telling as an Ethical Issue

All these perspectives on truth, together with your own insights, will be relevant as we look at cases in which truth telling is a major focus. The cases themselves will also raise some challenging controversies common to the intersection of journalism and truth:

■ *Truth and verification.* It's important that journalists end up with the truth as best they can ascertain it, but the processes of inquiry and verification they use to find out what's true are also ethically significant. As philosopher Lorraine Code (1987) notes, ethics are intimately connected to knowing because *what* we know (or *think* we know) affects what we *do*. As professionals who purport to seek the truth and report it, journalists are expected to be better at finding things out—so that citizens can act responsibly based on the knowledge journalists provide. Most of the time, you don't need to worry about the information for a news story. You have the documents. You have the interview on tape. And when the risk of harm is low, even having it in your notes may be good enough. But verification of information is especially crucial in a number of cases:

    – Using anonymous sources deprives you of a name to which you can attribute information. When that information is controversial (as it often is), readers and editors will want to know how you know what you say you know.

- Some information, such as the photos and videos now being submitted online to legitimate news websites, can't be easily verified. Yet these photos and videos may be the only good visual information you have. How do you decide whether such information can be used?
- Reporting rumors may seem like an easy call for journalists, as in, "Don't do it." But what do you do when the rumor is widespread? That's an increasing problem in an age when stories can be spread virally through email, Twitter, and websites. Does the extent of the rumor justify reporting it without confirming its accuracy? After all, the fact that the rumor is widespread is true and possibly consequential.

■ *Hard truths.* Some truth is painful. The permanence of print means a shocking photo stays on the breakfast table until you throw it way. But even though traditional visual media are more transitory, the combination of moving images and sound make the visual more emotional. Online media may be less troubling because the user is more in control of what is seen or ignored (you search for information, rather than having it stare at you from the news rack), but more troubling in their universal and long-term availability.

■ *Truths someone doesn't want told.* Information can be inconvenient or even harmful, whether we are disclosing some private fact about a local official or a brokered deal promising public money to support a new private company. Good reasons can sometimes be offered for keeping the information quiet. Journalists need to decide if those reasons are good enough.

■ *Truth and consequences.* What we do with information can have important consequences. For example, stories about teen suicides can cause other teens to mimic these death attempts. How we handle such stories—exactly what information we provide—is a critical ethical question.

Walter Lippman, one of the prominent journalists of the last century, wasn't convinced journalists were very good at providing people with the truth. The most journalists do, Lippman argued, was to "signalize an event" in one spot for a moment, leaving the area around it in darkness. That signalizing is like a spotlight that focuses on a few facts while the context of these facts, "the picture of reality on which men can act" remains hidden in the shadows. That's news, not truth, according to Lippman (1922: 226). In short, truth can be a challenging goal for journalists, despite its centrality to our profession. Let's see if we can wrap our minds around this concept with a few cases.

TRUTH-TELLING CASES AND WALK-THROUGH EXERCISES

Case 1: Reporting Rumors during Hurricane Katrina[5]

When Hurricane Katrina was done trashing New Orleans near the end of August 2005, it went into the record books as one of the five deadliest hurricanes in US history—part of the costliest hurricane season ever. When the levees collapsed under the pressure of the water's surge, 80 percent of New Orleans was flooded. More than 1,800 people died. But New Orleans wasn't the only part of the country that was flooded. In the early days of the disaster, much of the nation was also flooded—with rumors.

Situational Clues

■ According to the stories reported about Katrina:
- An infant's body was found in a garbage can.
- Sharks were swimming through the central business district.
- Roving bands of armed gang members were attacking the helpless at the Superdome.
- There were reports of "robberies, rapes, carjackings, riots and murder."
- National Guard troops were on rooftops looking for snipers while gunfire was heard in the distance.
- A man seeking help was shot by the National Guard, and another was run down and shot by New Orleans police.
- There were "bands of rapists, going block to block."
- Babies were being raped, 10,000 people were dead, bodies were being stacked in the Superdome (or in another story, dozens of bodies in the freezer at the Convention Center)

■ . . .The floodwaters of rumor were rising. Except that most of these rumors were—how shall we put this delicately?—bogus. Later reporting failed to confirm the claims made in countless news stories during the disaster.

■ Some journalists blamed the lack of accurate reporting on the breakdown of telephone service. With the city flooded, electricity out, and the city in chaos, it was hard to get good information.

■ Public officials complicated the problem. New Orleans mayor C. Ray Nagin went on *Oprah* days after the hurricane and talked about "hooligans killing people, raping people" in the Superdome.

Walk-through Exercise: Information in a Disaster

1. In a disaster, good information is vital, yet it can be tough to get. Is the journalist's obligation to verify information in disasters higher (because

knowing what exactly is happening is important) or lower (because reporting conditions are more chaotic and unpredictable)? In other words, what's the best paradigm for ethical reporting in a disaster?

2. The central ethical question here is about truth telling. But do you see other ethical norms that should be considered?

3. Several factors seeking to explain the flood of rumors are offered in the case. Which, if any, changes your assessment of the journalist's responsibility in publishing or broadcasting rumors?

4. Is the ethical responsibility of the journalist met if the information is identified as a rumor or as "unverified"?

5. What conditions would need to be met for you to report a rumor in a disaster like this one? When would you absolutely not report a rumor?

6. In evaluating the reporting on Hurricane Katrina, can you think of an analogous case (perhaps Katrina but with altered facts) that would change your decision about the reporting of rumor? For example, take the suggestion of Editor Jim Amoss of *The Times Picayune* and imagine that most of the people in the Superdome were white. Does that change your decision? If not, what altered facts could shift your position? What does that tell you about your ethical anchors?

One Last Look at Verification

1. One consequence of the rumors, according to *The Washington Post*, is that the stories of violence may have delayed rescue and evacuation efforts. Should journalists take responsibility for this delay because the rescue agencies were afraid to put rescue workers into the violent scene described by the mainstream news media? If you haven't factored in the consequences of reporting on rumors, now is a good time to do that.

2. Is it OK to report rumors if the consequences are less serious? Sports reporters regularly report rumors about who will become the new coach, what players will be traded where, or how much a player's new contract is worth. Anything wrong with that?

3. Are journalists responsible for the truth of what sources tell them or only for quoting the source accurately? In the 1950s, Sen. Joseph McCarthy labeled many prominent people as communists. One could accurately report what McCarthy said without verifying the accuracy of his claim. Is that enough? Was it enough to report what others were saying about conditions in New Orleans without verifying it? Did it make a difference if the information came from the mayor or a survivor?

Case 2: Outing a Confidential Source[6]

Many times, journalists are not sure if they have the facts right. In other cases, what's true is not in dispute; the issue is what truth needs to be told.

In a well-documented case from Minneapolis/St. Paul, journalists wrestled with a complex ethical question driven by exactly that concern.

Situational Clues

- Six days before the Minnesota gubernatorial election, Dan Cohen, an employee of an advertising agency working for Independent-Republican candidate Wheelock Whitney, approached reporters from four news organizations, including the *Star Tribune* of Minneapolis and the *St. Paul Pioneer Press*. He offered to provide documents relating to an opposition candidate for lieutenant governor in the upcoming election.
- Cohen had been encouraged by a group of Republican supporters to release the information.
- In exchange for a promise that he not be identified as the source of the documents, Cohen revealed to the reporters that Marlene Johnson, the Democratic-Farmer-Labor candidate for lieutenant governor had been convicted of shoplifting 12 years earlier, a conviction that was later vacated. Johnson stole $6 worth of sewing supplies. Her father had died right before the incident.
- After discussion and debate, the editorial staffs of the two papers independently decided to publish Cohen's name as part of their stories concerning Johnson. The *Star Tribune* made the decision after its reporter had contacted Cohen to ask whether he would release the paper from its promise of confidentiality. Cohen refused.
- In their stories, both papers identified Cohen as the source of the court records, reported his connection to the Whitney campaign, and included denials by Whitney campaign officials of any role in the matter. The same day the stories were published, Cohen was fired.
- The editors justified their decision on the grounds that: (a) Cohen's actions amounted to nothing more than a political dirty trick, and thus his motives were suspect; (b) Cohen's name was essential to the credibility of the story; and (c) reporters should not make promises of confidentiality without authorization from their superiors. The *Star Tribune* wrote strongly worded editorials about the incident and published a cartoon portraying Cohen as a garbage can.
- Cohen sued the papers for breach of contract and won a jury award of damages. The US Supreme Court eventually ruled 5–4 that such promises of confidentiality are legally enforceable. Although Cohen won his lawsuit, the ethical issues surrounding the newspaper's decision to break the promise of confidentiality and publish his name remain.

Walk-through Exercise: Source Attribution

1. What are the key facts on which an ethical choice turns in this case? What facts are *not* relevant for you?
2. Journalists do not need to attribute general information—facts that are widely known. However, the paradigm case for most information is that it should be attributed to the source. Can you think of a paradigm case (on which most, if not all, would agree) that would justify *not* attributing the information to a source?
3. What ethical norms should be considered in working toward a decision in this case? Be sure to relate these norms to the facts of the case in making your argument.
4. Can you think of any case (real or hypothetical) involving confidential sources in which you think most journalists would agree to violate the promise to the source?
5. If you could change one or more of the details in this case to shift your decision on what should have been done by the editors, what changes would you make?
6. Can you think of similar cases in which confidentiality would be justified? Again, these could be real or hypothetical cases. In other words, what kinds of conditions justify overriding the usual presumption that journalists will provide the source of their information?

One Last Look at Promises to Sources

1. Before he went into public relations, Cohen had been a public official. He was an alderman on the Minneapolis City Council and had been elected as the president of the council. He ran for mayor, but he was unsuccessful. He also wrote a weekly column in a major newspaper. Does Cohen's political past change your perspective on this case?
2. The incident described above was part of a political campaign, one arena of public life most open to free, unfettered debate. Does the setting of this case in a political campaign give more weight to exposing the "dirty tricks" side of the case than the "shoplifting" side? Or are they both fair game?
3. Bill Salisbury, one of the reporters who promised confidentiality, said that after Cohen was named by his editors, many of his other political sources dried up. One might have predicted this as a consequence of naming Cohen. Should this have been a factor in the editors' decision—or was the key ethical factor the promise itself?
4. The editors of the newspaper argued at trial that promising confidentiality was an unusual practice, that reporters knew it was discouraged, and that any promise of confidentiality was contingent on an editor's approval. In fact, written personnel policies clearly articulated the need for the editor's approval. But Cohen's lawyer showed that con-

fidential sources were regularly used in the newspaper. And reporters testified that they were often in a position where advance approval from editors was impossible. Finally, they said that this was the only time in anyone's memory that a promise of confidentiality to a source had been overridden. How do these facts affect your take on the case, if at all?

5. After he was promised anonymity, Lieutenant Colonel Oliver North discussed secret operations with *Newsweek* related to a 1986 political scandal in which top officials in the Reagan Administration authorized arms sales to Iran to finance anti-communist rebels in Nicaragua called the Contras. Then North testified at the Iran-Contra hearings in Congress that these leaks "seriously compromised our intelligence activities." After that testimony, *Newsweek* revealed that the source of the leaks was North himself. Was *Newsweek* justified in considering the promise of anonymity void because of North's testimony?

Case 3: The Pedophile Physician

At the heart of this case, taken from a Kentucky newspaper, is a question of when truth is relevant to a community. Word reached the newsroom that a physician who had been convicted of fondling children in his office had moved to the city. More facts on this case are given below. But before you read those facts, let's do a little casuistry.

1. On a piece of paper or in your computer, construct a paradigm case for a story like this that would lead most people to conclude the story must be published. In other words, make a list of the kinds of facts that would virtually guarantee that this story needed to be told. For example, you might feel a story had to be told if the physician were planning to open a private pediatric practice in the city. What other facts would be on your list? (This can be done on your own or perhaps with a group in your classroom.)

2. Now do the same for the opposing paradigm case. What factors would lead most people to decide this was *not* a story to publish?

3. Once you have made the lists, keep them at hand, but do not change them.

Situational Clues

A reporter for the newspaper dug into the story. Here's what he found:

- Dr P, a male physician, was licensed to practice medicine in the state of Kentucky.
- He was a general practitioner, serving as the primary care physician to patients of all ages in a major city in central Kentucky.
- Seven years ago, he was charged with molesting several children. The children were patients. The molestation took place in Dr P's office.

- Dr P pled guilty to the charges. He was stripped of his license to practice medicine in Kentucky and had to undergo court-ordered psychiatric treatment.
- He successfully completed his treatment, according to a supervising committee of physicians from the Kentucky Medical Association. The committee certified that Dr P was able to resume practicing medicine without risk to juvenile patients.
- Dr P's medical license was reinstated.
- He moved to the western part of the state (where the newspaper discovered him) and affiliated himself with a walk-in clinic. His role was primarily in administration. However, he was on call to fill in when another physician called in sick or went on vacation. It was unclear exactly how much time he would spend treating patients.

Walk-Through Exercise: Case Comparisons

Either on your own or in a small group in class, work your way through this case as a casuist might by answering the questions below:

1.   What do you think are the most relevant facts in this case? How do these facts match up with your paradigm cases? Does this case match your "must publish" paradigm better or worse than your "don't publish" paradigm?
2.   Are any critical clues that you need to make a decision missing? For example, you might check your list of key paradigm factors to see whether any are missing from the situational clues list.
3.   Now that you have identified what you believe are the relevant factors in the case, link these factors to one or more of the ethical theories we discussed in Chapter 2: consequences, character, duties, care.
4.   Finally, using the situational clues, create your own analogous cases by changing one or more of the factors. Compare the case at hand with your "new" case(s). Do the altered facts in your analogous cases move you closer to one or the other paradigm case? How does this help you identify the most critical factors in the case? How does this help you clarify where you might draw the line for or against publication?

One Last Look at Strength and Limits of Case-Based Reasoning

Normally, this is the spot where some facts are added to the case to complicate your decision. For example, we might have given you some data on the difficulty in treating pedophiles, casting some doubt on the conclusion of the psychiatrist that Dr P was cured.

But we'd like to look at this case from the opposite angle: focusing more on methodology. As you worked through this case-based process, what did this tell you about the strengths and weaknesses of casuistry? Are the weaknesses an inherent part of this process? Or can you think of ways to improve your skill as a casuist that would minimize or eliminate these problems?

Case 4: The AIDS Handbook[7]

The case of the AIDS handbook is a bit different than many of the cases in this textbook. The case takes you through a series of decisions, just as you have experienced in reporting and writing your own stories. Reporters and editors collaborate on the reporting of the story, from its beginning as an idea right to the final decision to publish.

The stages in this decision-making process can be seen as a series of analogous cases. Most facts stay the same, though a few may shift as better information is found. And new facts are added to the mix, even as the story begins to solidify. Each new decision point allows for a natural comparison with the case as we thought it was (the prior decision point) and the case as it is now. The corrected information and the new information may even shift the paradigm case, turning it from one kind of decision into another. In other words, several core steps in the casuistic process are at the core of standard journalistic routines.

If that's true, the key to making this case useful for you is to deal with each stage in the case independently. Identify the most relevant factors in each stage, link them to the relevant ethical norm(s) and force yourself to make a decision on what you would do, just as these journalists had to do. And keep asking yourself: What kind of case is this? What is the paradigm operating here? Has it shifted?

Don't look into the future of the case until you have done that. In fact, your instructor may want you to wait to read the case until you are in class. You are on the honor system here, but keep this in mind: doing it this way will be much more valuable—and you'll be able to compare your choices to those of seasoned editors.

The setting is Florida in the late 1990s. The newspaper is the *St. Petersburg Times.* An editor for the *Times* is presenting the case to you.

Stage 1: The Story Idea

The owner of a local typesetting and publishing firm came to us a few months ago with a story idea. He had collaborated with a local writer and a nearby physician serving on a medical school faculty to produce a handbook on AIDS. Would we be interested in producing a feature on the book?

The writer and the physician, we were told, had been working independently on AIDS ideas. When they met, they decided to join forces. The man with the typesetting-publishing firm had set copy for a cookbook by the writer. When he heard about the AIDS book project, he offered to get involved. Major book publishers were afraid of tackling an AIDS project, he told us, so the writer, the physician and the typesetter-publisher had joined forces and established a new book-publishing imprint in order to get their project under way.

Walk-Through Exercise: Judging Appropriateness

1. Do you see any problems?
2. Should the paper give money?
3. How about printing the pamphlet?
4. Should we pursue this story?
5. What additional information, if any, would you need before you feel we should invest the reporter's time in checking this out? In making your decision, keep in mind that this case takes place in the social climate of the late 1990s. Much less was known about AIDS, treatment options were limited, and the social stigma of infection was very high.
6. What are the relevant ethical norms in this story?

Stage 2: George, the Writer

The story looked good from several points of view: It was a human interest story about local people, a business story, a medical story, a public service story. We assigned a lifestyle reporter and photographer to the project.

The writer interviewed the subjects and produced a feature. The photographer got his photo, but he had a hunch he had seen the writer before, perhaps in court. Following his hunch, he stopped at the bureau office nearest the writer's home and shared his misgivings with the bureau chief and the office manager. Did they know this guy George, the writer?

They did. All of us did when our collective memory was engaged. This same George, we were reminded, had been convicted four years earlier on charges of rape of a male child under 16 and of distributing child pornography, and had been sentenced to a 20-year term in a state prison. Apparently he had been released after serving only two years.

Walk-Through Exercise: Judging Character

1. Does this change the situation?
2. Should the project go forward?
3. In terms of ethics, this information clearly raises questions of character. Is George's character relevant? In what way?
4. What are the alternatives now?

Stage 3: The Value of the Handbook

Immediately, our project was put on hold. We huddled. All of us agreed that we could not publish our story as written.

I contacted the typesetter-publisher who had approached us about the story. Yes, he knew of the writer's prison record, but he thought it was ancient history. And, in any case, he thought the man was a competent writer, and the AIDS project was a worthy one. It hadn't occurred to him, he said, that we might be angry or embarrassed to discover that one of the subjects of our AIDS-book feature was a convicted rapist-pornographer. If he had created a problem, he said, he was very sorry. He said he would like to discuss the situation with the writer. He called us back to report that the writer would be pleased to answer any and all questions in an interview. The man, he said, was trying to put his life back together. The book, he said, made a contribution to understanding. He said to do what we thought best—he'd trust us to make the right decision.

Walk-Through Exercise: Judging Relevance

1. What do you think of the typesetter-publisher's argument that the criminal record of the rapist-pornographer isn't relevant to his writing an AIDS handbook?
2. Does featuring George in a story about that handbook change the relevance of his criminal record?
3. What should the paper do? Why?

Stage 4: More about George, the Writer

We assigned a news reporter and said we'd await the outcome of the interview before deciding how to handle the story. Then the ex-pornographer writer backed off. No interview, he said; it could only hurt him and the AIDS project.

Meanwhile, I met with a local judge familiar with the case. At a few of our state prisons, the judge informed me, virtually everyone is paroled after serving one-tenth of his or her sentence: five-year sentence, serve six months; ten-year sentence, a year; twenty-year sentence, two years.

I talked to the assistant DA who had prosecuted the rape-pornography case. The scary thing with this writer-rapist at the time of the trial, he said, was that the man never felt he had done anything wrong.

Walk-Through Exercise: Judging Your Options

1. What are the alternatives now? A feature on an AIDS book authored by a convicted rapist-pornographer? A book review concerning the merits of the book with little or no comment on the authors? Or what?

2. As you think of each of these alternatives (or your own), think about how the relevance of the facts we now know may be different in each scenario. Do the ethical norms shift from one option to the next? Has the ethical paradigm shifted?
3. And would the case be different if the writer were a woman with a criminal record?
4. Does George's reported attitude toward his crime matter?

Stage 5: A Final Decision

We elected to probe the prison-probation system that releases prisoners routinely after they've served a tenth of their sentences.

A decent story was published. But it was not as provocative as it could have been. We didn't name our friend the author because we didn't feel it would be fair to single him out and not name a string of others who had been released early.

In a major feature on AIDS, we mentioned the local AIDS book very briefly and quoted the physician who had co-authored it. But we didn't review the book or produce a feature on those who produced it. We didn't want to destroy the book because of the history of one of its authors—and we didn't want to produce a feature on the book without going into that history.

That's where things stand at this moment. None of us is really sure that we acted wisely.

One Last Look: Looking Back

Knowing about the whole situation, should we have made a different decision at any of the earlier stages? What did you learn in seeing how the *St. Petersburg Times* handled the case?

Case 5: Tehran Video[8]

On Saturday, 20 June 2009, a young woman named Neda Agha-Soltan was shot in the chest at a demonstration protesting the outcome of the Iranian election. She was not the only Iranian to die in the aftermath of the election. But she quickly became an iconic figure because a 40-second video, taken with a cell phone, was uploaded to YouTube, quickly spreading to blogs and Twitter. Ironically, her first name means "voice" or "call" in Farsi.

MAKING HARD CHOICES IN JOURNALISM ETHICS

Situational Clues

■ It began this way, according to Nazila Fathi of *The New York Times:*

> It was hot in the car, so the young woman and her singing instructor got out for a breath of fresh air on a quiet side street not far from the anti-government protests they had ventured out to attend. A gunshot rang out, and the woman, Neda Agha-Soltan, fell to the ground. "It burnt me," she said before she died.

■ In the video, she is seen on the streets of Tehran, being helped to the ground with a pool of blood already at her feet. A man cries out, "She has been shot; someone come and take her." She is wearing jeans and running shoes. Several people, mostly men, surround her, trying to help.

■ As the video unwinds, we see her face, her eyes staring vacantly toward the camera. Blood begins to flow out of her mouth, then her nose. People scream and shout. Someone says, "Neda, don't be afraid" and "Neda, stay with me."

■ Caspian Makan, a photojournalist in Tehran claiming to be Soltan's boyfriend, was quoted by the Associated Press: "She only ever said that she wanted one thing. She wanted democracy and freedom for the people of Iran." The AP could not confirm Makan's relationship with Soltan, though he had pictures of himself with a woman he said was Soltan and Soltan was a Facebook friend of Makan.

Walk-Through Exercise: Citizen-Generated Images

1. One of the key issues in this case is whether we can trust the veracity of this video. What we don't know could hurt journalism's credibility. Was the woman killed by an Iranian soldier, a paramilitary Basij[9] sniper, or a stray bullet? Who recorded the video? Journalists can't control the posting of such material to public websites such as YouTube. But journalists do need to decide how to use this information on television newscasts, in newspapers, or on websites. In the immediate aftermath of this incident, what would you do in each of these settings (television, newspaper, online)?

2. Verification is increasingly problematic when citizens are producing the images. This is particularly so when the political conditions make verification difficult. What conditions would have to be met for you to confidently recommend using such a video (think "paradigm case")? What would cause you to refrain from using it?

3. Given these two extremes, would you use such a video with less than full confidence that it was genuine? Under what conditions can journalists lower the standards of verification in such cases?[10]

4. The central ethical norm in this case is truth telling. Are there other ethical concerns here?

Walk-Through Exercise: Images of Death

Showing death in photos or video images has always been a controversial issue for journalists. Below are some analogous cases. All contain one similar feature: death. Do the differences in each case make a difference to you in terms of what you would publish or broadcast?

1. *Death from a distance.* Video footage of the 1986 Challenger disaster shows the disintegration of the space vehicle as it streaks across the sky. Does the absence of bodies make it more acceptable? Or is imagining how the astronauts have died in those flames worse than actually seeing it? And how often should this video be shown? Is there an ethical problem in repeating this video on the loop of 24-hour news?

2. *Execution in Vietnam.* In 1968, photojournalist Eddie Adams captured Saigon Police Chief General Nguyen Ngoc Loan executing a Viet Cong prisoner with his handgun. Like the video of Soltan, this photograph took on iconic qualities that influenced public perception of the Vietnam War. But the facts surrounding the photo—unknown to many who saw it—told another story. Adams had great regrets about the effect of this photo, including its damage to the Loan family. Does this tell us anything about the power of visuals to overwhelm the context of such images?

3. *Death of a president.* When John F. Kennedy was shot, the public didn't get stills from the Zapruder film showing the assassination for days. The film itself wasn't shown for several years. Should the film have been shown sooner? After all, this was the death of a president. Or are we now too quick to broadcast moments of death?

4. *The beheading of Daniel Pearl.* When reporter Daniel Pearl of *The Wall Street Journal* was kidnapped in Karachi, Pakistan, and later beheaded, a video of the beheading was reportedly leaked to a jihadist site on the Web. Unlike the Soltan video, television news organizations did not broadcast the Pearl video. What do you think is the difference? Is it the gruesomeness of the beheading? Is it because the beheading was staged for video? Or is it the difference between showing the death of an American and the dying moments of an Iranian?

5. *The hanging of Saddam Hussein.* Go back to Chapter 1 and review "Case 2: Moment of Death." How does this case compare with the others listed here?

One Last Look at the Truth of Images

In 2008, Bill Mitchell of the Poynter Institute for Media Studies reviewed another image in another country in turmoil. The photo, first published in *The Times* of London, showed an 11-month-old child in the middle of the floor in a shelter for refugees of political violence in Zimbabwe. According to the story, the mother said young people in the governing party of President

Robert Mugabe shattered his legs to make her disclose the location of her husband, an opposition supporter. A number of news organizations linked to the story and photo in *The Times*.

1. Later, a *Newsweek* correspondent found the child, but his pictures showed the child without casts. *The Times* eventually reported that the child's legs had not been broken, though he had club feet. Does this new case affect how you feel about the issue of verification? Does it change your views about the decision to use the Soltan video on US networks such as CNN?

2. Before *The New York Times* ran this story, discussions were held about the veracity of the mother's account, according to Greg Winter, a foreign desk editor. Some factors lent credibility to her claims: her presence in the refugee shelter, her evident fear, and widespread attacks on opposition leaders in the country. But *The New York Times* was "careful to attribute everything she claimed to her directly," Winter said. Given the circumstances, was that the best ethical response available?

CHAPTER 5

▼ EVALUATING ETHICAL JUDGMENTS

Now that you've learned a bit about case-based reasoning, it's time to step back and critically assess the method. Case-based ethical reasoning raises similar questions to *CSI* investigations:

- How can the context of the decision-making process help or hinder case-based analysis?
- How much certainty can you have in the conclusions you reach with this method?
- How can you integrate theory with case-based reasoning?

To help us explore these questions, let's look in depth at a case involving the photo of a fatal wreck at *The Herald-Times* in Bloomington, Indiana.[1]

In Chapter 3, we considered the hypothetical example of an ethically problematic photograph intruding on a mother's grief. Just as in that case, the decision makers at *The Herald-Times* began the discernment process before they even had a chance to see the wreck photo in question. The victim was 23-year-old Brian Friedman, who died when the black BMW he was driving crashed into a guard rail. Although tragic for the family, this was a fairly routine fatal accident for the paper: just one victim, an adult, no extraordinary rescue efforts, no disruption to traffic, no major damage to others' property. The reporter phoned in and recommended the story run with other routine police news on page 2.

What made this a hard case ethically is that the family communicated to the paper, via a social worker at the local hospital, that they did not want *The Herald-Times* to run any pictures of the accident scene. The editor learned of the social worker's message just as he was meeting with his staff to make news decisions about that day's edition. The majority of the staff at the meeting, taken aback by the family's attempt to preemptively influence an editorial decision, recommended that the editor refuse. "I'm not sure it's quite that simple," the editor announced (Borden 1996: 70).

Now, instead of a routine wreck photo, the paper was confronting an ethically perplexing case requiring arbitration between two competing paradigms: "guarding professional discretion" and "respecting survivor privacy."

In true casuistical style, the editor initiated a fact-finding phase to get clearer on what exactly was at stake. He decided it didn't make sense to have further discussion until everyone had seen the image that the photo director was recommending. The photo showed the front of the BMW near the guard rail—the driver's side torn to pieces, the windshield broken and the roof smashed in. A white male state trooper was measuring road marks in the foreground of the photograph; another stood behind him and recorded the data. Two white male firefighters in the background were walking toward the wreck from their red fire engine, parked behind them. A yellow trooper car was also visible in the background, blocking the scene from traffic. The photographer avoided taking pictures of the body, which was lying, covered, on the road at the time.

Although there was some disagreement on the photo's news value, the majority of the group determined it was not newsworthy enough—request or no request—to run on the front of the "Region" section. However, in view of the social worker's message, the photo director said the image should run on page 2 of the Region section "to avoid sending the message to photographers that their work was less valuable than reporters'" (Borden 1996: 71).

By now, the news meeting had adjourned, and the police reporter was back in the newsroom. The editor got a second call requesting no photo from one of his acquaintances, who also happened to be the Friedman family rabbi. The discussion among the paper's staffers moved to the hallway. The editor continued seeking "probative evidence" in this case—the detail that would settle the decision definitively. How did this photo compare, he asked the others, with other fatal wreck photos we've run as far as details and newsworthiness? What's our policy for running such photos? For taking such photos in the first place? What's our actual practice?

The editor and police reporter searched the newsroom archives for precedents. They could only find two published fatal wreck photos in the previous nine months, even though the paper ran monthly stories on area traffic fatalities. Both photos ran on the front page, suggesting that the paper published such photos only rarely, when they were very newsworthy.

The paradigmatic example was one of these two photos, published a month earlier.[2] It showed a woman's car being pulled out of a quarry by a wrecker with firefighters at the scene. Because of its policy implications, the staffers agreed that it was newsworthy enough for page 1 and would trump any appeals to survivor privacy. The Friedman case, they acknowledged, was not so clear cut. Lacking the "dispositive evidence" of either high news value or

MAKING HARD CHOICES IN JOURNALISM ETHICS

a clear policy that would demonstrate relevance to the ethical decision, proponents of publication could not justify trauma to the Friedman family. They increasingly found themselves on the losing side of the argument.

The only applicable written policy was a general prohibition against running photos of the dead. This was the reason why the photo director recommended a shot excluding Friedman's body. As far as the policy for obtaining photos of traffic fatalities, the only policy in use was informal: it was catch as catch can. If an available photographer could get to the scene in time, the paper would have a photo. The photography department, of course, made more of an effort when unusual circumstances elevated the wreck's news value.

In view of these facts, the family's indirect request to "kill" the photo was the clincher that settled the editor's choice. The paper could not very well claim that the family would be fine with the photo, given its request.[3] The editor acknowledged to the others, now gathered in his office, that he was leaning against publication. The staffers voiced additional arguments for and against running the photo before the meeting ended with the decision still up in the air.

Influence of the Decision-Making Context

The story about Friedman's accident eventually ran on page 2 with nothing but a headshot. In the editor's view, nothing the paper would gain by publishing the photo was worth inflicting trauma on the family. However, the staff could have done more to assess the kinds of harms the photo might cause. For example, no one tried to find out exactly why the family might object to the photo or how strongly they might object to it. They simply took the word of the social worker and the rabbi that they didn't want anything in the paper. Neither did anyone question the police reporter when he said that turning down the family's request would inhibit his reporting. The only alternative that staffers discussed was the headshot option, which had been suggested by the police reporter.

In short, these journalists sought to establish the Friedman case's relevant characteristics responsibly. However, a combination of faulty reasoning and lack of thoroughness hindered their efforts.

A number of organizational factors were influential too. For example:

■ Staffers saw the editor's postponement of a decision at the news meeting as a sign that he had already decided against running the photo. Those who disagreed felt they had to prove why the photo *should* be published, rather than the other way around. This illustrates how the hierarchical structure of a newsroom—who's the boss and what his leadership style is—can steer the course of discernment about a hard case.

- For most of the two-hour decision process, only the editor argued against publication. Yet his framing of the case determined how it would be classified and what would count as morally relevant characteristics. This happened because of the editor's directive style and the paper's conflict-averse culture.

In Chapter 6, we make some recommendations for cultivating personal qualities and newsroom dynamics that contribute to excellence in case-based reasoning.

Certainty in Case-Based Reasoning

After the Friedman case, the staff deliberately avoided clarifying the paper's informal policy on publishing wreck photos or obtaining such photos. Interviewees reported a number of reasons for this, including the desire to preserve editorial discretion and a widespread perception that the editor had "caved." But it could just be that the staff found the Friedman decision so ambiguous that they didn't want it to set any kind of precedent.

Casuistry as an ethical decision-making method is, after all, "epistemologically modest" (R.B. Miller March 1996). Epistemology is the study of how we know what we know. Journalists' established procedures for reporting, verifying and telling news stories are epistemological procedures: They tell journalists how to find out about the world, how to vouch for their truth claims, and how to responsibly convey what they believe to be true. Journalists don't claim to know the whole truth or to have the final word on what is going on, or why. Casuists are like that, too—they avoid claiming too much. Remember, casuistry, like case law, claims to settle only the particular case at hand, not all cases for all time. Therefore, casuists claim their moral judgments are only *probable*. Their certainty depends on the case's ambiguity and the availability of a suitable paradigm.

However, such "epistemological modesty" makes some students of journalism ethics nervous; they worry that case-based judgments are inherently less reliable. But even in casuistry's heyday during the Middle Ages, the "probable opinions" of casuists were not recommended actions, let alone obligatory ones. "They were actions that the casuist judged to be morally permissible in certain special circumstances," according to Albert Jonsen and Stephen Toulmin (1988: 245–246). In other words, casuists have always dealt with the hard cases in ethics. It shouldn't be surprising that those are precisely the kinds of cases that would cause us to proceed with caution.

Those who worry that case-based conclusions are too tentative should also remember, as Jonsen and Toulmin (1988) remind us, that answers reached through casuistry are no more probable than those derived from theory. Perhaps we should question those who overstate the certainty of their moral

MAKING HARD CHOICES IN JOURNALISM ETHICS

judgments or overestimate the extent to which one case settles them all. After all, even science cannot achieve 100 percent certainty. The standard margin of error acknowledges that there's a 5 percent probability that scientific findings are nothing more than methodological mishaps or even random chance.

Forensic examiners, likewise, have no way to prove with absolute certainty that someone has committed a crime, but they do their best using tested pattern recognition methods. For example, the FBI has been collecting genetic profiles for years and has put them into a database that forensic examiners can use to match to DNA samples collected during criminal investigations. This program has helped investigators a lot. But, even with sophisticated databases as a tool, the best analysts can do is vouch for firm probabilities. That said, investigators can increase their odds of being right: the more reference samples they have, and the more experience they have with DNA analysis, the better they can make the algorithms and the more accurately they can calculate probabilities.

In the normative realm of ethics, we necessarily have less certainty than we do in the objective realm of science. Nevertheless, casuists can increase the odds of making competent moral judgments. Just as forensic examiners do, casuists can develop their case inventories and hone their expertise with hard cases.

THEORY AS A SAFEGUARD AGAINST SLOPPY THINKING

Some worry that casuistry brushes theory aside in favor of starting with cases. Although some casuists appear to take this view, we've advocated integrating theory and cases in our approach to case-based analysis. That's because case-based reasoning comes with a number of its own built-in limitations:

- The facts can be given more weight than ethical theory in resolving conflicts, especially for journalists concerned about objectivity. In a similar way, preference can be given to the status quo—"that's the way we do things here"—when one's focus is not on ethical norms.
- Journalists' pragmatic approach can lead them to do what they want, ethical theory be damned. For example, in an unpublished study of journalists and the naming of rape victims, journalists agreed with whatever ethical justification was offered (utilitarian, duty-based, etc.) as long as that ethical justification agreed with their belief that rape victims should (or should not) be named (Winch 1991). Casuistry's critics have referred to this temptation as *laxity*, a kind of moral oppor- tunism.
- Theoretical conflicts may be resolved by the details of the case, but casuistry offers no guarantees. In fact, people can argue about the

interpretation of the facts, their relevance to the case, or the importance of one or more of the ethical norms in conflict. W.D. Ross knew that when he advocated a system of variable-weight principles—each of which could come into conflict. Attention to the facts of the case may not resolve that conflict.

■ Similarly, complexity and ambiguity may resist resolution, even with careful attention to the facts. Attention to the case details could even accentuate the ethical complexity. Most of us have had an experience where we knew immediately what should be done. Then, as we dug into the issue, the information we discovered only made the right choice less clear. Black and white becomes gray.

■ Precedent and guidelines by nature are always up for revision. New cases—because they are different in some interesting way—raise questions. Does the precedent fit the new case? Should the guideline be modified or scrapped? And making those changes can be risky. In the Bowman/Smith case, several reporters felt the precedent set in the case wasn't about fairness at all. Said one, "It looks like the new guideline is, 'Don't have the bad luck to be raped by a celebrity.'" Hmmm.

In short, case details, paradigms and guidelines take us only so far. The best casuists use these strategies in tandem with theory. Theory, as we've noted, can help us to pick out the morally relevant characteristics of our case and to identify a suitable paradigm. By drawing our attention to key moral considerations we'll have to deal with in resolving any moral problem, theory helps us to get clear on what makes a case morally perplexing. Theory also puts a lid on rationalization by demanding a higher level of reflection and consistency than we can get by focusing on details alone.

Ethical theory performs the same function for case-based decisions that science performs for forensic examinations. As the National Research Council noted in a 2009 report, forensic labs lacking scientific rigor produce unreliable evidence for use in criminal investigations. Among the council's recommendations was setting up a National Institute of Forensic Science that would "establish and enforce standards of forensic science" (Hsieh 2009). Likewise, responsibly integrating theory and cases is important for using case-based reasoning well in journalism ethics.

Note, though, that you do not have to be a card-carrying Kantian or some other kind of theorist to be a good casuist. Ethical norms, such as autonomy and truth telling, function as useful "middle-level principles" (Kuczewski 1997: 6) that get the job done, whether or not they can be traced to this theory or that. They inform your choice of a paradigm case and what you consider to be its ethically relevant characteristics. They also set limits on the kinds of conclusions that you can reasonably reach using casuistry (Boeyink 1992).

For example, the norm of autonomy played an important behind-the-scenes role in the Friedman case. This ethical norm's theoretical origins can be traced to Immanuel Kant's imperative to treat people as ends in themselves, never merely as means (though there may be other theoretical candidates as well). For Kant, as you saw in Chapter 2, an important aspect of this principle is respecting people's autonomy, or right to make their own choices. For the "professional discretion" paradigm, newsworthiness was a crucial characteristic because professional journalists are supposed to make independent editorial decisions on the basis of newsworthiness alone (not outside pressure).

But another way for people to exercise autonomy is to control personal information. In the end, respect for autonomy set limits on how far these journalists would be willing to push their claim to professional discretion. After all, the family had claims to autonomy in this case, too; they had the right to exercise some choice about their son's memory. While a *lot* of news value might be worth violating the family's right to survivor privacy, a *little* news value might not. Further, if it could be shown that the family's request did not actually contradict the paper's own standards for making these types of editorial decisions —as embodied in policy and precedent—then a good case could be made that the staff's professional discretion was not being violated anyway.

Concepts such as autonomy can often be grounded in more than one theory— and this does not prevent people from agreeing on solutions to moral problems. In fact, casuists argue that their method has the advantage of cutting through moral disagreement based in theoretical differences (Jonsen and Toulmin 1988; Kuczewski 1997.)

Different theoretical outlooks seemed to be at work in the Friedman case. Although autonomy was the guiding ethical norm for those using the "professional discretion" paradigm, the editor's approach hinged more on an estimate of harms and benefits—the harms to the family resulting from a violation of their autonomy and from the trauma of seeing the scene of their son's death, and the benefits to *The Herald-Times*' readers and staff resulting from the image's news value and from asserting the paper's right to follow its own news standards for these kinds of photographs. In effect, he sought to weigh harms against benefits the way a utilitarian would.

If the two camps had approached this case theoretically, as a battle between Kant and Mill, it is very likely they would have ended up locked in an ethical battle with no way out. Approaching the problem first by determining precedent and establishing newsworthiness paved the way for common ground that could bridge these two frameworks.

Theory and Discernment

Far from rejecting ethical theory, then, case-based reasoning offers a way to give concrete meaning to general notions of autonomy or truth telling. Casuistry helps us do this by giving careful consideration to the specific social contexts in which we make decisions. The moral expertise we possess in these contexts helps us to go beyond what philosopher James Wallace (2009: 33) calls the *manifest content* of ethical norms—the surface meaning—and get down to their *latent content*—the deeper meaning.

As we've noted in Chapter 2, your role as a professional journalist will affect your idea of what it means to be autonomous and truthful. These ethical norms have to be understood within the entire web of moral commitments that you take on as a journalist. "Paradoxically, we cannot know what is expected of us unless we know what the situation demands of us, but we cannot know what the situation demands of us until we know what is expected of us" (Glasser and Ettema 2008).

Wallace (2009: 95) discusses how this works in soldiering: "Soldiers know that there are situations in which other matters properly take precedence over cleaning a weapon because they know how to follow the precept 'Keep your rifle clean and oiled' together with the other precepts comprised by soldiering." To make this determination, good soldiers have to understand, not just the manifest aspect of the norm in question ("Keep your rifle clean and oiled"), but its latent aspect, including the point of proper gun maintenance ("No point in having a functioning gun if you're not going to use it to defend yourself").

Wallace (2009: 97) takes pains to point out that we are not setting aside rationality for an "ineffable intuition" or an innate "faculty," like hearing, to understand a norm's latent content. Those who are immersed in an activity, such as soldiering or journalism, can explain a norm's latent aspect if they're "relatively articulate." However, they do not normally feel the need to do so. A thoughtful journalist, for instance, can explain the point of avoiding conflicts of interest and observing accuracy as part of his practice if given the time and opportunity. It's just that he understands these norms so well that he doesn't need to spell out their deeper meaning every time he uses them in an ethical decision.

In Chapter 2, we discussed discernment as a quality of character, or virtue. Aristotle thought there were two kinds of virtues: moral virtues (habits of the heart) and intellectual virtues (habits of the mind). Discernment is an intellectual virtue that gives us a competent understanding of what is reasonable given the full complexity of a case (Jonsen and Toulmin 1988). We cultivate this virtue by dealing with similar cases and by learning the ethical norms relevant to the various social roles and relationships at stake in a given situation (Kuczewski 1997). In journalism, this would include the norms of journalism, as well as norms associated with business, politics, family life, and other realms that intersect with journalism on a daily basis.

Just like "top-down" ethics, then, "bottom-up" ethics has its strengths and limitations. Moreover, finite human beings use these tools. Journalists bring their own experiences and beliefs to any controversy. That changes how they see the case. Facts may be interpreted differently; ethical norms may be defined differently. That's why casuistry pays attention to the qualities of the person doing the analysis. We'll discuss this more in Chapter 6.

Theory and Cases in Reflective Equilibrium

To bring it all together, the competence we have been calling *discernment* in casuistry is a kind of moral expertise concerning:

- The situation we face.
- Relevant ethical norms.
- The meaning of these norms within specific social contexts.
- Possible theoretical justifications for these norms.
- Situations that are analogous in terms of these norms.

These are not separate processes that occur in a specific sequence. Rather, we move back and forth among these components as we wrestle with difficult ethical decisions. This movement is similar to what philosopher John Rawls (1971: 20) called *reflective equilibrium,* a self-correcting process in which we move back and forth between the general and the specific to arrive at reasonable moral judgments. "It is equilibrium because at last our principles and judgments coincide; and it is reflective since we know to what principles our judgments conform and the premises of their derivation."

Let's look at an illustration of reflective equilibrium. At *The Herald-Times,* most of the journalists dealt with a controversial case by talking about the details of the case or others like it (what we called "analogous cases" in Chapter 4). One of the more experienced journalists dealt with the same controversies by quickly identifying what he thought were the norms relevant to the cases. When asked about this top-down strategy of applying norms to the cases, he said this reflected judgments he developed over the years. Faced with complex or controversial cases early in his journalism career, he gradually began to generalize from these experiences. He shaped guidelines that he applied to similar cases that came along later; he also identified the norms he thought most critical to these similar cases. In other words, he was a casuist at heart, using his bottom-up, case-based experience to develop guidelines (see Chapter 6) and norms that he then applied top-down.

For Rawls (1971: 48–51), reflective equilibrium was the interplay between the decisions we make each day and the norms that guide these decisions. It works like this: as you grow up, you develop basic operating principles, sometimes adopted from the social groups you live in or admire, sometimes from your own experiences. For example, you may have been raised in a family or religious group that believed homosexuality was a sin. Since most of the people around you were heterosexual, it was easy to sustain the judgment that homosexuals were bad. But then you went to college and became best friends with someone just down the hall. After about six months, your friend gets up the courage to tell you she is a lesbian. Your experience of friendship challenges your basic premise about homosexuality and sin. You are forced to reassess that principle in the face of this concrete personal case. Rawls argued that the moral life is characterized by this interplay between the concrete and the abstract, between our experience and our operating principles and beliefs.

Journalism ethics reflects the same interplay between controversial cases and theory. You may enter your career with a clear set of ethical norms you want to apply to the decisions you make as a journalist. But these will be challenged by your experience when the decision you must make involves a conflict of ethical principles or when the complexity of the case makes a textbook application of theory difficult. Like most journalists, you may develop your understanding of ethics as part of your work in the newsroom (Weaver, Beam, Brownlee, Voakes and Wilhoit 2007). But even when experience (case-based reasoning) is central, you will naturally develop broader guidelines to help you deal with similar cases. In fact, identifying the relevant details of any controversial case, as we saw in Chapter 3, can point you to the ethical norms and theories that make such details relevant. Moreover, the experience of the controversial case ultimately helps to define what we mean by ethical norms such as truth telling and directs our attention to theories that provide a philosophical rationale for them.

Let's take another look at the Bowman/Smith case to see how the decision-making process in this example relied both on theory and on cases.

Putting It All Together at *The Courier-Journal*

Courier-Journal staffers behaved like top-down ethicists in a couple of ways when deciding whether to identify Patricia Bowman in the paper. Managing Editor Steve Ford said his predecessor, Irene Nolan, was "more of a believer in just the rightness of the decision to name rape victims" and viewed the Bowman/Smith case basically as an excuse to implement this principle. In other words, Ford seemed to see this as nothing more than a top-down process of applying a general moral rule to a specific situation. Night editor Ben Post, meanwhile, seemed to equate making an exception to a policy with violating the policy itself: "I mean obviously we violated our guidelines in this, after discussion." His comment reflects a view of ethics in which moral rules reign, and they're absolute.

But we've already seen that the process at *The Courier-Journal* was not so cut and dried. The staffers did not rely primarily on theory, but proceeded by comparing the Bowman/Smith case to the kind of case on which the paper's no-naming policy was based. They viewed Bowman as a justifiable exception to the paper's policy shielding reported rape victims based on its differences from this paradigm. They treated the Bowman/Smith case as a precedent with presumptive force when the Tyson/Washington case arose. Judging the second case to be similar, they published Desiree Washington's name, too. However, most of the staffers viewed the Washington decision as another exception to the paper's general prohibition, not as a new policy that turned this prohibition on its head. The Bowman and Washington exceptions did not invalidate the paper's policy against naming rape victims; they refined it.

Just as some theorists might be tempted to overlook the way that cases and bottom-up reasoning influenced *The Courier-Journal*'s deliberations, some casuists might be tempted to overlook the roles of theory and top-down thinking. That would be a mistake. For one thing, we can assume that *Courier-Journal* staffers would have handled a typical rape case by simply applying the paper's standing policy, which reflected deontological concerns about autonomy, justice and non-maleficence. It is the hard cases, remember, that cry out for a close examination of the details.

When discerning the morally relevant features of the Bowman/Smith and Tyson/Washington cases, these journalists used general ethical norms. For example, Smith's celebrity became a critical component in their deliberations because it had implications for their views of justice.

Theories also shaped the newsroom debates about these two decisions. For example, those involved in the Bowman/Smith case suggested there was a push toward a new paradigm at *The Courier-Journal* allowing the naming of all rape victims. This change was suggested by those who interpreted the paper's commitment to harm prevention through a utilitarian framework. Nolan, in particular, seemed willing to sacrifice the well-being of individual victims during a transitional period in which they would be stigmatized by identification, but would, at the same time, help destigmatize rape in the long run. Ford recalled: "Irene became very insistent that . . . naming victims was the right thing to do and expressed a strong desire to get us to that point at some time, although I think she realized that this newspaper in this market — we couldn't suddenly start naming local rape victims, without their consent."

Meanwhile, a pull away from this new paradigm came from journalists who interpreted the commitment to not harm others through a deontological framework. Post, for example, took the dignity of individual victims more seriously than Nolan in the short run, preferring a policy that continued to shield most victims from identification in the newspaper: "It's not quite as easy if you're the woman out there who's afraid to come forward because you're going to be held up to some sort of shame or ridicule," he noted. Although casuistry's focus on particulars can often provide common ground where theories cannot, theoretical differences can undermine agreement whenever they lead casuists to follow different trails of evidence.

The Courier-Journal's decisions in the Bowman/Smith and Tyson/Washington cases could be justified theoretically, as well as casuistically. In the end, the decision-making processes used to resolve them illustrate how theory and cases complement each *other:*

- *Casuistry's* respect for the demands of particular circumstances allows journalists to make ethical decisions that are reasonable, as well as logical. Its common-law approach provides a realistic method for interpreting ethical norms in practice, while providing a measure of consistency absent from relativism.
- Theory, meanwhile, helps us to focus on the details that really matter and to avoid taking an overly narrow view of things. Its philosophical approach allows journalists to make ethical decisions that are logical, as well as reasonable.

You might think of theory as the reflective component of casuistry. Theory is more rigorous and thoughtful than our common sense about ethics. Cases are the practical component of casuistry. They alert us to the ethical norms at stake in a given situation and give them concrete meaning. Theory offers reasons; cases offer guidance (Glasser and Ettema 2008). Together, they result in the experience of reflective equilibrium, of "everything fitting together into one coherent view" (Rawls 1971: 21).

EYE ON SOCIAL JUSTICE

One area in which we may have to work hard to reconcile our practical experience and our operating principles is social justice. Social justice refers to the fair distribution of resources and opportunities needed to promote the well-being and development of persons. Unfortunately, the kind of world we'd like to live in and the actual world we inhabit are quite different.

Social Justice as an Ethical Issue

Although justice has a variety of meanings, we might agree that we should at least minimize gross social inequalities in democratic societies. This is where journalism comes in. The justice motive in journalism is most obvious in investigative reporting, which exposes "breaches in the moral order" to motivate public outrage against those who abuse their power (Glasser and Ettema 1991). But an argument could be made that much more reporting ought to be animated by the impulse to "comfort the afflicted and afflict the comfortable," as the old saying goes.

MAKING HARD CHOICES IN JOURNALISM ETHICS

Yet the press tends to cover the rich and powerful with much more zeal than the poor and other marginalized members of society. Donald Shriver (1997) cites several reasons for this:

- The news media, themselves owned by powerful corporations, reflect what critical studies scholars call *dominant ideas* about the world. An example is the myth that anyone can make it if she just works hard enough. The reality is that you are greatly advantaged or disadvantaged by your socioeconomic status from the get-go. Dominant ideas work in the interests of the powerful because they make the rest of us content to go along with the way things are. These ideas become "naturalized" until they come to be accepted, by journalists and citizens alike, as just "common sense." The result is that nothing is questioned—and nothing changes.

- A related reason is the journalistic tendency to let official sources set the news agenda. Official sources, such as school superintendents and police chiefs, have an interest in appearing competent and in control even when they're not. The world according to officialdom can be quite different from the lived experiences of "regular folks." But journalists treat regular folks—let alone countercultural folks—as being less believable than the people in charge. The result is an unrepresentative picture of society.

- The news tends to oversimplify ongoing social issues, such as housing discrimination or the plight of the uninsured, instead of exploring their complexities. For example, instead of focusing on the multitude of social issues around long-term care and end-of-life decisions for patients unable to communicate their wishes due to a stroke, a coma or some other medical condition, the news media focused on the legal jockeying and political posturing surrounding Terri Schiavo's feeding tube. The result is a lack of a public vocabulary for identifying and solving social problems.

- Journalists also tend to focus on timely events, such as congressional bills or attack ads, instead of giving social issues sustained attention even when there is no particular "news peg." The result is lack of momentum for policy change.

- The conventions of journalistic objectivity discourage empathy, insisting on a detached stance. The result is that humane responses to the suffering of others, especially others who are not "like us," are stifled.

Add to these the fact that newsrooms are not very diverse to begin with and that American culture as a whole is fairly individualistic and materialistic, and you have a recipe for coverage that often fails to reflect the priorities of the common good. Worse, sometimes journalists themselves act unjustly by circulating stereotypes, labeling dissidents as social deviants, and ignoring already marginalized communities. For example, NBC sent some "Muslim-looking" men to a NASCAR race in Roanoke, Virginia, in 2009 to see if any fans would react negatively. Besides stoking anti-Muslim sentiments, the segment planned for *Dateline NBC* potentially pigeonholed Southern car racing fans as rednecks (Kouri 2009).

Yet the press has the potential to be an effective instrument of justice. You've heard the expression "Knowledge is power." It means that those who are privy to certain kinds of intelligence (say, the ins and outs of trading) and expertise (how to invest in the stock market) have an advantage over others who are in the dark. In fact, the idea of "public enlightenment" in SPJ's ethics code is based on this view of knowledge as empowering people to act intelligently as citizens. Legal prohibitions against insider trading, monopolies and other "unfair" business practices recognize that the distribution of knowledge has ethical implications. So does public policy aimed at increasing access to higher education; we recognize that, in an information society, those who are more educated will fare better than those who are less educated.

Knowledge is the press' means for redistributing social power, says ethicist Elaine Englehardt (2006). But redistributing power through knowledge isn't always the right thing to do. Knowledge, Englehardt notes, empowers the receiver at the expense of the subject. So, journalists always need to consider whether there is *enough* benefit produced for those who are enlightened to justify the harm caused to those who are forced to let that light shine for all to see. For example, we saw in Chapter 1 that many Americans thought President Clinton's affair with Monica Lewinsky shed light on his trust-worthiness as a public official. However, the intense, intrusive coverage of the scandal caused considerable harm to Clinton, his family, Lewinsky, his administration, the Democratic Party, the country and the press itself. Exposing Clinton's bad choices certainly brought him down a few notches, but at what cost?

Here's another problem. Even when the information in question is positive, such as tips for preventing disease or advice on helping your kids excel in school, throwing that information out there for all takers doesn't necessarily even things out between the haves and have-nots. Mass communication theorists have demonstrated that those who are better off and more educated learn and retain more from reading the news, watching public service announcements, and so forth, than those who are less well off and less educated. So the "knowledge gap" actually widens when more information becomes available, rather than narrowing.

Clifford Christians, John Ferre and Mark Fackler (1993) argue that focusing on social justice is appropriate for journalists on the basis of the ethical norms of respect for persons and human solidarity: "The litmus test of whether the news profession operates justly over the long term is its advocacy for those abused or ignored by established power" (p. 92). What stories does justice require? Shriver (1997) makes the following suggestions:

- Give the same attention to the marginalized in society, such as the homeless and illegal immigrants, as you do to the establishment. "Every human being is newsworthy" (Shriver 1997: 143).
- Put a face on statistics and shun stereotypes to encourage empathy with others. Reducing people to a number or to a label alienates citizens from their plight.
- Strive for *sustained* attention to issues of social justice, such as healthcare reform and affordable housing. Don't just drop in for a news conference or a congressional vote; stay with the story as long as it takes.
- Cultivate grassroots sources with insights into social problems. The volunteer at the local food pantry will have a much better handle on the seriousness of hunger in your local city than the mayor.
- Look beyond the "great" and focus also on "supporting players." Don't interview the general at the Pentagon and forget to include the perspective of the soldier on the front line.
- Be willing to challenge audiences with uncomfortable truths. The only way to address problems is to confront them.

As you reason through the following cases, think of how they measure up to this list and whether you would add any recommendations to improve journalism's performance in the area of social justice.

SOCIAL JUSTICE CASES AND WALK-THROUGH EXERCISES

The cases in this chapter are designed to sensitize you to the ethical demands of social justice and provide practice in integrating theory and cases in ethical reasoning.

Case 1: The Littlest Victims[4]

Michael Nicholson had seen his share of horror as a veteran war correspondent for the British Independent Television News. But the Serbs' siege of Sarajevo after Bosnia declared its independence from Yugoslavia was worse than anything Nicholson had witnessed before. His experience covering the war in 1992, depicted in the movie *Welcome to Sarajevo*, raises questions about how far journalists should go in pursuing justice for the most vulnerable.

Situational Clues

- During the 2.5-year siege, snipers shot continually at the city's residents. Muslim girls and women were systematically raped, and boys and men were imprisoned and murdered as part of nationalist Serbian leader Slobodan Milošević's program of "ethnic cleansing."

- *Welcome to Sarajevo* portrays Nicholson's initial reluctance to cross the line of objectivity. But, as a father himself, he was struck by the plight of 200 children trapped in an orphanage just outside the city. He got to know the orphanage's director and some of the kids, who dodged shells to forage for food and supplies from bombed-out houses. They had been separated from their parents by chaos, death and circumstances. Thousands of others who weren't as lucky were shot by snipers or killed by bombs.
- Despite the efforts of Nicholson and other Western reporters to turn the world's attention toward the atrocities in Bosnia, there was little relief. The United Nations eventually imposed economic sanctions on Serbia and deployed peacekeepers in Bosnia, but the peacekeepers were under strict orders to remain neutral and not interfere militarily. Rather than report on what the UN and other official bodies were doing (or not doing), Nicholson kept going back to the orphanage, determined to get help for the most vulnerable victims of the war.

Walk-Through Exercise: Advocating for Justice

1. How do Nicholson's actions fare when compared against Shriver's suggestions for improving the news media's focus on social justice?
2. Another reporter who covered the Bosnian war, the *Guardian*'s Ed Vulliamy, said, "I believe that there are moments in history when neutrality is not neutral, but complicit in the crime" (cited in Good 2008: 156). Do you agree with his assessment? Did Nicholson go too far by getting involved in the story, or did other reporters not go far enough?

More Situational Clues

- One orphan in particular made an impression on Nicholson. "We'd picked out some children, going for the faces as you do on television, and we'd got ourselves a nice little story and were just packing up, when suddenly a little girl came and stood by me, pushing herself on me," Nicholson recalled in an interview with the London newspaper the *Independent* (Durrant 1993). "Now I know her, I realise she was very uptight that we hadn't filmed her. I said, 'Oh, she's rather a pretty little thing, let's do this one too.' Her name was Natasha."
- Nine-year-old Natasha—No. 388 to the orphanage—wanted more from Nicholson than a story. She made him promise her he'd save her. And he did. When it was time for him to return home to his wife and two sons in London, he arranged to get Natasha out of Bosnia as part of a convoy organized by a French charity.
- When he first learned of the rescue mission, Nicholson approached it as a reporter. "I thought, what a tremendous story, I'll go out on the convoy,

MAKING HARD CHOICES IN JOURNALISM ETHICS

too. And then I thought, here I've been, shouting my mouth off on TV every night about how disgraceful it is, well, I can actually take one out myself this way" (Durrant 1993). Nicholson left the convoy and took Natasha separately to the airport to keep his actions secret from his crew. He got her on the plane by lying on his passport, listing Natasha as his daughter, and buying her a ticket under the name "Natasha Nicholson."

■ The ploy worked, and Natasha went to live with Nicholson. Later, he returned to Bosnia to get her biological mother to give up her parental rights so that he could officially adopt Natasha. The woman had left her when she was a baby before the war; Natasha had grown up at the orphanage.

■ Nicholson himself was evacuated from Essex as a boy during World War II along with other children; he lived on a farm away from his parents for three years. Fifty years later, confronted by victimized children and genocide reminiscent of the Holocaust, he acknowledged that he was moved by the plight of his fellow Europeans in a way that he was not when witnessing the tragedies of war and famine in Africa and elsewhere.

■ Nicholson wrote about his rescue of Natasha in his 1993 book, *Natasha's Story*. Even though critics described the tale as heart-warming, many of his fellow journalists greeted his actions with scorn. As a journalist, they argued, he should have not switched from detached observer to involved advocate—making the news rather than reporting it, taking sides rather than remaining neutral.

Walk-Through Exercise: Becoming the News

1. Nicholson developed empathy for Natasha and other Bosnians because he was with them every day, getting shot at and crouching under furniture while Sarajevo was being shelled. How can journalists help their audiences feel empathy for the marginalized who are unjustly treated thousands of miles away?

2. Did Nicholson's situation possess the characteristics of a paradigm case? In other words, were his circumstances exceptional enough to warrant forgoing independence? Why or why not?

3. Four years after adopting Natasha, Nicholson rescued another girl while reporting in a foreign country. This time, it was 8-year-old Ana Sliva Mattias, whom he met while reporting from the Brazilian slums of Sao Paulo. She lived hand-to-mouth with her grandmother and was doomed to an early death unless she got an expensive operation to repair an abnormality in her bowels. Nicholson flew her to England, paid for her surgery and later secretly adopted her. Does this change your mind about the ethics of his actions in Bosnia? Why or why not?

Case 2: Katrina and the Social Contract[5]

The coverage of Hurricane Katrina, as you saw in Chapter 4, raised a host of ethical questions about the challenges of accurately reporting information after a natural disaster. But it also raised larger issues about social justice in the United States and how the news media address them.

Situational Clues

- Katrina was not a surprise. Sophisticated weather-tracking technology predicted the strength and path of the Category 5 storm as it approached. Years before that, safety experts and journalists had warned of the potential for widespread destruction should a strong hurricane make landfall in New Orleans.

- Indeed, the mayor of New Orleans ordered residents to evacuate as a safety precaution, but the city did not provide enough public trans- portation for those without the means to leave town. So, even if they wanted to comply with the evacuation order, they couldn't. Thousands converged on the Convention Center and Louisiana Superdome as instructed after the storm, only to find they had been abandoned once again. People waited for days to be rescued and died waiting.

- Once reporters started to realize how poorly the government had prepared for the disaster, the tone of the coverage changed dramatically. Reporters confronted officials on camera with pointed questions and contradicted official accounts with eyewitness reports and live footage that made middle-class Americans squirm in their seats.

- The most famous face-off was between CNN's Anderson Cooper and Louisiana Sen. Mary Landrieu. Landrieu started in with kudos for the Federal Emergency Management Agency and politicians managing the disaster. Anderson cut in:

    "Excuse me, senator, I'm sorry for interrupting," he said. "I haven't heard that because, for the last four days, I've been seeing dead bodies in the streets here in Mississippi. And to listen to politicians thanking each other and complimenting each other, you know, I got to tell you, there are a lot of people here who are very upset, and very angry, and very frustrated. When they hear politicians slap—thanking one another, it just . . . kind of cuts them the wrong way right now because literally there was a body on the streets of this town yesterday being eaten by rats because this woman had been laying in the street for 48 hours . . . Do you get the anger that is out here?"

    (de Moraes 2005: C01)

- The death and destruction were horrifying in themselves. But what audiences began to realize, along with journalists, is that Katrina's

MAKING HARD CHOICES IN JOURNALISM ETHICS

impact would have been considerably less had the nation been paying more attention to infrastructure, to security for the poor, to funding for police and other first responders. Although some affluent white neighborhoods were heavily impacted, damaged areas inside the city of New Orleans were disproportionately black and poor, occupied by tenants and the unemployed. As an Albany *Times Union* reporter put it in a story about the issues laid bare by Katrina: "What's more American: the public good? Or individual profit? Frankness? Or posturing? A safety net? Or tax cuts? The bloated corpses floating in the toxic New Orleans waters seem to demand an answer" (Gurnett 2005).

Walk-Through Exercise: Working the Fringes

1. *Columbia Journalism Review*'s managing editor, Brent Cunningham (2005), said more journalists need to "work the fringes" by seeking out sources with ideas outside the mainstream and producing stories that "connect the dots" among events and facts so that audiences can understand their significance. What are some of your ideas for doing this? Suggest at least one story idea and one follow-up.
2. A potential obstacle to "connecting the dots" is getting so close to your subjects that you lose a sense of the bigger picture. In other words, you don't see how things fit together. This has been a criticism of embedding journalists with military units in Iraq: we've gotten a sense of the war from the perspective of soldiers on the ground, but it's been harder to see how these individual experiences "add up." Develop a proposal for a series on homelessness in your community that includes suggestions for humanizing the statistics and focusing on "supporting players," but also provides perspective on the larger problem.
3. Scholars have suggested that journalists are influenced by cultural myths when they choose storylines for the news. These myths are seldom questioned and have the ring of truth. Cunningham suggests that the "gospel of wealth"—the idea that the rich deserve to be rich and the poor are to blame for being poor—gets expressed in stories that portray America's poor as "victims, perpetrators, or the face of failed social policies." How do you think this criticism applies to the coverage of Katrina? Give some examples. Which ethical norms are relevant to your critique?
4. The local paper in New Orleans, *The Times-Picayune*, was widely praised for its coverage of Katrina. The staff evacuated before the storm, but eight reporters and one photographer returned to the city to report on the aftermath.

> Living mostly in borrowed houses, often separated from friends and family, wearing donated clothes, and working with hand-me-down equipment and donated office space, the paper managed to

produce coverage of the disaster that serves to remind us all of just how deep is the connection between a city and its newspaper, how much they need each other.

(McCollam 2005).

Does engaging with your community as both a journalist and as a citizen help you to cover social justice issues better? Or are you better able to see the big picture when you limit your community involvement?

Case 3: Flooded by Stereotypes[6]

Surrounded by destruction and human suffering, journalists covering Hurricane Katrina were intensely affected by what they saw in New Orleans. Sharing the same deplorable conditions as the storm's victims, it was easy for journalists to get swept up in panic and fear in the first few weeks. Unfamiliar with the city, its residents and its history, many reporters flown in from elsewhere made erroneous assumptions about those who were trapped in New Orleans, resulting in reporting that reinforced stereotypes about blacks being poor, violent, dishonest and impulsive.

Situational Clues

- In Chapter 4, we looked at the rumors that circulated after Katrina. After all was said and written, the rumors about the Convention Center and Superdome turned out to be false. There were no rapes, and only 14 people were found dead in the two structures—of dehydration. Although there were some shootings, these were isolated incidents. "It's clear accurate reporting was among Katrina's many victims," according to a bipartisan report issued by a House committee several months later. "If anyone rioted, it was the media."

- So why did these rumors take wing and get repeated despite lack of confirmation? *Times-Picayune* editor Jim Amoss thought race played a role. "If the dome and Convention Center had harbored large numbers of middle class white people, it would not have been a fertile ground for this kind of rumor-mongering," he told the *Los Angeles Times*.

- Journalists also served up some powerful and enduring images courtesy of their language choices, which included calling victims "animals," "thugs" and "refugees." The contrast was striking when the caption for an Agence France-Presse photo showing people wading through floodwaters carrying groceries described two whites as "finding" food and an Associated Press caption described a young black man in a similar photo as "looting" a store.

Walk-Through Exercise: Getting the Big Story

1. When national news organizations send reporters on location to cover a big story, they are often criticized for engaging in "parachute journalism": National reporters parachute in just long enough to cover the event that brought them there, then they ship out to cover the next big story. Without the benefit of a long-range perspective, parachute journalism may contribute to overreacting. For example, New Orleans has a large black population, but not all black residents are poor. However, because the blacks left behind were those who couldn't afford to leave, news coverage created the impression that all blacks in New Orleans were poor, reinforcing a widespread racial stereotype, and obscuring the fact that New Orleans' problems with race and class are the problems of every major city in the United States. How good of a job do you think journalists have done in keeping the nation focused on poverty and inequality in New Orleans and other urban centers? How should local reporters cover these issues? How should national reporters cover them?

2. Katrina was a huge national news story, so the competition to get the latest was intense. How do you think this affected the reporting of rumors after Katrina?

3. Keith Woods and others at the Poynter Institute for Media Studies have argued that coverage of diversity (race, social class, gender, sexual orientation) is at the core of our responsibility as journalists. In fact, what we mean by truth telling in journalism is not just accuracy, but completeness, context and meaning. That's how the Katrina case in Chapter 4 framed the issue — as truth telling. Here the language has been about social justice. What are the implications of selecting one paradigm (truth) over the other (justice)? Are there any conditions under which both are relevant?

Case 4: Desecrating Muhammad[7]

When the conservative Danish newspaper *Jyllands-Posten* commissioned 12 cartoons of the Prophet Muhammad in 2005, it was trying to make a point about freedom of speech and religious irony. The paper published the cartoons in a full-page package on 30 September 2005 with a short editorial statement under the headline "The Face of Muhammad." Did the cartoons help us to reckon with the uncomfortable truth of religious intolerance, or were they a gratuitous insult to Muslims?

Situational Clues

■ Although there is no universal prohibition of images of Muhammad in Islam (certainly you can find images of Muhammad in Islamic literature), some Muslims believe that such images are blasphemous. As a result, a Danish children's author reported having trouble finding someone to illustrate a book about Muhammad's life for fear of attack by Islamic extremists. The paper's provocative gambit was a response to the author's predicament.

- The cartoons were accompanied by an editorial statement by *Jyllands-Posten*'s cultural editor that proclaimed a bias in favor of secularism as the rational alternative to religion in modern society; the implication was that religion is the natural foe of free speech and tolerance.

- The most controversial cartoon depicted Muhammad with a bomb-shaped turban. Others showed him as a terrorist and a devil. In one cartoon, he tries to turn suicide bombers away from heaven saying, "Stop. Stop. We ran out of virgins!" A couple of cartoons comment on the risky business of drawing the prophet, with one showing a cartoonist sweating profusely at the drawing table and another showing a turban-clad cartoonist holding a stick figure of Muhammad with what appears to be a grenade bearing the words "PR stunt" on top of his head.

- Muslims worldwide objected to the cartoons—some on principle, some because of the negative and stereotypical depictions. Arab governments in Saudi Arabia and Syria withdrew their ambassadors from Denmark and urged citizens to boycott Danish products. There were peaceful protests, but beatings of Danish workers and other violence were reported.

Walk-Through Exercise: Respecting Sensibilities

1. Which ethical norms are relevant to this case? Be sure to relate these norms to the facts of the case. How does being a professional journalist affect your understanding of these norms and these facts? How do your religious beliefs (or lack thereof) influence their meaning?

2. Trace these ethical norms to one or more of the theoretical frameworks from Chapter 2. Do any of the norms you identified have more than one theoretical basis? How does that affect their relevance to this case?

3. Historians note that people living in modern Western nations are used to thinking of pictures and art as symbolic abstractions to be analyzed, whereas traditional societies in the East think of images as partially embodying what they represent. In other words, to many Muslims, the images were not "just" images. How does this insight affect your estimate of the harms and benefits caused by publishing these cartoons? Is additional harm caused by the republication of the cartoons?

4. Islamic scholars have pointed out that there is, in fact, a diversity of viewpoints regarding pictorial representations of Muhammad among contemporary Muslims. Yet the Danish newspaper portrayed Muslims as a monolithic group, focusing on the minority who consider such

representations blasphemous by definition. Is it just to define an entire group by a minority of its members? Do stereotypes of Islamic fundamentalists have the effect of marginalizing *all* Muslims? Christians have made the same criticism, saying that the media harp on stereotypes of evangelical Christians. How can you overcome the tendency to stereotype Muslims, Christians and other religious groups?

One Last Look: Reporting Controversies

The story doesn't end here. US organizations had to decide how to handle the cartoons when reporting on the controversy going on in European and Arab nations. Before we look at how they actually handled things, let's see if we can come up with some paradigms:

1. On a piece of paper or in your computer, construct a paradigm case for an image like this that would lead most people to conclude the image must be published. In other words, make a list of the kinds of facts that would virtually guarantee that this image needed to be seen. For example, you might feel an image had to be seen if the audience had no other way to understand the controversy. What other facts would be on your list? (This can be done on your own or perhaps with a group in your classroom.)
2. Now do the same for the opposing paradigm case. What factors would lead most people to decide this was *not* an image to publish?
3. Once you have made the lists, keep them at hand, but do not change them.

More Situational Clues

- In solidarity with *Jyllands-Posten*, a number of European papers republished the cartoons. However, only a few American news organizations reporting on the controversy ran any of the images. ABC News and *The Philadelphia Inquirer* ran the cartoon of Muhammad wearing a bomb-shaped turban with an explanatory note.
- In the note, the *Inquirer*'s editors said they interviewed experts, including Islamic theologians, before deciding to publish the drawing. "The *Inquirer* published the image to inform our readers, not to inflame them," the note said.

Walk-Through Exercise: Providing Context

1. The *Inquirer* also printed a controversial photograph showing a crucifix in urine in 1987. Other controversial artworks that have been shown by news organizations include a portrait of the Virgin Mary made out of dung. How are these cases similar to the Muhammad cartoons? How are they different?

2. In its note to readers, the *Inquirer* placed its decision to publish the Muhammad cartoon in the context of other "troubling images" it had published, including the crucifix in urine and the mutilated bodies of Blackwater security contractors hanging from a bridge in Iraq. Do you agree with the editors that all these cases are of the same "type"? Why or why not? Are these cases comparable to the paradigm cases you developed earlier?

3. Does the cartoon of Muhammad with a bomb-shaped turban case match your "must publish" paradigm better or worse than your "don't publish" paradigm? What can you conclude about whether the *Inquirer* should have published it? Are there any characteristics that could have been changed to make publication more ethically acceptable besides the explanatory note?

One Last Look: Reflective Equilibrium

1. At some of the protests against the cartoons, protesters burned Danish flags. While that may not get your dander up, the image of Arabs burning American flags might. Rhetorician John Lucaites (2002) suggests that people who support flag burning based on the principle of free expression tend to look at the flag as an abstract symbol of American freedoms, whereas people who object to flag burning see the flag as a concrete embodiment of the blood that has been spilled by soldiers to protect American freedoms. How is the reaction of people who are offended by flag burning similar to the reaction of Muslims who were offended by the Muhammad cartoons? How is it different?

2. How do you reconcile abstract principles such as freedom and tolerance with felt experiences such as patriotism and religious devotion? What would you reassess in this case to achieve reflective equilibrium: your principles or your concrete experiences?

Case 5: Alternative Media[8]

Alternative media define themselves in opposition to mainstream media owned by commercial organizations and public media owned by the government. They usually present dissident views that do not get extensive coverage in mainstream media or that are presented as "radical" or "fringe" when they are covered. Some of the best-known alternative media today are *Ms.* magazine, *Utne Reader* magazine, *Mother Jones* magazine and *Slate* magazine, with many more appearing daily on both ends of the political spectrum online, on cable, in cities around the country, and on broadcast and satellite radio. Here are some more examples:

■ The editors of the first African American newspaper in the United States, *Freedom's Journal*, famously wrote in their inaugural issue in 1827,

"Too long have others spoken for us . . . We wish to plead our own cause." So began the black press at a time when most blacks were enslaved and their entire race was routinely denigrated in mainstream newspapers. Over the years, luminaries such as Frederic Douglass, W.E.B. DuBois, and Langston Hughes have advocated in the black press for equal rights and equal dignity for African Americans in US society. Today, the black press counts more than 200 newspapers under the umbrella of its trade organization, the National Newspaper Publishers Association; they are served by a wire service and linked through a web portal at BlackPressUSA.com.

■ *StreetWise* is a non-profit organization that provides employment assistance for the homeless in Chicago. It puts out a glossy magazine published in color every week with stories about the city and the challenges faced by its poor. Homeless people and residents at risk of losing their homes buy *StreetWise* for a nominal amount and earn an income by selling it at a profit. Since its founding as a monthly black-and-white newspaper in 1993, the *StreetWise* publication has helped more than 8,000 "vendors." The magazine, which has a circulation of more than 100,000, is funded by donations and advertising revenues. Besides providing income for homeless people, *StreetWise* provides them with a voice by inviting them to contribute stories to the publication. These contributors write with authority about poverty because they're living it and because they can write authentically about their experience without being stereotyped or otherwise being marginalized. More than 100 similar "street papers" empower the poor in other US cities and about 40 countries worldwide.

■ Perhaps the most famous newspaper for the poor, *The Catholic Worker*, still sells for a penny in New York, just as it did when journalist and activist Dorothy Day founded it with French immigrant Peter Maurin in 1933 during the Great Depression. Day published out of her kitchen and eventually opened up her house to the poor, who were welcome to stay and eat as long as they needed. More than 150 similar "houses of hospitality" belonging to the Catholic Worker Movement operate worldwide. Throughout its history, the *Worker* has advocated for civil rights and collective bargaining rights, consistent with Catholic teaching on social justice (though even Day's own church considered her a radical at times). The *Worker* has been most influential as an advocate for pacifism, recognized as a leading Catholic voice against nuclear weapons and the Vietnam War.

Walk-Through Exercise: Advocacy Journalism

1. Go to the websites listed in the endnotes and do a little more research on these alternative media. In what ways do they seem to practice journalism

similarly to mainstream media? In what ways do they seem to differ? Do they have more in common with each other than they do with mainstream media? Why or why not?

2. Alternative media are upfront about their advocacy for certain causes or communities. Does this give them more journalistic credibility or less?

3. Many alternative outlets are using open sourcing by freelancers and citizen journalists to generate and follow through on story ideas. What are the advantages and disadvantages to this approach?

4. To what degree is your assessment limited by your lack of membership in the communities these media represent?

5. What lessons can you draw about the difficulty that audiences must have sometimes in understanding how journalists interpret the meaning of ethical norms such as truth telling, independence and fairness in the context of their profession? Practice explaining your decision about the Muhammad cartoon to someone outside journalism.

CHAPTER 6

▼ CASUISTRY AND NEWSROOM POLICY

Case-based analysis has always had critics. Back in the seventeenth century, Blaise Pascal blasted the Jesuits for abuses of case-based reasoning. Casuistry can certainly be abused and misused by journalists today.

- Giving primacy to the details of the case, rather than rigid principles, makes the process vulnerable to rationalization. Offer journalists enough facts, and they can find reasons to do what they want—or to justify what they have already done. Pascal would have smoked out that problem among journalists in a heartbeat.
- Case-based reasoning also reeks of relativism. If every case is different in some way, then who's to say that decisions shouldn't always be made case by case? A decision made in one case can't be binding on the next case because the new case is different.
- And isn't casuistry just too time-consuming? What journalist has time in the course of a busy day and countless deadlines to follow the approach outlined in this book? In the age of online journalism, case-based reasoning, with its attention to gathering facts, finding paradigm cases, and exploring analogous cases may seem as overwhelming as the 20-page paper you don't start until the night before it's due.

Fortunately, the case for casuistry isn't that bleak. As we have shown, case-based reasoning—when used carefully—can undercut easy rationalizations. Moreover, most decisions journalists make don't raise these ethical questions; casuistry is only for the controversial cases. Most important, case-based reasoning is grounded in the desire for consistency and fairness. And cases often share key features that make them more alike than different. These similar cases should be treated similarly. This goal is embedded in the final step of casuistry: the development of guidelines.

Deriving Guidelines from Case-Based Analysis

CNN owns a user-generated news site called iReport. One can easily see iReport as an example of citizen journalism. Anyone is invited to post stories, photos or videos at iReport.com. These citizen reports "are not edited, fact-checked, or screened before they post," according to iReport's website. All those who file reports are encouraged to decide for themselves what constitutes "news" when considering a submission.

A handful of these user-generated reports—about 23 a day in May 2009—are "vetted" for CNN.com, the website for CNN. CNN doesn't say how it picks the reports. But you can imagine what a CNN editor faces. In early June 2009 someone in Tehran posted pictures of a political rally for one of the reform candidates. Who took the pictures? Does this person work for the reform candidate? Are the photos digitally manipulated? Are the people shown at the rally put in danger? What kind of process has this person used to select photos?

None of the usual checks CNN would have on the news it produces is in place. In effect, the raw cases provide the grounds for making decisions on which stories from iReport.com make it to CNN. Let's look at just one small piece of this vetting process: verifying the accuracy of the photos. We don't know the photographer's reliability, so we can't depend on that. But we could at least verify through other sources—say, the wire services—that such rallies are taking place in Tehran. We might even be able to see photos others have taken to see whether the scenes in these photos are similar. In other words, the guideline for verifying the accuracy of the photos would be different than with CNN's own photographers, but a guideline could still emerge.

That has clearly happened on the original iReport site. In 2009 iReport's slogan was "Unedited. Unfiltered. News." However, the site also lists the kind of information that isn't welcome: pornography, obscenity, hate speech, advocacy of violence and more. Viewers of the site can click on "report violation" if they feel a report violates "community standards."

The message: guidelines apply, even in a loosely regulated online environment where the citizen reporter is in charge. In news environments where no prior standards exist to regulate behavior, guidelines often emerge.

That's the essence of common law, a way of resolving legal disputes not clearly addressed by statutory law. In fact, case-based reasoning and common law are similar in the way controversial issues are resolved. A lawsuit is brought to court with the relevant facts presented by each side. Each of the lawyers in the case cites the precedents that are similar to this case, just as we used analogous cases. In many cases, the lawyers dispute what kind of case this is (what paradigm should be used to understand the legal issues). And when the judge decides the case, a precedent has been set. That precedent becomes a guideline for future (similar) cases.

Like many newspapers, *The Messenger-Inquirer* ran short stories reporting that a lawsuit had been filed. Not every lawsuit filing got a story. Some were not important enough. And filing of major lawsuits got more extensive coverage, complete with any interviews one could get from both sides of the case. But some lawsuit filings floated in the middle ground—not significant enough to merit extensive reporting at this stage (that would come later), but worth noting in the paper.

The standard formula for this story was simple: present the claims being made in documents filed by the plaintiff. But one day, John Hager, the editor and co-publisher, saw one of these stories and got upset. The story itself was accurate, but it represented only one side of the case. He worried that casual readers might infer that the plaintiff's side was right because that was the only side presented in the filing and, consequently, in the paper. After some discussion, he instructed the copy desk to include an editor's note with all stories like this. The editor's note would begin the story, telling readers that the report was based on the action of a plaintiff and represented only one side of the case. In other words, don't infer that the claims made by the plaintiff are correct or complete.

That guideline was placed in a policy manual on the copy desk. A copy of the offending story was attached to the guideline. A brief explanation of the reasoning behind the guideline completed the page.

This incident is a perfect illustration of casuistry's idea that a *taxonomy*, or storehouse of cases, can be the basis for developing sound newsroom policies about ethics. By carefully discussing problematic cases as they arise, as well as preserving the details of those cases for future reference (much as criminal investigators keep records of previously solved crimes), newsrooms can adopt living guidelines grounded in journalists' actual experiences.

It may be rare that we can witness the birth of a guideline in a news organization. However, we see the results of these decisions in policy manuals and codes of ethics. At times, ethical guidelines are also present in the unwritten culture of the newsroom: the practices that define "what we have always done." Such informal guidelines can even come with stories that illustrate the origin and the importance of the unwritten guideline.

These guidelines—written or unwritten—are critical to sustaining an ethical news organization in two ways:

- As a practical matter, guidelines save time. Working through a controversial case the first time can mean hours, even days, of research and reflection. The guideline that results can solve the next case in minutes.
- More critically, the guideline has the force of precedent. Following precedent provides consistency in decisions on similar cases. When Frank

Caperton of *The Indianapolis Star* argued that individual journalists with high ethical standards should be able to make their own decisions, those individual journalists made a variety of decisions on the use of anonymous sources. A careful reader could question why the paper had no consistency in the naming of sources.

The guideline is thus a check on those who argue case-based reasoning is an excuse for rationalization. In fact, any claim to abandon or alter the guideline must first overcome the presumptive force of precedent.

In a similar way, the guideline limits the claim that case-based reasoning is nothing more than ethical relativism. This should already have been clear when we saw the role that relevance plays in case analysis. Certain features of the case are relevant because they embody broad ethical norms. These norms shape our decisions in ways relativism denies. Guidelines are often linked to ethical norms in a similar way. A guideline about free gifts is grounded in a concern for autonomy and, ultimately, truth telling. A guideline about the naming of rape victims seeks to do no harm to the victim. Even the idea of the guideline is based in a concern for fairness.

Journalists have done reasonably well in developing and using guidelines. Codes of ethics are now commonplace at many news organizations. Journalists have been less successful in preserving a taxonomy of cases on which the guidelines have been built. It's useful to have a guideline. But without the details of the cases that were used to shape the guideline—and without the analysis of these cases—the guidelines are disconnected from the context that brought them into being. Like the guideline based on the report giving the plaintiff's side of the story at the *Messenger-Inquirer*, the taxonomy of cases provides an answer to the question, "Why do we do that?"

The court system has a way of capturing not only the decisions of the court (the precedent), but also the details of the arguments and, most critically, the reasoning of the judge in making a decision. Here journalism fails miserably. Only when the cases are kept alive in the oral tradition of the newsroom ("I remember the reporter who went to interview the owner of a diamond company. . .") does the rich detail of the case in which a guideline is grounded inform the journalists charged with following that guideline. In the current climate of shrinking newsrooms, even that part of the culture is threatened.

Barry Bingham, Jr, former editor of *The Courier-Journal*, created a taxonomy of sorts with his ethics newsletter, *FineLine*. Each issue presented the critical details on six to eight controversial cases, their ethical problems and the rationale for a particular decision. These cases are now part of Indiana University's journalism ethics online database. More taxonomies like this, especially inside news organizations, would fill an important gap in case-based reasoning.

We have been talking as if guidelines always came from the bottom up. In fact, editors have often created codes from the top down, formulating guidelines based on accepted norms of independence, truth telling and fairness. When the Society of Professional Journalists adopted a code of ethics in 1973, many editors and news producers adapted this code for their own news organizations. This is another example of the reciprocal movement between ethical theory and cases that we find everywhere in the way journalists operate. The key to success in resolving controversies is not where one begins, but whether all the critical components are part of the decision-making process.

But this is not the end of the story. We've been talking about living guidelines, not immutable rules. That means one must always be open to the possibility of change. If you read the first section of this chapter carefully, you know that guidelines promote consistency and fairness in decisions. But consistency and fairness are not always the same. Following a bad precedent can result in consistency; it may not result in fairness.

That's why new cases can challenge existing guidelines, threatening to overthrow them or, more commonly, revise them. It's to that challenge we now turn.

Revising Guidelines in Light of New Cases

In Chapter 3, you learned about Janet Cooke, the *Washington Post* reporter who wrote a story about Jimmy, an 8-year-old heroin addict. Jimmy's identity was kept a secret from everyone, ostensibly to protect the child. But, as you know, Cooke fabricated the character of Jimmy. When this hoax was exposed, many editors developed a new operating guideline: At least one editor must also know the identity of the source (*After Jimmy's World* 1981).

A case-based approach remains open to revisiting guidelines as necessary in light of new cases. We saw how this happened in the Bowman/Smith case at *The Courier-Journal*. The policy of not naming rape victims was challenged by the novel nature of this allegation of rape, resulting in a new guideline: rape victims would not be named except in cases where the accused assailant was well-known and the trial coverage was likely to be extensive.

Why should we expect changes in guidelines? For lots of reasons. As we noted earlier, casuistry provides no certainty in always finding the best solution. Cases can be complicated and the facts incomplete. Fallible humans may not consider all the possible applications of the guideline. A new case exposes our limited policy, requiring a revision. Think of it as a kind of "marketplace of guidelines." As more cases are considered, we'll get closer to a guideline that can stand up to repeated challenges.

New cases also add unforeseen elements. At *The Herald-Times,* it was standard practice to publish all reports of violent crimes, including key details, such as the identity of who was attacked, the name of the attacker (if known), and other key evidence about the crime from the police report. It was a simple policy based on full reporting of law enforcement activity. But one day, a woman called the paper to complain. She was scared. The newspaper named her, gave her address, and the attacker was still at large. Now he knows where I live, she said. No one thought about that problem when the earlier policy was put in place. So the policy changed in ways that would protect the identity of someone whose attacker was still at large.

Sometimes, the new circumstances may even warrant a "paradigm shift," a radical reframing of the policy. That almost happened at *The Courier-Journal* when Irene Nolan argued for the naming of all rape victims. If we named all rape victims, we would be treating rape as a crime of violence, not a sexual crime. Naming the victim would implicitly assert that the injured woman had no cause for shame, that society should shift its attention from the victim to the alleged assailant, just as it does in other crimes of violence. Implementing that policy would have shifted the paradigm from "protecting individual rape victims" to "changing social attitudes toward rape."

Or consider this example: research of crime coverage in Chicago showed that local television stations consistently aired footage of the first public appearances of those accused of crimes. The problem was that the suspects who were less educated and poor often made their first appearance in front of the cameras in prison garb and handcuffs, flanked by police officers. Those with more education and money were more likely to appear first in street clothes, flanked by their lawyers. Guess whose visual images said, "guilty"? The coverage also had a racial bias: More blacks appeared as prisoners; more whites appeared as citizens (Entman and Rojecki 2001: 81–84). It seems likely that removing the presumption of guilt will require a new paradigm for how the accused are visually portrayed. Like opening a "cold case" in light of new evidence on *CSI*, we may need to admit we got it wrong the first time. It's time for a new way to frame the evidence and seek a better solution.

Before we leave, a word of warning: watch out for vague exceptions to guidelines. Sometimes journalists will anticipate the kinds of challenges to guidelines we have discussed here. *The Courier-Journal* did that in many of its reporting guidelines, including the one on naming rape victims: "Victims of rape will not be named, unless there are exceptional circumstances." This escape hatch may be helpful in suggesting that this guideline is open to revision. But without knowing what unnamed circumstances might justify an exception, the wiggle room isn't helpful. In fact, it seems to allow journalists to do what they want and rationalize it later. And the "exceptional circumstances" clause didn't help the editors when they were addressing the

Bowman/Smith case. Only laying out the details of that case and crafting a revised guideline accounting for celebrity cases did that.

More important, one could argue that the language of exceptions is misplaced. It assumes that one can ignore the guideline in one "exceptional" case, then return to the original guideline as if nothing had happened. But the "exception" actually means the new case contains features that need to be addressed in a new or revised guideline—just as *The Courier-Journal* did.

CHARACTER AND GOOD REASONING

The focus of this chapter is on the critical final step in casuistry: establishing guidelines. Guidelines are valuable because they create a standard against which journalists can compare and test future cases. If they treat similar cases similarly by applying guidelines, they can achieve a level of consistency in newsroom practice.

Unfortunately, consistency in pursuit of a bad policy is hardly a virtue. Journalists with the power to establish guidelines and precedents can do so for the worst kinds of reasons. One small newspaper took up the practice of publishing a front-page photo of every person convicted of driving under the influence. Another had a detailed policy regulating Bigfoot sightings. Still another set a standard for free gifts that mocked the goal of an independent journalist: all you could eat or drink within two hours.

Human beings make decisions in newsrooms. Working in a competitive environment, constrained by dwindling resources, limited in time—all these conditions can yield standards more concerned with doing it fast than with doing it right. A great deal has been made of the wholesale fabrication of stories by Stephen Glass at *The New Republic*. But let's look through Glass and focus on the editors. The editors at *The New Republic* took pride in having a fact-checking system as rigorous as *The New Yorker*. Yet editors (and reporters who checked each other's stories) often used a reporter's notes as the ultimate verification of a story's facts. This was true even when Glass' stories were riddled with references to companies and people that could easily have been checked independently—and exposed as non-existent. It took a journalist from another organization to focus on this blindspot among Glass' editors. Glass was deficient in the moral virtue department, but his editors were lacking in intellectual virtue.

That's why casuistry—in addition to focusing on methodology—also advocates the need for good character. The good casuist needs to be committed to the moral life—to doing what is right, rather than what is expedient. Moreover, the good casuist needs a set of virtues that will foster good decisions and good guidelines. Here is a list of virtues particularly suited to helping journalists make ethical decisions in controversial cases (Borden 1999: 97–98):

- *Truthfulness.* In a profession dedicated to the truth, the value of having journalists "disposed to habitually tell the public information they believe to be true, relevant and complete" (Borden 1999: 97) may seem obvious. But is it? We've had too many examples of people like Jayson Blair to take this virtue for granted. And it's precisely when the casuist faces ethical controversy that we need to make sure we get the facts and the complete context of the case right.

- *Diligence.* The virtue of truthfulness commits a journalist to getting the story right. But diligence may be needed to accomplish that. Diligence is working hard to get the story right—double-checking information, finding diverse sources, and pushing against attempts to hide information. For the casuist, diligence is not rushing to judgment, but spending the time to develop all the relevant details of the case. When the pressure of deadlines pushes journalists to publish fast, diligence demands that they keep digging, not only for facts about this case, but for the paradigm cases and analogous cases that will guide them to the best decision.

- *Empathy.* When *The Journal Gazette* of Fort Wayne, Indiana, covered the brutal murder of its own editorial page editor and his family, editor Craig Klugman had to decide whether to include in its stories information about the molestation of the surviving toddler. Against the advice of nearly everyone in the newsroom, Klugman withheld the information from *Journal Gazette* readers, arguing that this child did not need people to know what she had experienced as she grew up in that community. Klugman tried to see the world through her eyes and decided to spare a child who lost her entire family at least that much hurt. That's empathy. The empathetic casuist should be guided by how everyone is affected by a decision or guideline, not only the competitive, pragmatic newsroom.

- *Fairness.* In the context of casuistry, the virtue of fairness predisposes journalists to consider the common good, the interests of all—including the weak and voiceless. In the same way that a judge is asked to be fair to all parties in a legal case, the casuist is asked to be equitable in considering everyone's interests in a controversial journalism case.

- *Temperance.* The virtue of temperance for the journalist is not a call to drink less alcohol—though that might be good advice for some college students you know. Temperance is about curbing the journalist's appetite for fame, prizes, or power. The reason is simple: Unfettered ambition gives a priority to self-interest, rather than to the interests of others. Cooke fabricated the story of Jimmy in part because of her well-documented career goals. Blinded by ambition, Cooke would have made a rotten casuist. One can even see the value of temperance in cases where the issue is not about self-interest. Geneva Overholser, then editor of the *Des Moines Register*, wasn't exactly temperate in her views about reporting rape. She wanted to name all rape victims to destigmatize this crime of violence against women—a potentially radical shift in policy.

But when she wrestled with what to do in the *Register,* she took a moderate approach. She published the story of Nancy Ziegenmeyer, a woman who wished to be identified, but the *Register* continued to withhold the names of other rape victims. Overholser's own views were tempered by the social reality of the stigma women who were raped still felt.

- *Courage.* One of the key elements of character is the will to do what is right. Virtue directs us toward what is good and away from what is bad. Although all virtues involve the will, the importance of will power is front and center in the virtue of courage. Courage is not just about placing oneself in danger in war reporting. Courage is also standing up against a whole newsroom to allow an orphaned infant to grow up without the community's knowledge of her molestation. Courage is the decision of then editor Jay Harris not to enforce the newsroom cuts for the *San Jose Mercury News* mandated by the chain's corporate executives.

- *Discernment.* If this book has taught you anything, it's that casuistry can get complicated. Sorting through that complexity in order to come to a good decision takes what has classically been described as "wisdom." We want people who make decisions to be wise. The word we have been using to describe that wisdom in casuistry is discernment. The discerning casuist will be able to sort the relevant from the irrelevant details of the case, be able to find the right paradigm and reason through the challenging analogous cases. And from all that, the discerning casuist can draw a guideline that will provide direction for the future.

That sounds easy enough in the abstract. But discernment is tested every election cycle when decisions are made on how to cover the candidates. Do competing candidates get equal time on television each day, no matter how much more breaking news is coming from one campaign? Or is it only necessary to provide balanced coverage over time—even if we can't guarantee that viewers see every show? Does Sara Moore, who arrives at the newsroom with a rusting car and a hand-lettered business card, deserve a story about her gubernatorial race? Or should candidates be "viable" before they get lots of ink? And if we exclude fringe candidates such as Moore because they have not attracted sufficient financial support or political endorsements, are we really living up to our obligation to give citizens the information they need in a democratic society—or are we settling for information about political candidates who already represent powerful groups? This kind of wisdom won't come easily. It will come gradually with the kind of moral training this book seeks to provide. And it will develop with the moral training that results from doing: "Journalists will learn to be virtuous journalists by doing virtuous acts *as journalists*" (Borden 1999: 101).

It should come as no surprise that the Bowman/Smith case illustrates the role of character in case-based reasoning. We have been able to explore this case throughout the book in part because of the ethical culture in the newsroom of *The Courier-Journal*. Barry Bingham, Jr, brought a transformational leadership to that newspaper that made ethics a core concern of the newsroom. Rigorous standards governing conflict of interest were implemented to protect the independence of the journalists and the newspaper they served. These standards applied equally to top management.

At the same time, the editors encouraged discussion and debate about controversial cases in the newsroom, both as cases were developing and in brown-bag lunches where post-mortems could dissect and challenge the decisions that were made. The paper's editors exhibited the kind of character journalism desperately needs.

In a way, the newsroom culture at *The Courier-Journal* had good character too. As important as individual virtues are, journalists who want to achieve moral excellence need to work in healthy news organizations that provide them with the moral training and support they need to pursue the practice's mission with integrity.

Final Thoughts

As you page through the policy manual developed over the years at *The Courier-Journal*, you will find a striking division between two types of operating practices. Some of the practices, primarily those focused on conflict of interest, are absolutes. No free gifts from sources. No free books from publishers. No free space at the statehouse for newspaper staff. No exceptions. Nada. *Courier-Journal* editors didn't think any particular circumstances merited a case-based approach to freebies. The principle of autonomy was clear and applied top-down to everyone.

But when it came to guidelines on reporting practices, the picture changed. Nearly every guideline contained language that suggested one could consider alternative strategies if the particular circumstances of cases demanded it. The world on which journalists reported was simply too complicated for any top-down, one-size-fits-all reporting policies. We've looked at one of these practices, on the naming of rape victims, throughout this book. But the policy manual was sprinkled with other examples that assumed journalists would have to engage in case-based reasoning on controversial cases.

Simply put, that's the argument of this book. Many times, it's easy to identify an ethical norm, apply it to a case, and move on. You don't need an ethics textbook to know that you can't fabricate a story or a quote, take diamond earrings from a source, or interview a 7-year-old girl without her guardian's consent.

But practicing journalism gets more complicated than that. And when it does, ethical norms alone may not provide the best ethical answers. In these cases — when ethical norms are in conflict, when the case is complicated, when the scenario is ambiguous — a different kind of approach is needed: case-based analysis. Beginning with the case, one can explore a rich narrative that will inform one's ethical decision. And following a clear strategy — searching for relevance, paradigm cases, analogous cases, guidelines and ethical norms — can offer hope that a reasonable decision has been made. Perhaps, if you have done your job well, the best decision possible.

EYE ON GUIDELINES

In previous chapters, we have focused on a particular issue, such as privacy or deception. In this final chapter, the focus is on methodology, specifically the development of guidelines.

Guidelines are the counterpart of paradigm cases for casuistry. The paradigm anchors the analysis in its early stages, providing the unambiguous case on which one expects nearly universal agreement. Guidelines anchor the conclusion of the analysis, providing a tentative standard for cases that are more problematic. In a sense, guidelines are like the conclusion you reach after you have looked at the evidence and constructed an argument.

CASES AND WALK-THROUGH EXERCISES

The cases that follow will give you some practice in constructing guidelines, both with cases we have already discussed in the book and several new ones. Let's have a go at it.

Case 1: What the Q@$%^%#$#@?[1]

You work for *The Courier-Journal* in Louisville, Kentucky. Like most newspapers, *The Courier Journal* has a code of ethics (actually a policy manual with a variety of guidelines, some of which are ethical). One of the guidelines governs the use of offensive language (in news stories, not newsroom arguments!). Before you learn what this policy is, think about what you would like it to be if you were the editor.

Step 1: Write a Preliminary Guideline

To begin this case, write a guideline governing the use of offensive language in quotes from sources. Compose a clear, concise guideline on the inclusion of offensive language in this context (assume no reporter or editor will include offensive language if it is not a source's quote). Be ready to defend your guideline, arguing why you adopted it. Use hypothetical examples to illustrate your argument. This should require no more than a page, but your instructor can provide more specific instructions.

Here are a few questions to get you thinking:

1. What words are too offensive to be used in the newspaper?
2. Should the newspaper ban the use of all words that are declared offensive?
3. Under what conditions, if any, should offensive words NOT be banned (again, the principal concern here is offensive language used by sources in quotes)?
4. How, if at all, does context make a difference?
5. Who should decide when it is allowed?
6. If an offensive word is to be used, how should it be written?
   a. Spell it out?
   b. Replace the word with 4 dashes, no matter how many letters the word has?
   c. Use dashes to indicate the exact length of the word?
   d. Replace all but the first letter with dashes?
7. We hope you have other ideas for your policy. Your instructor may ask you to bring this policy to class so you can discuss the case as a group.

Step 2: Explore Other Guidelines

Find at least two examples of guidelines on the use of offensive words in quotations in print or online publications. Print out these guidelines. Your instructor may ask you to bring them to class.

Step 3: Compare Guidelines

Discuss your guideline and the guidelines you found with members of your class, perhaps in a small group. See if your group can write a single guideline to present to the class.

Step 4: Compare Your Guideline with The Courier-Journal

Here's *The Courier-Journal*'s policy:

> The following will be our style for handling obscenities. The editors in charge of the news desks will be responsible for judging what words or expressions are too offensive to be printed in the newspaper.
>
> Any word or expression which he does not think we should print will be replaced by four short dashes. This will represent the full expression. We will NOT use "----ing," nor will we use "mother----er," etc.

In other words, the total expression, regardless of its length, will be represented by the ----.

It is the policy of these newspapers to use offensive words — including such mildly offensive words as "damn" and "hell" — ONLY when the ranking editor on duty rules that the words are material to the story.

What do you think of this guideline? Is it different from your guideline? How would you change this guideline? How would you change yours? Discuss it in a small group in relation to your earlier discussion of guidelines.

Step 5: A Case that Challenges the Guideline

You now have a case that might call this guideline into question. Your newspaper has been investigating the Sheriff's Department of Jefferson County for some time. Jim Greene, who is known in the community as a genial old-time political figure, runs the department.

- You have been doing stories about his mismanagement of the office for several months. Some employees are unhappy. Employees have also filed several sexual discrimination suits.
- You have come into possession of a taped conversation between Sheriff Greene and his former deputy. The tape came from the deputy, who taped Greene surreptitiously. The deputy was working for the Sheriff's Department at the time. (Such taping was legal in Kentucky as long as one party to the taping knew about it.)
- In the tape, Greene discloses information about his attitude toward competitive bidding (he rejects it, though he is on record as supporting it), toward blacks and women, and toward *The Courier-Journal*. It also contradicts the image Greene cultivated in his political career (in Kentucky, sheriffs are elected) as a harmless, good old boy. The recording shows him to be mean, vindictive, and vulgar, using his power against people to get special favors, such as free tickets to the Kentucky Derby.
- The tape is laced with offensive language. A few samples are provided below. Because you need to know what the words are to decide whether they should or should not be used, the offensive words are printed as spoken.
  - On competitive bidding: "But what it's going to end up doing is they are probably going to pass some legislation in Frankfort when we got to go out and bid every fucking thing and, boy, I don't want any fucking part of that, my friend. . ."
  - On a judge's call for an investigation of his office's financial procedures: "The fucking. The goddamn. All that [story] did was give that judge credit. Fuck. That judge didn't ask for anything. I'm

the one to ask for the son of a bitch. Goddamn them. I get so fucking mad."
— On an employee who said Greene's career was over: "She's a no good son-of-a-bitch. If I get re-elected, I'm not going to hire her ass back. Fuck her." Told this woman only likes two of the deputies in the office, Greene says: "She's probably sucking both of them."

What would you do with Greene's language? Why?

1. Refuse to use any part of the tape because Greene was taped unethically, even if it was legal?
2. Paraphrase the quotes, focusing on the substance of Greene's stated positions on public policy issues without mentioning the offensive language?
3. Paraphrase the quotes, but also mention the frequency of the offensive language in the conversation?
4. Follow the stated policy, replacing the offensive words with the four short dashes (----)?
5. Follow the policy you (or your group) formulated?

Step 6: Evaluate What The Courier-Journal Did

Editors at *The Courier-Journal* debated how to handle the offensive language. Two major concerns emerged from the discussion. The editors thought the offensive language was an essential part of the story, as it exposed the gap between Greene's public image and his private character. The offensive language also added a level of intensity to his stated opinions on important public issues, such as competitive bidding and race relations. The statement would not have the same meaning (truth) without the offensive language. At the same time, the editors did not want to shift the public's focus from Greene to *The Courier-Journal.* The risk was that people would become upset with the publication of the offensive language and make the newspaper the focus of their anger, not Greene.

In the end, the editors decided not to follow their guideline. They thought it was important for readers to know what words were said. So they began the words with the appropriate consonant, filled in the spaces with dashes equal to the number of omitted letters, and included some of the end letters, e.g. "f---ing." The quote about the female employee who criticized Greene included the word "sucking" in full because editors said it was the only way readers could be sure what he said.

Do you think the editors were justified in abandoning the guideline in this case? Why or why not?

MAKING HARD CHOICES IN JOURNALISM ETHICS

Step 7: Rewrite The Courier-Journal *Guideline*

You may not agree with what *The Courier-Journal* did. But its actions clearly demonstrate that the editors thought this case fell outside the existing guideline. How would you rewrite the guideline to match the editors' conclusions for similar cases that might arise in the future?

One Last Look at The Courier-Journal*'s Guideline*

1. After the story was published with the explicit language clearly identified, *The Courier-Journal* received only 12 complaints about the handling of the language. The editors concluded they had struck the right balance in their decision, keeping the focus on Greene, not *The Courier-Journal.* Do you agree?
2. Prior to this story, *The Courier-Journal* had run a number of stories focusing on Greene's mismanagement of his office. In an interview about this story, editor David Hawpe said that the conclusion of this story was that Greene needed to go. Does this change your evaluation of what was done in this story?

Case 2: Anonymous Sources and the Judge[2]

A district county judge told the local television station that he was retiring from the bench for reasons of health. The station broadcast a brief story about his resignation on the nightly newscast. Shortly after the broadcast, the news director got two calls from inside the police department. Both callers said that the station got the story wrong.

Situational Clues

Here's what the callers said happened:

- Over the course of several years, the judge had been propositioning female defendants who appeared before him in court. He would ask the defendants to see him in his chambers after 5 p.m., when the staff had gone home. He then told the defendants that he could assist them in their cases in return for sexual favors.
- However, one female defendant who was asked to meet with the judge contacted a friend in the police department. The police wired her for sound and recorded her encounter with the judge. Shortly after the police collected this evidence, they contacted the state's Judicial Retirement and Removal Commission. The commission worked out a deal with the judge. In return for his retirement, he would not be prosecuted.

Walk-Through Exercise: Judge the Story

1. Is this a story you want to pursue? The story you initially broadcast may have been bogus. But now the judge is not in a position to use his power over any more defendants. What's your justification for pursuing this story?
2. If you think you have a legitimate story, is it ready for broadcast? Neither of the police officers who called is willing to appear on air. In fact, neither is willing to be named as the source of this information. Though you don't know the police officers well, you know the police don't always agree with the actions of judges. Are you ready to broadcast this story with two anonymous sources?

More Situational Clues

- The news producer and the staff all believe this is a story the station should try to get. For one thing, the judge had misled them, and they had published a story that was not true. And, several argued, this story documented how people had been treated by an important public institution. Although this was the lowest court in the judicial system, it was where most people sought a fair hearing.
- Moreover, not doing the story would leave other victims powerless. A story could trigger lawsuits seeking redress for their mistreatment.
- Finally, a great deal was not known about the deal the judge had made. Would he be able to run for election in the future? Would he still be able to practice law?
- No one thought the story was ready for broadcast. They had no sources on the record, something they thought was critical to an important story such as this one. And they had other alternatives to pursue. One was to seek other sources in the police department and prosecutor's office. That produced nothing.
- Another strategy was to request the police records. In the state where this case developed, police investigations are subject to the open records law when the investigation is closed. So, on a Wednesday, the station filed an open-records request for a copy of the investigation. Under state law, the police department had three days to comply.
- On Friday, officials from the Judicial Retirement and Removal Commission flew into town and requested all records of the police investigation, including the originals. The police gave up their records. The police called the TV station later that day, saying they were not able to comply with the open records request because they no longer had the records. The state commission, now in sole possession of the documents, is not subject to the open records law.

Walk-Through Exercise: Judge the Sources

1. Are you ready to broadcast the story, based on your two anonymous sources?
2. Or do you have other ideas for confirming the accusations being made anonymously?

More Situational Clues

■ The station's management decided it was not ready to broadcast the story. Although this was an important story in their view, the charges being made were serious. The reputation of the former judge was at stake. And even if the judge might deserve public scorn, innocent family members would be hurt. So the station went to court, filing a suit against the police department for its violation of the open records law.

■ The station won its lawsuit against the police. The judge in the case concluded that the police should have turned the requested documents over to the station, not the commission. However, the judge also refused to force the commission to return the documents. So the station, while vindicated, could not confirm the truth of the charges against the judge.

Walk-Through Exercise: Judge the Options

1. Should the station drop the story, knowing they don't have anything on the record against the judge?
2. Should the station run the story, quoting two anonymous sources?
3. Should they pursue some other strategy? What would that strategy be?

Final Clues

■ At this point, the station decided to broadcast the story. The journalists there thought they had exhausted their options. The story was worth doing. And they had two independent (though anonymous) sources.

■ The story was broadcast shortly after the end of the lawsuit.

■ The judge never ran for public office again. But he did not lose his law license and, despite the negative publicity, he practiced law in the county for a number of years.

Walk-Through Exercise: Judging the Decision

1. With the facts of this case in mind, reach a final judgment on what you would have done had you worked at this television station as this case developed. Here's a checklist of things a casuist might do. Check to see which steps you have missed in the process:

a. Identify the relevant facts that shape your decision(s).
b. Sketch out a paradigm case that would clearly justify the use of anonymous sources. Does this case fit your paradigm case, or are there important differences? Do the similarities lead you to the same conclusion in this case? Or are the differences too great to conclude that this case should be treated in the same way?
c. Find at least one other real analogous case on the Web, and compare this case to it. Also, shift some of the facts of this case to make it into a hypothetical analogous case. What can you learn from the comparisons to these real and hypothetical cases?
d. Make a quick list of the ethical norms that play some part in this case. Rank these in terms of importance.
e. Finally, write a guideline for this television station that would establish a working standard for the use of anonymous sources. Make a list of the conditions that would need to be met before you would use information from anonymous sources in a story like this one. Rank-order these conditions, beginning with conditions that are always required, then those that are important, then those that may be relevant, but not critical. Be ready to justify each of the conditions on the list.[3]

Case 3: Naming Rape Victims

At this point, you know more about the case of Patricia Bowman and William Kennedy Smith than most living journalists—and all dead journalists as well. If we asked, you might say you know much more than you want to know, but we're not asking. In fact, we want to take advantage of your knowledge of the case and apply it to the question of guidelines. And just in case you think you have thought of everything, this exercise has a little twist at the end to test your skills. Let's begin with *The Courier-Journal* policy that was in force when the Bowman/Smith case surfaced:[4]

> Please don't identify the victims of attempted rape. A survey by Frank Hartley of selected editors. . .(male and female) showed there is wide agreement on this point.
>
> The policy is the same as it is for victims of rape and other sex crimes. We don't identify them, directly or indirectly, except in the most extraordinary circumstances.
>
> Don't name the victim of attempted or actual rape, and don't give the victim's home address or even block number. If the alleged incident occurred in the victim's home, give a general location, such as East Louisville or Southwestern Jefferson County.

Walk-Through Exercise: Does the Guideline Work?

1. This is the first time you have seen the actual guideline. Does anything surprise you about this guideline?
2. Earlier in this chapter, we noted how many of the reporting policies at *The Courier-Journal* included an "exceptions" clause. Do you think this is a useful clause to have in such a policy?
3. Back to the Bowman/Smith case. The facts in that case will not be reviewed here; you know them. Imagine yourself as one of the editors seeing this case with widespread national interest being covered in the pages of your newspaper. Though you know Patricia Bowman's name, the Associated Press stories on the trial do not name her. Apply *The Courier-Journal*'s guideline to the circumstances of the case. When you use this guideline, what decision do you reach about the use of Bowman's name?
4. Does this case meet the "extraordinary circumstances" exception or not? What's the basis for your conclusion?
5. If you make an exception for extraordinary circumstances, do you think you need to change the guideline for future cases? Or is it better to keep the guideline the same and make exceptions on a case-by-case basis?

Walk-Through Exercise: Draft a Revised Guideline

As you know, the editors thought this case merited an exception. In particular, they argued that the key difference in this case (compared to other rape cases) was the obsessive public curiosity about this incident and the resulting daily coverage of the trial. That introduced a new ethical factor, according to the editors: justice. Naming Smith over and over as the alleged rapist while Bowman remained in the shadows of media coverage did not seem fair. The exception was made. Several journalists at *The Courier-Journal* saw this in a slightly different way. They saw celebrity as the pivotal issue, not fairness. The editors, of course, could concede that prominence (celebrity) precipitated the intense interest, but that the result was still unfair.

1. Using the existing guideline as a beginning point, revise the guideline on naming rape victims to include the specific exception made in the Bowman/Smith case.
2. Remember that your goal is to craft a guideline that will be useful for similar cases. Use language that will be precise enough to handle the Bowman/Smith case, but broad enough to handle similar cases. You can use the Tyson/Washington case as a test of the guideline.
3. Look for a real case that would challenge the guideline you have written. If you can't find one, create a hypothetical example, such as a rape trial that has captured significant publicity—perhaps because of excessive brutality—but does not involve celebrity. (The multiple rape of a woman

on the pool table at Big Dan's Tavern in New Bedford, Massachusetts, fits this model. Details can be found on the Web.)

One Last Look at the Bowman/Smith Case

Unlike *The Courier-Journal* and NBC News, many news organizations kept Patricia Bowman's name out of their coverage of the trial. The jury in that trial found Smith "not guilty." In follow-up stories after the verdict, several news organizations continued to keep Bowman's name out of their accounts. This outcome raises several interesting questions:

1. Does the "not guilty" verdict change your perspective on the decision made by *The Courier-Journal*? Does it give more credence to the fairness argument the editors used?
2. What is the justification for not naming Bowman after Smith has been found "not guilty"? Bowman eventually went public in interviews with the media. But assume that she had not. Can she still claim to be a "rape victim" (and her anonymity protected) when the courts conclude (at a minimum) that the prosecuting attorney did not show that he was guilty? How is this different from a case in which a woman claims she was raped, then takes her story back?
3. Write an addendum to the guideline on naming rape victims that clarifies what the paper's policy will be in post-trial coverage on naming a woman who says she was raped, but whose alleged assailant is found "not guilty."

Case 4: CNN's iReport and Policies on Verification[5]

In 2007, a student at Virginia Tech used the video camera on his cell phone to shoot footage outside the building where the shootings were taking place. Gunshots are heard on the video. That video was posted to iReport, a citizen-journalist website where individuals can post material without prior approval or editing. CNN bought the exclusive rights to the video because it did not have comparable footage.

Situational Clues

■   The link between CNN and iReport.com got closer the following year when CNN purchased iReport.com, making CNN the first major news organization with an official space for citizen reports. Other news sites, including MSNBC and ABC, now offer such sites.

■   The iReport site continues to operate much as it did before, though it is now a linked page on CNN's site. Editors from CNN search unvetted iReport submissions on that page for stories they want to include on CNN.com's main news pages. On CNN's home page, you can find iReports that CNN editors have reviewed and marked with the "CNN iReport" tag.

Walk-Through Exercise: Sample iReport

1. Visit the CNN.com site. Find examples of vetted iReports ("CNN iReport") to get a better idea what kind of material CNN editors select. It would be helpful to make a brief list of some stories as examples of the kinds of material chosen.
2. Now sample the unvetted iReports on the iReport page at CNN.com. Can you see any differences in either quality or content between the raw, unfiltered iReport stories and the stories selected by CNN?

More Situational Clues

Now that you have some idea of the material these citizen journalists are posting, let's focus on guidelines, beginning with iReport.com.

- In June 2009 the banner on iReport.com proclaimed: "Unedited. Unfiltered. News."[6] At the entry level, access for people wanting to post to the site *is* unedited and unfiltered. However, iReport does have a set of "Community Guidelines,"[7] reproduced here, that rejects certain kinds of material:
  - Pornography/sexually explicit content
  - Obscene/lewd content
  - Content that advocates violent behavior
  - Content that contains violent images of killing or physical abuse that appear to have been captured solely, or principally, for exploitative, prurient or gratuitous purposes
  - Content that advocates dangerous, illegal or predatory acts or poses a reasonable threat to personal or public safety
  - Hate speech/racially or ethnically offensive content
  - Content that infringes somebody's copyright
  - Repeated uploads that flood the site with duplicate versions of the same or similar content
- Users can flag material that violates the community guidelines by clicking the "report violation" tag at the bottom of each article. Moderators of the site review offending material and can remove it from the site. The account of any individual whose material must be removed under these guidelines more than three times is disabled.

Walk-Through Exercise: Assess the Community Guidelines

1. What's your assessment of the Community Guidelines? Which of the guidelines would be easy to enforce? Which would be difficult for site moderators to apply consistently (fairly)?

2. Should a citizen-journalism website that is "unedited" and "unfiltered" screen material for this kind of content? Do you see any content from this list that deserves to be shared in the Web's "marketplace of ideas"?
3. What ethical norms do you see being applied in these guidelines?

More Situational Clues

Ironically, CNN provides even less guidance (publicly) on the standards it uses to select material from iReport for display on CNN's website. iReporters are offered six guidelines in the "iReport Toolkit" to enhance the chances that CNN might pick up their submission. These guidelines (except for the first) are paraphrased:

- "First things first: your story needs to include the basics. That's who, what, where, when, why and how. It needs to be true, and it needs to be fair."
- Help people connect with the story. Be a storyteller, and make people care.
- Tell the story simply and clearly so everyone can understand; imagine explaining it to a best friend.
- Maintain pace, build interest and tension with narrative, quotes and natural sound.
- Include emotion—think about how to use images, sounds, and words to convey emotion.
- Map it out—storyboard, include text with video and photos, and include the most important material first.

As you can see, only the first guideline has explicit ethical content. The rest are more tied to storytelling techniques. Beyond the injunction to tell the truth and be fair, CNN does not provide ethical guidance. In fact, three iReporters contacted for this case (people who submitted content for iReport that was later selected for use on CNN.com) said that CNN editors didn't ask questions aimed at assessing the accuracy of the information.

Here's the interesting dilemma: Should the material on CNN.com be considered in the context of citizen journalism or traditional journalism? The video, photos, stories, and opinions on iReport.com begin their lives as the work of individuals representing only themselves. But when CNN captures one of these entries and "elevates" it to the status of material created for its own website, some kind of judgment has been made on the piece's merit. CNN offers no clues about the basis for that judgment other than what we can infer from its guidelines for iReporters (see above). And it continues to segregate the iReport material in a clearly labeled special section of the website.

At the same time, CNN can edit this material to suit its own needs. One contributor said his 3.5-minute piece on outsourcing was edited to 20 seconds when it made the move to CNN.com. (Responsibility for unedited blogs usually rests with the contributor; responsibility for edited material also falls on the owners of the site.) Moreover, CNN can use photos and video for its own stories when it has none. That happened when one interviewed iReport contributor posted video footage of a Turkish plane crash.

So, back to the question: When CNN vets iReport material for presentation on its own site, uses this material to supplement its own coverage, and edits the material, is this citizen journalism, traditional journalism, or something in between? And what ethical norms should apply?

Walk-Through Exercise: Compare iReport Standards to SPJ Code

1. Do you believe iReport material selected by CNN for the CNN.com website is more like: a) citizen journalism; b) traditional journalism; or c) something in between?
2. Based on your answer, how should we think about guidelines for this material?
3. Using guidelines (in quotes) from the Code of Ethics for the Society of Professional Journalists, should CNN.com accept, reject, or modify these guidelines in evaluating iReport material?
   a. "Test the accuracy of information from all sources." Should CNN verify the accuracy of iReport information that it uses on the CNN website?
   b. "Never distort the content of news photos or video." Should CNN ask iReporters about how the photos and videos were produced and whether any editing was done?
   c. "Avoid undercover or other surreptitious methods of gathering information." Should CNN ascertain how information was gathered?
   d. "Remain free of associations and activities that may compromise integrity or damage credibility." One iReporter interviewed for this case said the CNN producer asked questions about his financial status and background. Should CNN regularly check on the associations and activities of iReporters to guarantee their independence?
   e. "Distinguish between advocacy and news reporting." Much of the material on iReport is opinion-based. Should CNN label this content as opinion?
   f. "Clarify and explain news coverage and invite dialogue with the public over journalistic conduct." Should CNN publicize the standards it uses to vet iReport material?

As we noted above, CNN does *not* discuss how it selects iReport material for the CNN website. Even if the ethical guidelines are different than those set by the Society of Professional Journalists, one could argue, as the *Online*

Journalism Review does, that online journalists should "disclose, disclose, disclose."[8]

Walk-Through Exercise: Develop Guidelines for iReport Material

Write a set of guidelines for CNN.com's use of iReport material. The absence of disclosure from CNN provides an open field for creating standards. Here are a few things to keep in mind before you begin:

1. Make sure you have a good feel for the content on iReport.com and on CNN.com. You might even want to find a few specific examples that would help you frame your guidelines.
2. Think about the types of material that will need to be vetted:
    a. Photos, video and text are all part of the mix. You may want to craft different guidelines for different media forms.
    b. News vs opinion: some guidelines may cover both; other guidelines may be needed for one, but not the other.
    c. iReport only vs CNN: some iReport material will only be available on the iReport pages at CNN. Other iReport material may be part of CNN.com's own coverage. Think about whether the guidelines for these two uses should be different.[9]

More Situational Clues[10]

This case focuses on guidelines for online use of citizen-generated material. Should we up the ante for CNN's television broadcasts?

■ In the coverage of the 2007 election in Iran (see Case 5, Chapter 4), CNN introduced a new graphic. At the bottom-right corner of the screen, the graphic read: "Unverified material. CNN Live." The graphic was clearly a response to CNN's dependence on information generated by Iranian citizens in the absence of Western journalists on the scene. Said one CNN reporter, "Because of these new restrictions, what we're doing now at CNN is we're relaxing our usual vetting process a bit." Another CNN reporter put it more directly: "We cannot verify readily some of this material we are going to show you."

■ This prompted comedian Jon Stewart of *The Daily Show* to ask, "And that is different from what you normally do, how?" Stewart followed that comment with a collection of clips from CNN on a variety of stories that included information pulled from social networking sites, including iReport, MySpace, Twitter, and Facebook.

Walk-Through Exercise: Different Standards Online?

1. Should a different standard apply to CNN's network coverage than to its website? Does the shift from the online environment to a traditional television news environment signal a need for a higher standard? If so, what would that standard be?

2. Does the "unverified material" graphic solve the problem of CNN's inability to check the accuracy of the video? Would the same argument hold for identifying information as rumor?

CHAPTER 7

▼ THE JANIE BLACKSBURG CASE: CASUISTRY IN ACTION

As you have practiced working through the cases in this book, you have become increasingly skilled at using case details to make case-based decisions. The following case will challenge your ability to analyze and resolve a number of questions in a realistic newsroom setting.

Our goal in the Janie Blacksburg case is to give you the kind of rich complexity that journalists often face when they have to make tough decisions. You can use this case material in a number of ways. We've written the case chronologically, allowing you to move with the journalists from decision to decision. As you read each section, you can make a decision before moving on to the next section. We've provided questions to offer some guidance. But the real question is simple: What would you do and why?

As a part of this process, we'd like you to use the tools of case-based reasoning whenever appropriate. Examine the details, sorting out the relevant facts from irrelevant information. Consider what might be paradigm cases that could set an ethical boundary on the choices. Explore analogous cases, real and hypothetical, to test your judgment. Establish a clear guideline that you think could be used in similar cases in the future. Identify the ethical norms that you see at stake.

Another option is to read the entire case all at once and think through its ethical implications with all the facts in front of you. This strategy has the advantage central to case-based reasoning: knowing all the relevant facts. However, as you make judgments in this context, you have a perspective the journalists in the case did not: You can see the future. And the case could easily have evolved differently. If you take this holistic approach, you will probably want to focus less on the daily decisions that needed to be made and more on the broader issues of decision-making strategy, guidelines, and the role of ethical norms.

Though some details have been changed, the abduction and death of Janie Blacksburg is real. The case is reconstructed here based on a series of interviews conducted with journalists at a major metropolitan newspaper. More than 100 pages of taped interviews provide the basis for the case narrative. The identities of the newspaper and key subjects in the case have been changed to protect the anonymity of the people involved. All names of journalists have also been changed.[1]

THE JANIE BLACKSBURG CASE

The Cast of Characters

Because this is a complex case, a large number of people are involved. Below is a list of the people involved in the case. The case narrative will try to make each person's role clear, but if you have questions, you can refer to this list.

The Family, a Friend, and the Abductor

- Janie Blacksburg, an 11-year-old girl abducted as she walked home from a sleepover at a friend's house.
- Frank Blacksburg, Janie's father. Frank and Janie's mother are separated and live in different parts of the country. Janie has limited contact with her father.
- Betty Trimble, Janie's mother. Betty has primary custody of Janie.
- Brian Sorrell, Janie's stepfather. Brian lives with Betty Trimble and Janie.
- Andrew Trimble, Trimble and Sorrell's 6-year-old son.
- Frieda Van Dyke, the woman in whose home Janie spent her last night before being abducted.
- Peter Sand, live-in boyfriend of Frieda Van Dyke.
- Ron Jones, an unemployed auto mechanic who will be accused of abducting Janie Blacksburg.

The Journalists

- Joe Fiorella, a general assignment and social services reporter. Fiorella was the first reporter to pick up the Blacksburg story.
- Edna James, the police reporter with primary responsibility for investigating the story of Janie's abduction.
- Jamal Granger, TV/media critic.
- Cindy Carroll, reporter regularly involved in the Blacksburg abduction story.
- Victoria Brand, reporter who took primary responsibility for the Janie Blacksburg profile story.
- Nan Healy, assistant metro editor with responsibility for daily coverage.
- Charles Logan, metro editor responsible for overall editing of the Blacksburg stories.

- Raul Hernandez, managing editor in charge of the newsroom operation.
- Julia Franks, editor and president of the company.

THE JANIE BLACKSBURG STORY

Case Narrative

Tuesday, Day 1

Joe Fiorella, general assignment and social services reporter for the *Metropolis Messenger*, is one of the first reporters on the Blacksburg story. On Tuesday, he is on an assignment in Stratford, a city near Metropolis, but outside the primary circulation area of the *Messenger*.

Fiorella is covering a serious traffic accident. Normally, the paper would not have much interest in a traffic accident in a city where it has few readers. But initial reports called for a rerouting of traffic on a major highway that could impact commuters heading into Metropolis. That promised major traffic problems for the newspaper's readers in the days ahead.

After some initial investigation, Fiorella calls back to the newspaper. "I'm not sure we've got a story here," Fiorella tells Nan Healy, the assistant metro editor. Traffic disruption the next day will be minor.

"We might have something else for you," replies Healy.

"Oh, it's that girl who's been videotaped, isn't it?" Fiorella asks.

Fiorella remembers a wire story in Monday's paper about Janie Blacksburg, an 11-year-old child reported missing on Sunday. She had been on a sleepover the night before. Around 6 p.m. Sunday Janie called home to say she was walking home from Frieda Van Dyke's house, the site of the slumber party. Her stepfather, Brian Sorrell, decided to drive the route so she wouldn't have to walk the whole way. Sorrell didn't see her along that route. The police were called, but Janie could not be found. One of the most extensive searches in the history of the area was launched.

Healy knows about the videotape, taken by a surveillance camera at a local carwash on the route Janie took home. Healy has not seen the tape, but she knows the visual evidence suggests that this was an abduction, not a family dispute or a runaway child.

As it happens, Fiorella's traffic story places him in Stratford, the city where Janie lives. The police there are about to have a press conference on her disappearance. Healy wants Fiorella to cover it, go to the family's house and find out anything he can about developments in Janie's disappearance.

Fiorella does that. But he has some doubts about whether this is a story for the *Metropolis Messenger*. Stratford is not part of the primary coverage area of the *Messenger*. He is only there because the traffic problem might have some impact on Metropolis. He isn't sure if this story of a missing girl is really relevant to his readers. "It was really a borderline case," Fiorella says.

"The first day [Monday] was not crazy," Fiorella says. It still isn't a big national story, though that is about to change. He attends the Tuesday press conference, where Janie's mother, Betty Trimble, pleads for Janie to call home. Over national television, Janie's mother tries to get a message to Janie: "If you can call, I have this phone on me all the time. Please call. You are loved. You are missed. We need you."

But Fiorella knows Janie is not likely to call. At the news conference, Fiorella sees a series of digital photos taken by a surveillance video camera at a nearby carwash. The photos show Janie being led away by an unidentified man. The discovery of the videotape transforms this from a missing child story to an abduction story. Police issue an Amber Alert.

Fiorella visits Janie's home, but he is not able to talk to the family. He does interview a family friend. And he finds other people congregating at the carwash where the surveillance video was taken. After a few more interviews, he goes to the office to write his story.

He writes about the search, the involvement of the FBI and the anguish of the parents. And he writes about Janie, a blue-eyed, blond girl who likes music, friends, and shopping—last seen wearing jeans, a red top and a pink backpack. And he writes about the unidentified man, shown in a photo leading her away.

The video showing the abduction changes the dynamic of the story in the newsroom. With the presence of visual evidence that confirms the abduction and can be run on television, Janie's story goes national quickly.

"It was a really competitive story," Fiorella said. "That always colors a story like this because, I mean, we're reading stuff about Janie Blacksburg in the New York *Daily News* and the *New York Post*.

"So there's always this sort of fear in the back of everybody's mind that the story is going to appear in some other paper, so that adds to the pressure cooker atmosphere."

What facts about this developing case do you think are critical in deciding whether to devote Fiorella's time to this story?

Should the *Metropolis Messenger* devote significant resources to doing this story about Janie Blacksburg, given its location in a city outside the primary circulation area of the *Messenger*?

Does the national attention because of the visual evidence of the abduction change the news value of the story for the *Messenger*?

Finally, are any ethical sensors tingling, or is this just a straight news decision?

Wednesday, Day 2

Fiorella's story on Janie Blacksburg's abduction runs in the *Messenger*. Fiorella focuses on the visual evidence and the way this has transformed the abduction into a national story.

The story is turned over to Edna James, a *Metropolis Messenger* police reporter. Together with Jamal Granger, the television critic, James plans to report in Thursday's paper about the news frenzy the video has created on cable channels and national networks. The video makes this abduction big news. And for the first time, a suspect, Ron Jones, 37, is identified by police. Jones is being held on unrelated, unspecified charges.

But more is going on in the newsroom that doesn't appear in the newspaper. Reporters and editors wonder what a small girl was doing coming home by herself at night, crossing busy streets, unsupervised by any responsible adult.

"I think a question a lot of readers might have is, 'Why was that little girl walking so very far all by herself?'" says Victoria Brand, a reporter who will become heavily involved in the case.

Brand may not have realized that Janie did call home before she left the Van Dyke house. But the question remains: Why did Sorrell or Janie's mother think letting her walk even part of the way at sunset was safe? Why didn't they insist that she stay put until she could be picked up?

Does the newspaper have a responsibility to pursue the question Brand raises about why Janie tried to walk home alone on busy roads late in the day?

To get that information, journalists might have to ask Janie's mother and stepfather some tough questions at a difficult time. Are there competing ethical claims here?

Despite the media invasion—50 reporters and 16 television cameras, including CNN, Fox News and America's Most Wanted—Edna James doesn't feel much aggressive reporting is going on. The sheriff is trying to keep the lid on the investigation, telling the reporters not to pester the police for any more information and not to contact the family. Most of the media stay at least 100 feet away from the command center set up by the police near the carwash. "No one was really being aggressive," James says. "No one was firing, like, tough questions." James concludes everyone is intimidated by the sensitivity of the event.

Meanwhile, James and the newspaper library are tracking down information on the Blacksburg family. According to Healy, one angle from the beginning is finding out about the family. "We can cover the search, we can document what's being done to find her, but we also need to know who are the people in her life," Healy says.

The *Metropolis Messenger* has a standing policy, according to reporters, to do a "full body search" on all sources in the newspaper's stories. That means a thorough check of all public records on Betty Trimble; Frank Blacksburg, Janie's father; and Brian Sorrell, Janie's stepfather. When the librarian does that background check on the family, he discovers the people in Janie's life have been in trouble with the law:

- Janie's mother, Betty Trimble, was arrested for an attempt to purchase crack cocaine five years earlier, though the charge was dropped. She was convicted on misdemeanor charges of domestic battery less than a month before Janie's disappearance.
- Frank Blacksburg, Janie's father, living in New York, was arrested on a charge of loitering and prowling.
- Brian Sorrell, Janie's stepfather, pleaded "no contest" to a charge of issuing a bad check. He was also convicted of driving under the influence twice and of driving while his license was suspended. All these convictions occurred four or five years earlier.

At the same time, the police are not hinting that the family is suspected or involved. Nor does the newspaper find any evidence of neglect. Based on interviews with neighbors and school friends, Janie was happy and well cared for by her family. "I was hearing, you know, mom was always there for every choir practice, etc." Fiorella says. "They cared a lot about their daughter, they spent a lot of time with their daughter, she had lots of friends, etc. I wasn't hearing a picture of neglect, although you know, those are certainly red flags that would make you look into it at the same time."

Healy agrees: "Whenever you see that, it raises suspicions." So in addition to checking the court records, reporters talk to people who know the family, visit places Janie had been, and talk with anyone who can shed light on what might have happened to her.

Victoria Franks thinks this could be relevant to the question of why Janie was walking home alone. "I think that both her mother and her stepfather's criminal histories might have lent some insight into that," Franks says.

If you think about the standard practice of the "full body search," it isn't hard to imagine that the reporters will frequently be faced with the challenge of deciding when to use such information in stories. Can you construct a paradigm case that you believe everyone would agree justifies the use of negative information about the subjects and sources in news stories? How about a paradigm case in which the negative information should never be used? (Hint: consider both the kind of information you already have and the information you would like to have.

At this point, the editors and reporters have to decide if these details about the family's criminal record are relevant to the abduction story. This problem is challenging because of another guideline at the paper. The paper's fundamental obligation is to the reader, not the subject of a story, Julia Franks, editor and president of the company, says. In that context, the commitment of the *Metropolis Messenger* is to give readers the truth, as accurately and completely as it can, letting the readers make judgments about the relevance of the information. Nan Healy, the assistant metro editor, remembers wondering if that wasn't her obligation: "I remember at least thinking to myself, 'Look, we've got the information, we're in the business of putting information in the paper. That's what we do, and we'll let the readers decide.'"

Is this a useful guideline in this case? Should the *Messenger* give readers the information about the criminal background of Janie's family and let readers decide whether the information is relevant? Or should the ethical judgment of relevance be in the hands of the editors? Is the presence of this basic guideline helpful in shaping the responsibilities of the journalists? Does it fit the circumstances of this case?

Despite this strong commitment to full disclosure, none of the front-line editors is ready to publish that information. "I was in favor of getting the information and putting it in the paper in a responsible way," says Charlie Logan, the principal editor on the Blacksburg stories. "On the other hand, I think it's important for a newspaper to be sensitive to things like this."

As Edna James notes, many reporters are not being aggressive on this story, perhaps because they don't want to harm a family whose daughter has been abducted and is still missing. Healy clearly feels that way. "I think one factor would be the potential harm that the information could inflict on a family that was already struggling and grief-stricken," she says.

Raul Hernandez, the managing editor, has another concern: "Our publishing that information might have been signaling something that was not supported by our reporting, which is that her [mother's] drug history may be connected to Janie's death." Despite her inclination to publish, Healy agrees: "If we had put that information in the paper, many readers would have believed that we were publishing the family's background because we thought they had done something wrong."

What do you think of the practice of investigating the background of all sources? Such background provides important context for stories, but it also raises questions about what to do with controversial information once you have it. Would it be better for the "full body search" to be more targeted: for example, looking only for homeowner information on real estate stories and looking for criminal records only for suspects in crime stories, not the victims? Or would that miss important information that you might want to use?

See if you can think of some analogous cases that would help you decide what sort of standard the newspaper could use when searching for information about subjects and sources.

Meanwhile, Ron Jones, an unemployed auto mechanic, is named by police as a suspect in the Blacksburg abduction. Identified through one of 400 tips received by the police as a result of the photos and video, Jones is arrested and held on unrelated charges. Cindy Carroll, another reporter on the case, digs out the information on Jones. Jones is married with three daughters. He has been arrested 13 times, mostly on drug charges (heroin, oxycontin, cocaine), but once for kidnapping and false imprisonment. Despite all the arrests, Jones has only served 16 months in prison for prescription fraud and probation violation.

Thursday, Day 3

Two stories on the Blacksburg case run in the *Metropolis Messenger*. James, the police reporter, and Granger, the TV reporter, do the story about the way the video footage has propelled the Blacksburg case to the national spotlight. The story also identifies Jones as a suspect. Carroll's story on Jones' background also runs. In the story, Brian Sorrell, Janie's stepfather says, "None of us recognize him."

MAKING HARD CHOICES IN JOURNALISM ETHICS

The relevance of the family information takes a new twist. Reporters and editors are asking questions about who Ron Jones is. They especially want to know whether he knows Janie. And is there a connection between Jones and Janie's family? The reporters hit the streets.

- They hear that Janie's mother and the abductor may have frequented the same bar; one source thinks they may have had the same drug supplier. James, the police reporter, learns that Betty Trimble and Ron Jones bought drugs in the same neighborhood—on the same street corner. However, no personal ties between Janie's mother and Jones can be confirmed.
- Peter Sander, the live-in boyfriend at the home where Janie spent her last night, tells the New York *Daily News* that he knows Ron Jones. Jones, a mechanic, may have worked on the boyfriend's car.
- Sander also has a criminal record, including drugs and violent crime.

Meanwhile, James, the police reporter, has had a response to her request for information on other police calls (those not involving arrests) to the Blacksburg house. One report from the previous year says that Janie's mother called home from a payphone, perhaps while on a crack binge, asking her husband to tell the kids goodbye. James clearly wants to get some of this information about the Blacksburg family into the paper, especially the information that can be confirmed.

Given the emerging picture of Janie's family—and the extensive local and national coverage being given to her abduction—what would you do with this controversial information? What facts, if any, are newsworthy about the Blackburgs, the live-in boyfriend where Janie spent her last night, and Ron Jones? What facts are morally relevant because of their relation to ethical norms?

Using the paradigm cases you constructed earlier, how does this case fit those paradigms? Is it closer to the "don't publish" paradigm or the "must publish" paradigm? What facts in the case, if changed, would shift the case closer to one or the other?

At this point, conduct a brief ethical inventory. What ethical norms push you toward publishing the negative information about the Blacksburgs? What ethical norms push you away from publishing that information?

Several people in the newsroom begin to discuss doing a profile story on Janie Blacksburg, who is still missing. Edna James, the police reporter, says that the Blacksburg case has sparked more attention than some notorious murder cases she has worked on. Clearly, the images of an 11-year-old girl being led away into a car by a stranger touched the hearts of most who saw the video.

Conversations about Janie bubble through the community. And the level of interest nationally is almost as intense.

Despite all the coverage, one sentiment in the newsroom is, "We haven't told people who Janie Blacksburg really is." The decision is made to do a profile story, spurring a new round of reporting, including conversations with classmates, friends, and neighbors. Again, the controversial details of Janie's family become a topic of debate.

Should the *Messenger* do a profile on the life of Janie Blacksburg? Is it an appropriate part of the coverage of a case that is at the core a story about her abduction? If you were in the newsroom, how would you make your argument for or against the profile? What ethical arguments would you use?

If we are telling the story of Janie Blacksburg's life, is the information about her family and her relatives' encounters with the law needed for her story to be complete and coherent? Ethically speaking, should we use that information? Beyond the intense desire of readers to know more, can you offer a strong ethical reason for including the information?

Key editors make the decision to run a profile story on Janie Blacksburg. Reporters are able to combine their previous reporting with new contacts to present a well-documented picture of Janie. Her principal describes Janie as "the all-American girl." She's a good student and popular with most of her classmates. She's known for great hugs and creating nicknames for her friends. She dresses based on her mood.

Final editing on the story is under way in preparation for publication on Saturday. At a 4 o'clock meeting, Charlie Logan, the metro editor, raises the issue of "the other side of the story" that has not been reported. He has typed up a couple of paragraphs that talk about the family members of Janie who have had brushes with the law. Julia Franks, the *Messenger*'s editor and president, suggests putting the information in the profile story. After that discussion, the editors make plans to include information in the story about the family's criminal past.

Do you agree with this decision? If so, where would you place the information in the story? How would you contextualize it? If you don't agree, why not? Justify your decision by making reference to relevant ethical norms.

In the eyes of Healy, the assistant metro editor who has been with the story from the beginning, some of the material on the family is now relevant. "What was her world?" Healy asks. "Well, her little friend who had a sleep-over, her mom's boyfriend was arrested for cocaine possession. That would have been part of her world as was her mother."

Edna James complains about being left out of the negotiations when editors decide what information might go in the story. James is the most aggressive in wanting to publish the information about the family: "This family wasn't perfect, and the headline was something like, you know, 'All-American Girl' or something, you know?"

James knows television crews are buying them dinner at Outback. She hears how the family fights over the popcorn shrimp. One reporter tells James how Janie's mother, when she found out the reporter was on the way, asked, "Can you pick up a box of donuts from Publix on the way?"

The sheriff's office has set up a fund, and people are donating money, according to James. "Maybe somebody may not be so inclined to donate to someone who has a drug problem," James says.

Does this emerging portrait of Janie's family affect your decision about how the profile should be structured? Are questions of their character relevant to the decision? And how would you factor in the public's growing investment in the funds being established?

Charles Logan, metro editor, has a different concern. He wants to make sure the commitment of the newspaper to publishing the truth is honored. "There was a piece of the story we haven't reported and it's a part of the whole picture," Logan says. "But we haven't found a vehicle to get it in the paper." The profile provides that vehicle for Logan.

Victoria Brand, one of the profile writers, agrees. "We wanted to give the readers the most accurate picture we could of who she was," Brand says.

"Life isn't pretty," James says. "And if you start to try and make it look pretty and keep out certain facts, you're not presenting the whole picture."

For Nan Healy, that whole picture becomes more relevant as the community becomes more involved in the story. "If we got to a point where children were leaving their after-school activities to conduct search parties in parks and parents were donating their time in bringing money and food to the sheriff's officials who were combing the Atlanta area, more people have a stake in Janie Blacksburg," Healy says. "That opens the door for us to give them more information and some different information about who this is."

None of the reporters or editors wants to lead the profile story with the controversial material. They agree that the key is to put that material in the broader context of Janie's life. But they all believe they can find some place to tuck the information: "There was some paragraph," James says, "where you could have said, 'In fact, her mother was arrested in 1999 for trying to buy crack, and her stepfather has three DUIs.'"

Raul Hernandez, the managing editor, feels the key difference in putting the controversial information in the profile story is context. In the stories about the abduction, the information would have implied that the mother or stepfather could have been responsible for her abduction. The same information in the profile story isn't linked directly to the crime, only to the life of Janie.

Do you agree with the editors' plan to include the controversial information in the profile? Do you agree with the reasons they offer for the relevance of this information to the story? What is the relevance of this information to ethics?

Friday, Day 4

In Friday's edition, another Edna James story on Ron Jones runs in the paper, including information that Jones had previously attacked two women.

But the real news of the day surfaces early in the morning. At 7 a.m., the county sheriff announces that "the body of a beautiful, lovely little girl, Janie Blacksburg, has been found." Janie's body is discovered beneath a pile of brush at a local church, reportedly because Jones told police where to look. One of the sheriff's top investigators adds: "We have found Janie and the person responsible for her murder. Law enforcement will work to ensure that he will pay the ultimate price for what he did to her."

The profile of Janie Blacksburg is in its final editing stages with a small section in the center of the story to be devoted to the troubled past of the family. Publication is scheduled for the next day.

Should the story of Janie Blacksburg and her less-than-perfect family be told the same day her body is reported found, when her mother, father, and stepfather are grieving? And if not that day, when? Finally, does the knowledge that Janie is dead, almost certainly murdered, require changing the content of the story? Does it change the newspaper's justification for doing a profile on Janie? How has the ethical landscape for the profile changed?

MAKING HARD CHOICES IN JOURNALISM ETHICS

Saturday, Day 5

Two stories run in Saturday's edition. One story covers the grief of the community and the family. An evening church service shows a community of sorrow, mourning the death of Janie Blacksburg.

The second story of the day is the profile of Janie Blacksburg, the *Messenger*'s attempt to tell the community more about who this little girl was and what her life was like. The dominant message in the story is of an "all-American girl," smart, popular, and funny.

Deep in that story—in the seventeenth paragraph—is a single sentence alluding to all the information the reporters had gathered on the family's criminal past: "Even at her young age, Janie had experienced some hardships." Readers never learn what the story means by "hardships."

Nan Healy wanted to do the profile on Janie Blacksburg. With a richer texture of Janie's life a profile provides, Healy thought the criminal information would have been appropriate. "But the circumstances changed," Healy says.

Victoria Brand, one of the writers of the profile, had another concern about using the negative material. "Janie didn't want to become a public figure," Brand says. "Her mother had no desire to become a public figure. It's just through this one man's act that they became so."

"You have to weigh the invasion of that family's privacy against a reader's right to know," Brand says. "What's the greater good that you're serving by publishing the mother and the stepfather's criminal histories?"

In addition to the two stories, a one-paragraph brief also appears in the newspaper that day: a memorial fund in Janie's name has been set up at a local bank. Readers are told where they can send contributions. (In less than one month, a number of such funds collect more than $70,000. The funds are to be used for children's education programs. At this point, Janie's family is still working on the details.)

> Several ethical arguments were raised by reporters and editors, justifying the deletion of most of the negative information in the profile story. Which of these ethical positions do you find more persuasive? Which are problematic? Are there other ethical arguments they should have considered?

Sunday, Day 6

Two stories on the Blacksburg case appear in the Sunday edition. Victoria Brand reports on the way that several tragedies, including the death of Janie

Blacksburg, have disrupted the serenity of Stratford, a normally quiet community. Meanwhile, James, the police reporter, follows up on new details about the car driven by Jones. The suspect's car shows signs of a struggle.

Monday, Day 7

For the first day since the report of Janie's disappearance, the Blacksburg story is not part of the day's news.

Tuesday, Day 8

Janie Blacksburg is dead, but the *Metropolis Messenger* continues to follow the fallout from the crime. James and Fiorella join forces for a story about a judge's decision to keep Jones on probation instead of in jail, despite evidence of parole violations.

Friday, Day 11

Victoria Brand reports on a memorial service for Janie. More than 1,500 people attend the service at the Community Church of God. Her family does not belong to the church, but it is selected because of the size of its auditorium.

Remembrances of Janie are shared; many tears are shed. In the story, Brand reports that Ron Jones, the unemployed mechanic, has been charged with her abduction and murder. His next court appearance is one month away.

Tuesday, Day 29

More than two weeks after the massive memorial service, the *Stratford Press*, Janie's hometown newspaper, runs a story outlining for the first time in print the legal troubles of Janie's mother. The story recounts in detail the drug arrests, the domestic battery incident, and repeated visits to Janie's house by the police—all material the *Messenger* has known for weeks.

Frank Blacksburg is the centerpiece of the *Stratford Press* story. The *Press* quotes Blacksburg responding to information about Betty Trimble's criminal record: "Had I known," he says, "I would have gone through some type of action to protect my child."

Of course, the reason Blacksburg knows now is that the reporters from the *Press* have told him, framing the story around his reaction to the information they provided.

Blacksburg says he doesn't blame Janie's mother for Janie's death, only that he would have wanted custody. "Would any parent want their child in that environment?" he asks.

Was the *Stratford Press* justified in running its story about the legal troubles of the family? In the end, which newspaper took the more ethically defensible position regarding the negative information?

The Aftermath

One Year After Janie

Janie Blacksburg's name keeps coming up in the news. Dozens of stories mention her in the context of other abductions, community safety, and efforts to pass new laws to prevent such abductions.

But a handful of stories in the *Metropolis Messenger* focus on the latest troubles of Janie's family:

- Janie's stepfather, Brian Sorrell, is arrested after a night of drinking. He pushed Janie's mother into a stove and grabbed her throat, though Betty Trimble refused to press charges. A wire story outlining the incident mentions Trimble's 1999 arrest for domestic violence after a fight with Janie's father.
- Two months after the Sorrell incident, Trimble loses custody of Andrew, her 7-year-old son, after failing a drug test. Janie's mother acknowledges her drug problems, including the time she was on a crack cocaine binge and was missing for two days the year prior to Janie's murder.
- Meanwhile, Frieda Van Dyke, the woman in whose home Janie spent her last night before being abducted, pleads guilty to felony drug possession.

Does this new information about Janie's family change your mind about the *Messenger*'s decision not to include what it knew about the troubled family in its early coverage of the abduction? What about the decision not to use it in the profile story? Do you think the deterioration of the family was caused by the trauma of Janie's abduction, rape and murder? Or could this deterioration have been predicted based on the history of the family that the *Messenger* already had? Was the pressure of the *Messenger*'s commitment to publishing the truth right after all?

A year after Janie's death, the *Metropolis Messenger* reviews the legacy of the last year for Janie's family. The story mentions Ron Jones and his broken life. But this story is really about those who loved Janie and their unraveling lives. The image of Janie's all-American life that permeated the profile story the day after her body was found is now radically altered. "Janie came from a broken home," a county commissioner says in the story. "She came from an atmosphere of drug abuse."

What readers of this story do not know is that some of the story's information on the family's history—and more—was known by *Messenger* reporters and editors at the time of Janie's abduction and murder.

In the *Messenger* story reviewing the spiraling decline of the principals in the Blacksburg case, should the newspaper have told readers that *Messenger* reporters knew about the criminal history of Janie's family a year earlier but did not publish it? If so, how do you think this could have been done?

Should the paper establish a guideline regarding such situations? If this situation doesn't warrant setting a precedent for future cases, what sort of situation would?

What do you think about the practice of the "full body search" for all subjects of news stories? Does this case suggest that the practice should be revised in any way? Or does the practice provide an ethical assist to the paper's commitment to discovering the whole truth? Do readers have a right to the whole truth?

Twenty Months After Janie

Ron Jones goes to trial 20 months after he killed Janie. He is linked to Janie by the video, by DNA, and by his brother's testimony that Jones admitted to the rape and strangulation. As Jones is tried for Janie's murder, visitors file by a memorial garden and monument featuring an angel and small children on the spot behind the church where Janie's body was found. Jones is convicted on all counts. Two years after Janie's death, he is sentenced to death.

Less than one week after a judge hands Jones the death sentence, Betty Trimble is ordered to spend 90 days in jail after pleading no contest to drug and prostitution charges.

While in jail, she learns that her brother has died in a car accident. Her brother was previously arrested four times for driving under the influence and has nine arrests for a variety of offenses, many including drugs. Trimble posted bail for her brother after his most recent run-in with the law, using an $800 check, part of a cache of money and jewelry she stole from her father.

MAKING HARD CHOICES IN JOURNALISM ETHICS

FINAL QUESTIONS

Now that you have learned all the critical details of the case and its after-math, you might want to consider several larger questions surrounding the case:

- Culture (collective decision making) and character (high standards for the practice of journalism) are evident in this newsroom. Interviews with reporters and editors exposed a commitment to collaborative ethical decisions. How do you think the frequent conversations among reporters and editors at the *Messenger* affected the outcome?
- The case illustrates the dual nature of ethical deliberation in the news-room: operating inductively from the bottom up in concrete reporting and editing decisions, while also enforcing a commitment to truth telling (at almost any cost) from the top down. Several of these guidelines and norms, including the "full body search" and the commitment to pub-lishing the truth, play important—and controversial—roles in the case. How do you see these top-down strategies interacting with the case-based strategy the journalists also employed? Is this combination of top-down and bottom-up ethical reasoning useful?

Our goal in the Janie Blacksburg case is to open a window into the complexity of the decision-making process in this case, a complexity not often present in ethics cases found in textbooks. Yet it is precisely this complexity that is a regular part of the daily life of a journalist—and one for which case-based reasoning is uniquely suited.

We welcome your observations on the case, the questions we have raised, and the strategy of case-based reasoning. Send your comments to David Boeyink (boeyink@indiana.edu) or Sandra Borden (sandra.borden@wmich.edu).

▼ NOTES

CHAPTER 1: HARD CASES IN JOURNALISM ETHICS

1 The categories of objectively, subjectively and normatively knowable are borrowed from a lecture given by philosopher Martin Benjamin in August 2000 at Miami University of Ohio.
2 The live coverage of the Thomas hearings arguably set the stage for the celebrity trial coverage that the Bowman/Smith case would later receive, giving birth to a new genre of cable news in which no chivalry was to be shown toward its female subjects, now apparently fully capable of overcoming any residual sexism that might be lurking in society.
3 We are using the language of ethical norms to include the range of ethical factors that can influence a decision, whether it is consequences, principles, care, character or some other ethical concept.
4 As Haas (2003) notes, there also is tension between acting independently and being accountable because making yourself answerable to someone else automatically limits your freedom.
5 Facts compiled from BBC News.com.
6 The events summarized here come from the timeline compiled by CNN News available at http://www.cnn.com/ALLPOLITICS/1998/resources/lewinsky/timeline/.
7 Facts compiled from Bennett (2009).
8 Facts compiled from CNN.com and Brown and Murray (2005).

CHAPTER 2: THE ROLE OF ETHICAL THEORY

1 These differences are also found in subjects from tribal societies tested by Kohlberg. One could also explore ethical differences based on Western vs Eastern cultures; urban vs rural communities; liberal vs communitarian perspectives. Clearly, other theoretical approaches could supplement those we have chosen to cover. Students with an interest in these perspectives should find that, though the outcomes might differ, a case-based approach can still be a valuable methodology.

2 For more examples, see Harris (2000).

3 Facts compiled by Dybel, Levin, Smith and Tesser (unpublished manuscript).

4 McBride's (2008) article provided the initial framework for this case. Used with permission. Additional resources cited include a 2004 staff memo from executive editor Phil Bronstein, a letter from the San Francisco Human Rights Commission to Bronstein, a 2004 *San Francisco Chronicle* column by reader representative Dick Rogers, and a story from the San Francisco Bay *Guardian* Online (Brahinsky 2004).

5 Facts compiled from Malone (2002), Tash (2002), Tobin (2002), and Varian (2002a and 2002b).

6 Facts compiled from Stevens (1998/1999).

CHAPTER 3: THE PARADIGM CASE AS ETHICAL STANDARD

1 Facts compiled from *Gazette* stories posted at http://www.mlive.com/kalamazoo/.

2 The women did not file charges against Smith and were not allowed to testify at his trial.

3 In the latest survey of American journalists, David Weaver and his associates (2007) reported that the percentage of journalists who said that violating a confidentiality agreement with a source could be justified has ranged from 5 to 8 percent over the last 20 years.

4 However, Libby was charged with obstruction of justice and providing false statements to investigators. She was later convicted.

5 Miller told National Public Radio's *Reliable Sources* that she would have never actually published any information using that attribution, but would have gone back to Libby to try to negotiate a more accurate description.

6 Although *The New York Times* did not single out Miller for criticism when it acknowledged deficiencies in its pre-war and early war reporting, critics have noted that she was prominent among those whose stories lent credibility to the unfounded claim by the Bush Administration that Iraq possessed weapons of mass destruction. The newspaper attributed its dubious coverage of the WMD claim to a scoop mentality and a "pattern of misinformation" by Iraqi exiles, intelligence sources and administration officials ('The *Times* and Iraq' 2004).

7 Facts compiled from Fakazis (2003).

8 Facts compiled from Silverstein (2007a) and Silverstein (2007b).

9 Facts compiled from Horwitz (1994) and Paterno (1997).

10 Facts compiled from interviews conducted by one of the authors at *The Philadelphia Inquirer*.

11 Facts compiled from Green and Ith (2003).

12 Facts compiled from Kolbert (1993).

13 Facts compiled from Elliott (2004).
14 Facts compiled from Elliott (2004).

CHAPTER 4: USING CASE COMPARISONS TO MAKE ETHICAL CHOICES

1 This case is based on unpublished interviews by one of the authors.
2 See "Jeffrey M. Masson, Plaintiff-Appellant, vs. The New Yorker Magazine, Inc."
3 Information on this story was developed in interviews at *The Courier-Journal*. See also Boeyink 1998: 176–177.
4 This incident occurred when one of the authors was working at the *Messenger-Inquirer*. See also Boeyink 1994: 898–899.
5 Facts compiled from stories in the *Los Angeles Times*, *The Washington Post*, and the *Guardian*.
6 Facts compiled from the Rothenberg court files of Cohen vs. Cowles, "Newsweek says North was a source of leaks" (1987), and Salisbury 1991.
7 This case was obtained from Andrew Barnes, former editor of the *St. Petersburg Times*. Some of the original language was modified.
8 This case was built on an analysis by Bill Mitchell (2009).
9 The Basij is a volunteer militia created in 1979 by the Ayatollah Khomeini. This militia was active during the protests of the 2009 Iranian election.
10 Questions of the authenticity of the video circulated on the Internet, some charging that the video was a fake; that she had a vial of fake blood in her hand, and that the blood at her feet before she was lowered to the ground was inexplicable. CSI and journalism can't get much closer than this. By the time you read this, you will be able to find out how many of these questions have been resolved.

CHAPTER 5: EVALUATING ETHICAL JUDGMENTS

1 All the facts about the Friedman case come from Borden (1996).
2 The other was a wreck that had killed two people the previous summer.
3 Today, the newsroom's harm assessment would have to consider that any images uploaded to its website could be downloaded, shared, doctored, and viewed repeatedly.
4 Facts compiled from Durrant (1993), Finley (1997) and Hoyle (2008).
5 Facts compiled from de Moraes (2005), Gurnett (2005) and Logan (n.d.).
6 Facts compiled from O'Keefe (2005) and Gray (2006).
7 Facts compiled from "Inquirer Editors Explain" (2006), Kimmelman (2006), Kumar (2006), and Maykuth (2006).

8 Facts compiled from Brinkley (1983) and the websites for *StreetWise* (http://www.streetwise.org/index.html), the International Network of Street Papers (http://www.street-papers.org/), and the National Newspaper Publishers Association (http://www.nnpa.org/News/default.asp).

CHAPTER 6: CASUISTRY AND NEWSROOM POLICY

1 Facts for this case were compiled by one of the authors in interviews at *The Courier-Journal*.
2 Facts for this case were compiled by one of the authors as a participant in the case. Some of the facts have been changed to protect the identity of the subjects, especially the family of the judge.
3 Here's a bonus for careful readers who check out obscure endnotes. A list of conditions that could justify anonymous sources can be found in Boeyink (1990).
4 Taken from "News Policies" (1986: 44).
5 Much of the unpublished research for this case was done by Samantha Weiss, Risha Kohli, and Jeremy Lacey.
6 One interesting side issue is iReport's claim that its content is news. In traditional definitions, much of the content of iReport.com is opinion, not news. But iReport encourages its contributors to create their own definition of news. This blurs the traditional boundary between opinion and news, an ethical issue worth pursuing.
7 "What Isn't Welcome" from "Community Guidelines" (n.d.).
8 "Tell your readers how you got your information, and what factors influenced your decision to publish it." Quoted in "What are the ethics of online journalism?" (2007).
9 Your instructor may want to give you more detailed instructions on how to develop the guidelines. For example, individuals might be assigned to only one of the categories above (visual vs text, news vs opinion, or iReport only vs CNN.com). Your individual guidelines can also be used as the basis for small-group and class discussions.
10 Information for this segment was taken from Stewart (2009).

CHAPTER 7: THE JANIE BLACKSBURG CASE: CASUISTRY IN ACTION

1 Anonymity was guaranteed to the journalists as part of the research protocol.

▼ BIBLIOGRAPHY

"1978: Bribes were only real thing at Mirage," (2008) *Sixty Years of History*, Chicago: Sun Times News Group. Online. Available: http://www. suntimes.com/news/metro/history/798307,CST-NWS-high17.stng (accessed 29 June 2009).

After Jimmy's World: Tightening up in Editing, New York: National News Council, 1981.

Andron, S. (1997) "Food Lion versus ABC," *Quill*, 85 no. 2: 15–16, 19–21.

Aristotle (1925) *The Nichomachean Ethics of Aristotle*, London: Oxford University Press.

Arras, J.D. (1991) "Getting down to cases: the revival of casuistry in bioethics," *The Journal of Medicine and Philosophy*, 16: 29–51.

—— (1993) "Thinking about hard cases: lessons from Baby Johnson," *Ethically Speaking*, 2 no. 1: 1–3.

—— "Casuistry in medicine," paper presented at Theory and Practice, a symposium on casuistry held at the annual meeting of the Association for Practical and Professional Ethics, St Louis, Missouri, March 1996.

"Arthur Ashe vows to go forward despite his AIDS disclosure," (27 April 1992) *Jet*, 10.

Associated Press (20 May 2003) "Ex-reporter Blair 'couldn't stop laughing' at one deception," The Associated Press State & Local Wire.

Beam, A. (2009) "How the wrong Neda photo became Iran's face of freedom," Online posting. Available: http://wipoun.blogspot.com/ (30 June 2009).

Belenky, M., Clinchy, B., Goldberger, N., and Tarule, J. (1997) *Women's Ways of Knowing: the development of self, voice, and mind*, New York: Basic Books.

Bennett, J. (4 May 2009) "A tragedy that won't fade away: when grisly images of their daughter's death went viral on the Internet, the Catsouras family decided to fight back," *Newsweek*, 38–40.

Bentham, J. (1948) *An Introduction to the Principles of Morals and Legislation*, New York: Hafner.

Boeyink, D.E. (1990) "Anonymous Sources in News Stories: justifying exceptions and limiting abuses," *Journal of Mass Media Ethics*, 5 no. 4: 233–246.

—— (1992) "Casuistry: a case-based method for journalists," *Journal of Mass Media Ethics*, 7 no. 2: 107–120.

—— (1994) "How effective are codes of ethics?" *Journalism Quarterly*, 71/4: 893–904.

—— (1998) "Codes and culture at *The Courier-Journal*: complexity in ethical decision making," *Journal of Mass Media Ethics*, 13/3: 165–182.

Bok, S. (1979) *Lying: moral choice in public and private life*, New York: Pantheon Books.

—— (1989) *Secrets: on the ethics of concealment and revelation*, New York: Vintage Books.

Borden, S.L. (1996) "Choice processes in a newspaper ethics case," *Communication Monographs*, 64: 65–81.

—— (1999) "Character as a safeguard for journalists using case-based ethical reasoning," *International Journal of Applied Philosophy*, 13 no. 1: 93–104.

—— (2007) *Journalism as Practice: MacIntyre, virtue ethics and the press*, Hampshire, England: Ashgate Publishing.

Brahinsky, R. (2004) "Bliss and bias," *San Francisco Bay Guardian*. Online: Available: http://www.sfbg.com/38/25/cover_bias.html (accessed 1 July 2009).

Brinkley, A. (13 February 1983) "Catholics on the Left," *The New York Times*, book review of M. Piehl, *Breaking Bread: the Catholic worker and the origin of Catholic radicalism in America*, 1983, Temple University Press. Online. Available: http://www.nytimes.com/1983/02/13/books/catholics-on-the-left.html (accessed 4 July 2009).

Bronstein, P. (2004) "Chronicle bans two female journalists from same-sex marriage story for marrying each other," *Grade the News*. Online. Available: http://www.gradethenews.org/pages2/marriage.htm (accessed 29 June 2009).

Brown, C. (1998) "Listening to subjects' concerns about news photographs," unpublished thesis, Indiana University.

Brown, D., and Murray, S. (16 June 2005) "Schiavo autopsy released: brain damage was 'irreversible,'" *The Washington Post*, A01.

Carvajal, D., and Mifflin, L. (17 November 1998) "Diana's biographer and ABC's Walters get Lewinsky deals," *The New York Times*, A1.

Christians, C. (1997) "The ethics of being in a communications context," in C. Christians and M. Traber (eds) *Communication Ethics and Universal Values*, London: Sage.

Christians, C.G., Ferre, J.P., and Fackler, P.M. (1993) *Good News: social ethics & the press*, New York: Oxford University Press.

Code, L. (1987) *Epistemic Responsibility*, Hanover: Brown University Press.

"Community guidelines" of iReport.com. Online. Available: http://www.ireport.com/guidelines.jspa (accessed 28 June 2009).

Conover, T. (n.d.) "Afterword," www.tedconover.com. Online. Available: http://www.tedconover.com/afterword.html (accessed 23 June 2009).

Cunningham, B. (29 November 2005) "Working the fringes," *Columbia Journalism Review.* Online. Available: http://www.highbeam.com/doc/1G1-138859854.html (accessed 3 July 2009).

Deaver, F. (1990) "On defining truth," *Journal of Mass Media Ethics,* 5 no. 3: 168–177.

de Moraes, L. (3 November 2005) "Anderson Cooper, CNN's man of the hour," *The Washington Post,* C01.

Downie, L. (2004) "Ask the Post." Online. Available: http://www.washingtonpost.com/wp-dyn/articles/A59087-2004Sep29.html (accessed 29 June 2009).

Durrant, S. (3 October 1993) "How we met: Michael Nicholson and Natasha Mihaljcic," *Independent.* Online. Available: http://www.independent.co.uk/arts-entertainment/how-we-met-michael-nicholson-and-natasha-mihaljcic-1508390.html (accessed 30 June 2009).

Dybel, S., Levin, M., Smith, L., and Tesser, D. (2008) "The Borgata Hotel and Casino grand opening event," unpublished manuscript, Indiana University.

Elliott, D. (1986) "Foundations for news media responsibility," in D. Elliott (ed.) *Responsible Journalism,* Beverly Hills: Sage.

—— (2004) "Reading and seeing: when words and pictures collide," *News Photographer.* Online. Available: http://commfaculty.fullerton.edu/lester/writings/words_pictures.html (accessed 23 June 2009).

—— (2007) "Getting Mill right," *Journal of Mass Media Ethics,* 22 nos 2&3: 100–112.

Englehardt, E. (2006) *Media Ethics: the powerful and the powerless,* publication of the Center for the Study of Ethics in Society, Western Michigan University, Kalamazoo, Michigan.

Entman, R. and Rojecki, A. (2001) *The Black Image in the White Mind: media and race in America,* Chicago: University of Chicago Press.

Fakazis, E. (2003) "How close is too close?: when journalists become their sources," in H. Good (ed.) *Desperately Seeking Ethics: a guide to media content,* Lanham, MD: Scarecrow Press.

Finley, B. (21 December 1997) "Natasha's story," book review published in *The Denver Post.* Online. Available: http://extras.denverpost.com/books/book102.htm (accessed 29 June 2009).

Geertz, C. (1994) "Thick description: toward an interpretive theory of culture," in M. Martin and L. McIntyre (eds) *Readings in the Philosophy of Social Science,* 5th edn, Cambridge: MIT Press.

Gilens, M. and Hertzman, C. (2000) "Corporate ownership and news bias: newspaper coverage of the 1996 Telecommunications Act," *The Journal of Politics,* 62 no. 2: 369–386.

Gilligan, C. (1993) *In a Different Voice: psychological theory and women's development*, Cambridge: Harvard University Press.

Glasser, T. (1984) "Objectivity precludes responsibility," *Quill*, 72 no. 2: 13–16.

Glasser, T.L., and Ettema, J.S. (1991) "Investigative journalism and the moral order," in R.K. Avery & D. Eason (eds), *Critical Perspectives on Media and Society*, New York: Guilford.

—— (2008) "A philosophy of accountability for journalism," *Media Ethics*. Online. Available: http://media.www.mediaethicsmagazine.com/media/storage/paper655/news/2008/12/31/AnalysesCommentary/A.Philosophy.Of.Accountability.For.Journalism-3639324.shtml (accessed 1 July 2009).

Goldberg, J. (2007) "The media's Katrina malpractice," *Los Angeles Times*. Online. Available: http://articles.latimes.com/2007/sep/04/news/oe goldberg4 (accessed 29 June 2009).

Good, H. (2008) "Journalism and the victims of war: Welcome to Sarajevo," in H. Good (ed.) *Journalism Ethics Goes to the Movies*, Lanham, MD: Rowman & Littlefield.

The Good Work Project (2007) Online. Available: http://www.goodwork project.org/ (accessed 20 April 2009).

Gray, M. (30 August 2006) "The press, race and Katrina," *TIME*. Online. Available: http://www.time.com/time/nation/article/0,8599,1471224,00.html (accessed 3 July 2009).

Green, S.J., and Ith, I. (18 April 2003) "Ethics of paper's fake arson story debated," *The Seattle Times*. Online. Available: http://community.seattle times.nwsource.com/archive/?date=20030418&slug=sherer18e (accessed 21 April 2003).

—— (1986) "Grief photo reaction stuns paper," *News Photographer*, 41 no. 3: 17–18, 20.

Gurnett, K. (9 September 2005) "No shelter from storm of issues: observers say Katrina disaster could be time to reflect on societal values," *Times Union*. Online. Available: http://archives.timesunion.com/mweb/wmsql.wm.request?oneimage&imageid=6356783 (accessed 30 June 2009).

Haas, T. (2003) "Reporters or peeping Toms?: journalism codes of ethics and news coverage of the Clinton-Lewinsky scandal," in H. Good (ed.) *Desperately Seeking Ethics: a guide to media content*, Lanham, MD: Scarecrow Press.

Hansen, C. (13 March 2007) "Reflections on 'To catch a predator,'" transcript posted to NBC *Dateline's* website. Online. Available: http://www.msnbc.msn.com/id/17601568// (accessed 23 June 2009).

Harris, J. (2000) "What is missing from your news?" in William Serrin (ed.) *The Business of Journalism: ten leading reporters and editors on the perils and pitfalls of the press*, New York: The New Press.

Heinicke, M. (2004) "Letter to Phil Bronstein," Human Rights Commission, City and County of San Francisco. Online. Available: http://www.ci.sf.

ca.us/site/uploadedfiles/sfhumanrights/docs/0422%20Item%2014%2
0att.pdf (accessed 20 June 2009).

Hitchens, C. (7 January 2007) "Lynching the dictator: on Saturday morning, the United States helped to officiate at a human sacrifice," *Slate*. Online. Available: http://www.slate.com/id/2156776/nav/tap2/ (accessed 4 June 2009).

Horwitz, T. (1 December 1994) "9 to nowhere—these six growth jobs are dull, dead-end, sometimes dangerous; they show how '90s trends can make work grimmer for unskilled workers," *The Wall Street* Journal. Online. Available: http://www.pulitzer.org/archives/5744 (accessed 23 June 2009).

Hoyle, A. (15 June 2008) "The girl TV reporter Michael Nicholson brought to Britain, adopted as his daughter. . .but didn't write a book about," *Daily Mail*. Online. Available: http://www.dailymail.co.uk/femail/article-1026 543/The-girl-TV-reporter-Michael-Nicholson-brought-Britain-adopted-daughter—DIDN-8217-T-write-book-about.html (accessed 30 June 2009).

Hsieh, S. (18 February 2009) "New report by National Research Council criticizes reliability of forensic evidence," *Lawyers USA*. Online. Available: http://www.allbusiness.com/science-technology/experimentation-research/11790200-1.html (accessed 2 June 2009).

Iggers, J. (1995) "Journalism ethics: right name, wrong game?" Minnesota News Council. Online. Available: http://www.news-council.org/archives/95igg.html (accessed 16 June 2009).

"Inquirer editors explain why they published Danish cartoon," (6 February 2006) *The Philadelphia Inquirer*. Online. Available: www.philly.com (accessed 7 February 2006).

"iReport" at CNN.com. Online. Available: http://www.cnn.com/ireport/ (accessed 30 June 2009).

Jaksa, J.A., and Pritchard, M.S. (1994) *Communication Ethics: methods of analysis*, 2nd edn, Belmont, CA: Wadsworth.

"Jeffrey M. Masson, Plaintiff-Appellant, v. The New Yorker Magazine, Inc.; Janet Malcolm; Alfred A. Knopf, Inc., Defendants-Appellees." (1996) United States Court of Appeals for the Ninth Circuit. Online. Available: http://altlaw.org/v1/cases/1051799 (accessed 4 July 2009).

Jonsen, A., and Toulmin, S. (1988) *The Abuse of Casuistry: a history of moral reasoning*, Berkeley: University of California Press.

Kant, I. (1956a) *Critique of Practical Reason*, Indianapolis: Bobbs-Merrill.
—— (1956b) *Groundwork of the Metaphysic of Morals*, New York: Harper & Row.

Kimmelman, M. (8 February 2006) "Critic's Notebook: A startling new lesson in the power of imagery," *The New York Times*. Online. Available: http://www.nytimes.com/2006/02/08/arts/design/08imag.html?scp=1 &sq=Kimmelman%20startling%20new%20lesson&st=cse (accessed 17 November 2009).

LEEDS TRINITY UNIVERSITY COLLEGE

King, M.L. (1963) "I Have a Dream." Online. Available: http://www.american rhetoric.com/speeches/mlkihaveadream.htm (accessed 29 June 2009).

Kirk, K. (1999) *Conscience and Its Problems: an introduction to casuistry*, Louisville: Westminster John Knox Press.

Kohlberg, L. (1969) "Stage and sequence: the cognitive-developmental approach to socialization," in D. Goslin (ed.) *Handbook of Socialization*, New York: Rand McNally.

Kohli, R., Weiss, S., and Lacey, J. (2008) "iReport: a case study," unpublished manuscript, Indiana University.

Kolbert, E. (10 February 1993) "NBC settles truck crash lawsuit, saying test was 'inappropriate,'" *The New York Times*, A1.

Kouri, J. (7 April 2009) "NBC's Dateline caught in new scandal?" *American Chronicle*. Online. Available: http://www.americanchronicle.com/articles/view/7805 (accessed 28 June 2009).

Kuczewski, M.G. (1997) *Fragmentation and Consensus: communitarianism and casuist bioethics*, Washington: Georgetown University Press.

Kumar, S. (2006) "Religious tolerance versus tolerance of religion: a critique of the cartoon controversy in Jyllands-Posten," *Flow*, 4 no. 1. Online. Available: http://flowtv.org/?p=150 (accessed 14 July 2009).

Kurtz, H. (17 October 2005) "Reporter, Times are criticized for missteps; media analysts question decisions by Miller, newspaper's editors regarding leak," *The Washington Post*. Online. Available: http://www.washington post.com/wp-dyn/content/article/2005/10/16/AR2005101601040.html (accessed 14 May 2009).

Lambeth, E. (1992) *Committed Journalism: an ethic for the professional*, Bloomington: Indiana University Press.

Lancioni, J. (2003) "Survivor in the vast wasteland: the ethical implications of reality television," in H. Good (ed.) *Desperately Seeking Ethics: a guide to media conduct*, Lanham, MD: Scarecrow Press.

Lickona, T. (1992) *Educating for Character: how our schools can teach respect and responsibility*, New York: Bantam Books.

Lippman, W. (1922) *Public Opinion*, New York: Harcourt, Brace and Co. (2008) "Living with a hole in your pocket," Twin Cities Public Television. Online. Available: http://video.cfed.org/hole_in_your_pocket.html (accessed 3 July 2009).

Livingstone, S. (2008) "Taking risky opportunities in youthful content creation: teenagers' use of social networking sites for intimacy, privacy and self-expression," *New Media & Society*, 10 no. 3: 393–411.

Logan, J.R. (n.d.) "The impact of Katrina: race and class in storm damaged neighborhoods," report posted on Brown University's website. Online. Available: http://www.s4.brown.edu/katrina/report.pdf (accessed 3 July 2009).

Lucaites, J., and Hariman, R. (2002) "Performing civic identity: the iconic

photograph of the flag-raising on Iwo Jima," *Quarterly Journal of Speech*, 88: 263–292.

Malone, M. (5 September 2002) "With this place comes a new sense of name," *St. Petersburg Times*, 1B.

Maykuth, A. (5 February 2006) "U.S. media debate showing controversial cartoons," *The Philadelphia Inquirer*, A05.

—— (6 February 2006) "*Inquirer* editors explain why they published Danish cartoon," *The Philadelphia Inquirer*. Online. Available: www.philly.com (accessed 7 February 2006).

McAdams, K. and Yopp, J. (2003) *Reaching Audiences: a guide to media writing*, 3rd edn, Boston: Allyn and Bacon.

McBride, K. (2008) "Searching for the Threshold," *Poynter Ethics Journal*. Online. Available: http://www.poynter.org/column.asp?id=53&aid=62768 (accessed 20 June 2009).

McCollam, D. (November/December 2005) "Uncharted waters," *Columbia Journalism Review*. Online. Available: http://www.highbeam.com/doc/1G1-138859851.html (accessed 3 July 2009).

McFadden, K. (1 April 2005) "Cable news' coverage of Schiavo death was obscene," *The Seattle Times*. Online. Available: http://community.seattle times.nwsource.com/archive/?date=20050401&slug=kay01 (accessed 9 June 2009).

MacIntyre, A. (2007) *After Virtue: a study in moral theory*, Notre Dame: University of Notre Dame Press.

McMasters, P. (1997). "It didn't have to come to this," *Quill*, 85 no. 2: 18–19.

Mill, J.S. (1956) *On Liberty*, Indianapolis: Bobbs-Merrill.

Miller, J. (16 October 2005) "My four hours testifying in the federal grand jury room: a personal account," *The New York Times*. Online. Available: http://www.nytimes.com/2005/10/16/national/16miller.html?pagewanted =1 (accessed 18 May 2009).

Miller, R.B. (1996) *Casuistry and Modern Ethics: a poetics of practical reasoning*, Chicago: University of Chicago Press.

—— "Applied ethics, narrative ethics, and casuistry: some distinctions," plenary address given at *Theory and Practice*, a symposium on casuistry held at the annual meeting of the Association for Practical and Professional Ethics, St Louis, Missouri, March 1996.

Mitchell, B. (2009) "Iconic video from Tehran protests demands new skills of journalists," Poynter Institute for Media Studies. Online. Available: http://www.poynter.org/column.asp?id=101&aid=165524 (accessed 30 June 2009).

Mitchell, G. (15 October 2005) "After 'NY Times' probe: Keller should fire Miller—and apologize to readers," *Editor & Publisher*. Online. Available: http://www.editorandpublisher.com (accessed 17 October 2005).

Murrow, E. and Friendly, F. (24 November 1960) "Harvest of Shame." "CBS Reports", television program.

Nelson, D. and Henderson, B. (2009) "Slumdog child stars miss out on the movie millions," *Daily Telegraph*. Online. Available: http://www.telegraph.co.uk/news/worldnews/asia/4347472/Poor-parents-of-Slumdog-millionaire-stars-say-children-were-exploited.html (accessed 30 June 2009).

"News policies," (1986) Louisville: Louisville *Courier* and Louisville *Times*, unpublished manuscript.

"Newsweek says North was a source of leaks," (1987) *The New York Times*. Online. Available: http://www.nytimes.com/1987/07/20/world/newsweek-says-north-was-a-source-of-leaks.html (accessed 4 July 2009).

"The New York Times Company policy on ethics in journalism." (2005) Online. Available: http://www.nytco.com/press/ethics.html (accessed 16 June 2009).

"*The New York Times*: guidelines on our integrity" (13 December 2000). Judicial-Discipline-Reform.org website. Online. Available: http://judicial-discipline-reform.org/6TextAuthorities%20Cited%20toeC71/J%20Prof%20respon%20lawyrs%20journlis/18NYTimes%20on%20Integrity%20sep4.pdf (accessed 20 November [SB1]2009).

Niles, R. (14 January 2007) "What are the ethics of online journalism?" *Online Journalism Review*. Online. Available: http://www.ojr.org/ojr/wiki/ethics/ (accessed 28 June 2009).

O'Keefe, K. (1 December 2005) "Ethical firestorm: a month after one of the greatest natural disasters in American history, experts grade the media on their coverage of Hurricane Katrina," *Quill*. Online. Available: http://www.accessmylibrary.com/coms2/summary_0286-12080973_ITM (accessed 3 July 2009).

Overholser, G. (1989) "Why hide rapes?" *The New York Times*. Online. Available: http://www.nytimes.com/1989/07/11/opinion/why-hide-rapes.html?scp=3&sq=Geneva%20Overholser%20rape&st=cse (accessed 25 May 2009).

Pascal, B. (1941) *Pensees* and *The Provincial Letters*, New York: The Modern Library.

Paterno, S. (May 1997) "The lying game," *American Journalism Review*. Online. Available: http://www.ajr.org/Article.asp?id=598 (accessed 23 June 2009).

Patterson, P. and Wilkins, L. (2007) *Media Ethics: issues and cases*, 6th edn, New York: McGraw-Hill.

Pierce, R. and Gerhart, A. (5 October 2005) "News of pandemonium may have slowed aid," *The Washington Post*, A8.

Plato (1961) "Laws," in E. Hamilton and H. Cairns (eds) *The Collected Dialogues of Plato*, Princeton: Princeton University Press.

Pollitt, M. (2008) "Applying traditional forensic taxonomy to digital forensics," in I. Ray and S. Sheno (eds), *Advances in Digital Forensics IV*, Boston: Springer.

Rawls, J. (1971) *A Theory of Justice,* Cambridge, MA: Harvard University Press.

Reinson, K.F. (2010) "Quasars: silent celebrities, ethical implications" in H. Good and S.L. Borden (eds) *The Ethics of Entertainment* (working title), Jefferson, NC: McFarland & Co.

Rogers, D. (2004) "When the news is personal," *San Francisco Chronicle.* Online. Available: http://www.sfgate.com/cgibin/article.cgi?file=/chronicle/archive/2004/03/22/EDGLU4UDSL1.DTL (accessed 1 July 2009).

Rosen, J. (2000) *The Unwanted Gaze: the destruction of privacy in America,* New York: Random House.

Rosenblatt, S. and Rainey, J. (2005) "Katrina takes a toll on truth, news accuracy," *Los Angeles Times.* Online. Available: http://articles.latimes.com/2005/sep/27/nation/na-rumors27 (accessed 29 June 2009).

Ross, W.D. (1930) *The Right and the Good,* Oxford: The Clarendon Press.

"Rothenberg, Elliot C. case files from Cohen v. Cowles Media Company, 1982–2001: finding aid." Online. Available: http://oasis.lib.harvard.edu/oasis/deliver/~law00128 (accessed 30 June 2009).

Salisbury, B. (1991) "Burning the source," *American Journalism Review.* Online. Available: http://ajr.org/Article.asp?id=1553 (accessed 1 July 2009).

Shriver, D.W., Jr (1997) "News of the neglected," in D. Arant (ed.) *Ethics, Issues and Controversies in Mass Media,* St Paul: Coursewise Publishing.

Silverstein, K. (30 June 2007a) "Undercover, under fire: the Washington press corps is too busy cozying up to the people it covers to get at the truth," *Los Angeles Times.* Online. Available: http://www.latimes.com/news/opinion/commentary/la-oe-silverstein30jun30,0,2313728.story (accessed 20 November 2009)

—— (July 2007b) "Their men in Washington: undercover with D.C.'s lobbyists for hire," *Harper's Magazine.* Online. Available: http://www.harpers.org/archive/2007/07/0081591 (accessed 20 November 2009).

Solove, D. (2007) *The Future of Reputation: gossip, rumor, and privacy on the Internet,* New Haven, CT: Yale University Press.

Steele, B. (26 June 2000) "Protecting lives and principles," Poynter Online. Available: http://www.poynter.org/content/content_view.asp?id=3677 (accessed 20 November 2009).

Stevens, E. (1998/1999) "Mousekefear," *Brill's Content,* 1 no. 5: 95–103.

Stewart, J. (16 June 2009) "The Daily Show," Comedy Central, television program.

Tash, P. (15 September 2002) "Why the St. Pete Times Forum?" *St. Petersburg Times,* 1D.

Thomas, E. (with Yousafzai, S., Moreau, R., Hussain, Z., Conant, E., and Horesh, A.) (23 May 2005) "How a fire broke out," *Newsweek.* Online. Available: http://www.newsweek.com/id/52117/page/1 (accessed 10 June 2009).

"The *Times* and Iraq," (26 May 2004) *The New York Times,* A10.

Tobin, T. (4 September 2002) "Ice palace renamed St. Pete Times Forum," *St. Petersburg Times*, 1E.

Tucher, A. (1994) *Froth & Scum: truth, beauty, goodness and the ax murder in America's first mass medium*, Chapel Hill: University of North Carolina Press.

Varian, B. (7 September 2002a) "Naming rights deal valued at $30 million," *St. Petersburg Times*, 1B.

—— (6 September 2002b) "Official demands Times deal details," *St. Petersburg Times*, 1B.

"Virtues and values", *Wikipedia*. Online. Available: http://en.wikipedia.org/wiki/Virtue#Virtues_and_values (accessed 25 May 2009).

Wallace, J.D. (2009) *Norms and Practices*, Ithaca, NY: Cornell University Press.

Weaver, D.H., Beam, R.A., Brownlee, B.J., Voakes, P.S., and Wilhoit, C.G. (2007) *The American Journalist in the 21st Century: US news people at the dawn of a new millennium*, Mahwah, NJ: Lawrence Erlbaum.

Weston, A. (1997) *A Practical Companion to Ethics*, New York: Oxford University Press.

Winch, S. "On naming rape victims: how editors stand on the issue," paper presented at the Association for Education in Journalism and Mass Communication conference, Boston, August 1991.

Woo, J. (2006) "The right not to be identified: privacy and anonymity in the interactive media environment," *New Media & Society*, 8 no. 6, 949–67.

Younge, G. (2005) "Murder and rape – fact or fiction?" *Guardian*. Online. Available: http://www.guardian.co.uk/world/2005/sep/06/hurricanekatrina.usa3 (accessed 30 June 2009).

▼ INDEX

ABC News 143, 166; and Disney 50, 60; and Food Lion 10, 12
access *see* undercover reporting
accuracy *see* truth telling
advocacy journalism 43, 136–9, 144–6, 169
AIDS, reporting on 28–9
alternative media 144–6
analogical reasoning *see* comparing cases
analogous cases *see* comparing cases
anonymous sources *see* sources, anonymous
Aristotle 41, 50, 55, 96, 128
Ashe, Arthur 27–9
attribution *see* anonymous sources
autonomy 3–4, 8, 31–2, 89–90, 98, 126, 141–2, 146, 150; relation to conflicts of interest 46–9, 72, 93, 169; relation to privacy 14–15, 185; relation to professional ethics 127, 136–7, 169; relation to truth telling 78–9, 93–4; relation to watchdog role 86–9, 124, 191

Bentham, Jeremy 36
bias 48, 55–7, 78; and class 145, 152, 155; and gender 7–8, 159–64, 191; and race 31, 58, 90–1, 108, 140–1, 144–5, 152, 159, 167; and religion 141–4; and sexual orientation 55–7 *see also* conflicts of interest *and* objectivity
Blacksburg, Janie: aftermath 187–8; narrative of case 175–87; people involved in case 174–5
Blair, Jayson 65–6, 71–2, 74, 76, 154
bottom-up ethical reasoning *see* casuistry
Bowman, Patricia 1, 7–8, 11, 13, 45–6, 67, 70–2, 76, 96, 101, 103, 126, 130–2, 151–3, 155–6, 191–2
Bush, George W. 26, 74

care ethics 38–41, 55
case-based reasoning *see* casuistry
casuistry: contrasted with applied ethics 70; contrasted with situation ethics 70; historical background 2, 147; limits of 12–13, 125–6, 147; processes involved in 66, 112–13, 129, 151, 157, 163, 173, 189; similarities to forensic investigations 1–2, 13, 31–2, 46,

freebies 39, 47–9, 51–3, 63, 93–4,
156 *see also* conflict of interest
friendship: as a virtue 50, 55; with
sources 49–50, 53–5

Geneva Conventions 19–20
Gilligan, Carol 38–9
guidelines: and paradigms 95, 99,
157; and policies 71, 86, 123–4,
147–9, 167–8, 178–9, 188; and
precedents 96, 122, 126–7, 131,
148–51, 188; contrasted with
moral rules 11; development of
66, 129, 148–50, 153, 157–61,
170–1, 194; exceptions to 103,
152–3, 156, 159, 165; revision
of 86, 99, 126, 151–3, 161,
165, 188

hard cases 1–2, 11, 67–8, 72, 76,
80, 103, 123–4
harm: avoiding 3, 7–8, 13, 34, 43,
45, 72, 76, 106, 123, 150;
estimating 8, 27, 36, 98, 105,
123, 142; justifying 7–8, 17, 25,
37, 98–9, 127, 131, 134,
179–80; making up for 34;
minimizing 3, 17–18, 24, 77
Herald-Times (Bloomington,
Indiana) 46, 72, 93–4, 104,
121, 127, 129, 152
hidden cameras *see* surreptitious
taping
human dignity 8–9, 134, 145; and
Kant 33, 47, 127; relation to
privacy 14–15, 72, 131
Hussein, Saddam 19–22, 24

images: blasphemous 142–4;
deceptive 89–91, 93, 118, 148,
152, 166–70, 193; embarrassing
19–20, 103–4; graphic 20–1,
26, 118, 121–3, 166; of grief
36–7, 72–4, 121; on the Internet
20, 24, 26–7, 106, 116–18,
148, 166–71, 193; unpatriotic
144
impartiality 33, 36, 39, 42
independence *see* autonomy
inductive reasoning 31 *see also*
casuistry
integrity 42, 56
Internet 88, 103–4, 106, 148,
166–71, 194
intuition 11, 35, 128
iReport *see* CNN

justice: 43–5, 68, 72, 74–5, 77–8,
96, 98, 101, 116, 126, 146,
150–1, 154, 165–6, 168,
178–80 *see also* social justice
justification, ethical 80, 101; and
laxity 125; and theory 126;
certainty of 124–6
Jyllands-Posten 141–3

Kant, Immanuel 32–5, 43, 47,
126–7 *see also* Categorical
Imperative
Kennedy Smith, William; *see*
Bowman, Patricia
Kohlberg, Lawrence 38, 191

law: case 10; statutory 11 *see also*
precedent
law enforcement *see* autonomy
laxity *see* justification, ethical
Lewinsky, Monica 15–16, 22–4,
68, 134 *see also* Clinton, Bill
libel *see* defamation
lies, lying 33, 35, 41, 44, 78–9, 89,
151, 153; as paradigm of
deception 78; contrasted with
errors of fact 78; definition of
78 *see also* deception in
reporting
logic *see* reason
Los Angeles Times 78, 83, 193

MacIntyre, Alasdair 41–2
memberships *see* community
  involvement
Mill, John Stuart 37, 127 *see also*
  utilitarianism
Miller, Judith 74–6, 192 *see also*
  New York Times
minimizing harm *see* harm
Muhammad 141–4, 146
Murrow, Edward R. 40–1
MySpace 25, 170

New York Times, The 1, 8, 49,
  74–6, 91, 116, 119, 192
news organizations 148–50, 155,
  189
Newsweek 3, 22, 25, 90–1, 111,
  119
norms, ethical 11–13, 32, 43–6;
  conflicting 98–9, 101, 126, 146,
  169–71; definition of 191;
  meaning of 70, 128, 130, 132,
  142, 169–71; relation to ethics
  codes 70–1, 76, 151, 169–70;
  relation to relevance 68,
  113–14, 116, 127–9, 131–2,
  142, 150, 164, 173, 181,
  182–3; revision of 70; violation
  of 71, 79–80, 156 *see also* rules,
  ethical

objectivity 39–40, 43, 77–8, 125,
  133, 136–40, 169–71, 194
obligations *see* rules, ethical
obscenity 26, 156–61, 167; *see also*
  images
online journalism *see* Internet
open records 162–3, 178
organizational culture *see* news
  organizations

paradigms: classification of 68–9,
  74, 76, 86–8, 144; conflicting
  12, 122, 131–2, 141;

explanation of 65–6, 69–70;
finding 72–4; flawed 69, 75–6,
99, 151; hypothetical 73–4,
90–1, 110, 111, 143, 158,
164–5, 179; identification of 68,
74, 76–7, 79–82, 84–6, 93–4,
101, 157, 181; shifts in 74, 101,
104, 113–16, 152, 181;
similarities to legal precedents
10–11, 96, 100, 148, 150;
similarities to samples in forensic
investigations 65, 97; types of
70–1, 81–2, 103, 112
Philadelphia Inquirer, The 85,
  143–4, 192
photographs *see* images
plagiarism *see* deception in
  reporting
police *see* autonomy
policies *see* guidelines
Poynter Institute for Media Studies
  86, 118, 141
precedent: explanation of 10–12,
  148; relation to paradigms 76
  see also guidelines
Prime Time Live 10, 12, 72, 85,
  103
Principle of Veracity 79–80 *see*
  also truth telling
principles, ethical *see* rules, ethical
privacy: achievement of v.
  protection of 15–16, 127; and
  health 28; and surveillance 25;
  cases of 19–29, 82; explanation
  of 14–15; survivor 25, 122–3,
  127; violations of 14, 17, 37,
  73, 104, 106, 179, 185
professional ethics 43–4, 49, 63,
  105, 127–8, 137, 168–9
promises 49, 59, 77, 98, 101–2,
  109–11, 136, 192
propaganda 65, 79
public relations 51–2, 83–4,
  109–10, 142